LIVING WITH THE DEAD

Ancestor Worship and Mortuary Ritual in Ancient Egypt

Nicola Harrington

I0892904

OXBOW | books
Oxford & Philadelphia

First published in the United Kingdom in 2013. Reprinted in 2021 by
OXBOW BOOKS
The Old Music Hall, 106-108 Cowley Road, Oxford, OX4 1JE

and in the United States by
OXBOW BOOKS
1950 Lawrence Road, Havertown, PA 19083

Paperback Edition: ISBN 978-1-84217-493-7
Digital Edition: ISBN 978-1-78297-090-3

A CIP record for this book is available from the British Library

Library of Congress Cataloging-in-Publication Data

Harrington, Nicola.
Living with the dead : ancestor worship and mortuary ritual in ancient Egypt / Nicola Harrington.
p. cm.
Based on the author's thesis (doctoral)--Oxford University, 2010.
Includes bibliographical references.
ISBN 978-1-84217-493-7
1. Funeral rites and ceremonies--Egypt. 2. Ancestor worship--Egypt. I. Title.
BL2450.F8H37 2013
393.0932--dc23
2012040015

For a complete list of Oxbow titles, please contact:

UNITED KINGDOM
Oxbow Books
Telephone (01865) 241249
Email: oxbow@oxbowbooks.com
www.oxbowbooks.com

UNITED STATES OF AMERICA
Oxbow Books
Telephone (610) 853-9131, Fax (610) 853-9146
Email: queries@casemateacademic.com
www.casemateacademic.com/oxbow

Oxbow Books is part of the Casemate Group

Front cover illustration: Sennedjem, his wife and two young children, offered a libation by his eldest son. Burial chamber of the tomb of Sennedjem (TT 1), Deir el-Medina, 19th Dynasty. © Heidelberger Ramessiden-archiv, 40107. Reproduced with the kind permission of Eva Hofmann.
Back cover illustration: Widow weeping and throwing dust onto her hair at the foot of her husband's anthropoid coffin. Tomb of Nebamun and Ipuky (TT 181), Khokha, 18th Dynasty. After Mekhitarian 1978: 128.

Dedicated with love to my Mother
Catherine Harrington

Contents

List of Figures and Tables

Disclaimer

Images are by the author unless otherwise stated. All reasonable attempts have been made to contact copyright holders where appropriate.

Introduction

Although the relationship between the living and the dead has been touched upon in several general studies and some more specific articles, the phenomenon of ancestor cults and associated activities in Egypt have not been covered in great depth. In this book, which evolved from my doctoral thesis, I address the issue of ancestor worship, drawing together a diverse range of sources in order to present as complete a view as possible.

Funerary remains have to a large extent shaped our understanding of Egyptian culture, and evidence is biased towards those who had the means to create lasting monuments. The specialised nature of sites such as Deir el-Medina and Amarna may mean that the beliefs and practices of their inhabitants were entirely incompatible with those of people living in non-elite settlements about which comparatively little is known, and anthropological data is useful in shedding some light on gaps in our knowledge that can only be satisfactorily filled by future excavations. The purpose of incorporating ethnographic examples is to show that the ancient Egyptians were not alone in their behaviour in relation to events such as death and childbirth, and to offer insights from other cultures where relevant evidence is lacking.[1] This concern with presenting a less westernised view of ancient cultures has been expressed over the last generation in *Egyptology and the Social Sciences*[2] and *Anthropology and Egyptology: a developing dialogue*[3] among others. For example, Gerhard Haeny noted:[4]

> … as long as we continue to view Egyptian art through our usual looking glasses, studying it by methods and judging it by standards derived from our modern civilization, our endeavours can give an answer only to the question of what aesthetic or other satisfaction Egyptian art may bring to us … New approaches have to be tried, new methods have to be developed. It almost demands that we jump over our own limitations.

In incorporating a range of ethnographic data, I hope to place ancient Egyptian culture in a wider perspective, to build on attempts to engage Egyptology with anthropological methodology and materials,[5] and to further understanding (or stimulate debate) about the role of the dead in society in general.

Previous studies

In her 2001 doctoral thesis, *Aspects of the interaction between the living and the dead*, Clare Plater discusses letters to the dead, reserve heads, warnings to visitors and appeals to the living, medical texts, magical practices, and the role of saints, across a wide spectrum of Egyptian history, from the Old Kingdom to the Late Period. She does not consider funerary or mortuary

---

1 *Cf.* Baines 2007: vi; Weeks 1979: 21.

2 Weeks 1979.

3 Lustig 1997.

4 1979: 94.

5 E.g. Meskell 1999.

cult. Lynn Meskell has worked extensively with Deir el-Medina material, publications of which include *Private life in New Kingdom Egypt* (2002), and *Object worlds in ancient Egypt* (2004). The domestic religion of the other well-known workmens' settlement was analysed by Anna Stevens and published as *Private religion at Amarna: the material evidence* in 2006. Sylvie Donnat in her thesis *La peur du mort* (2003) uses the corpus of letters to the dead as a basis for exploring the relationship between the living and the dead, especially its more negative aspects: ideal versus "revengeful" funerals, and the blessed versus the damned; some aspects of these phenomena had been discussed by Jan Zandee (1960) in *Death as an enemy according to ancient Egyptian conceptions*.

Jan Assmann has covered the topic of death and the afterlife most comprehensively in several books and articles, particularly *Tod und Jenseits im alten Ägypten* (2001) translated in abridged form as *Death and salvation in ancient Egypt* (2005); his studies are mostly text-based. Christina Adams also takes a text-based approach in her work on communication between the living and the dead:[6] *Appeals to the living and letters to the dead: the interface between the living and the dead in ancient Egypt* (2004, BA dissertation); *The living and the dead: contact and communication as exemplified in Coptic texts of the 4th to 11th centuries AD* (2005, M.St. thesis); *Between two worlds: the interface between the living and the dead as evidenced in texts of the Late, Ptolemaic and Roman periods* (D.Phil. thesis, in progress). Comparative studies of beliefs in ancient and modern Egypt have been made by Nadia el-Shohoumi in *Der Tod im Leben: Eine vergleichende Analyse altägyptischer und rezenter altägyptischer Totenbräuche. Eine phänomenologische Studie* (2004), Rawya Ismail in her PhD entitled *Aspects of household cults in New Kingdom sites in ancient Egypt compared with such practices in modern Western Thebes* (2004),[7] and Elizabeth Wickett in *For the living and the dead: the funerary laments of Upper Egypt, ancient and modern* (2010).

The most extensive study of ancestor busts is Jean L. Keith's *Anthropoid busts of Deir el Medineh and other sites and collections* (2011). Other studies of the busts include Karen Exell's article in the UCLA Encyclopaedia of Egyptology (2008), and Anne Friedrich's MA thesis (Berlin, 2010). The classic work on ancestor cults, based around the analysis of *akh iqer* stelae, is that of Robert Demarée (1983). Robert Ritner has presented an overview of household religion (2008), as well as a study of *The mechanics of ancient Egyptian magical practice* (1993), and John Baines and Peter Lacovara (2002) have analysed the ambivalent attitudes of the Egyptians towards their dead. The death and burial of, and afterlife provision for, children and infants appear not to have been extensively studied for ancient Egypt.[8] The principal works covering this aspect are Erica Feucht (1995: 121–34), Joyce Filer (1998), Françoise Dunand (2004), Cathie Spieser (2007), and Ruth Zillhardt (2009). The most recent publication that touches on the cult of the dead is Emily Teeter's (2011) *Religion and ritual in ancient Egypt*. Ron Tappy (1995: 63), in discussing mortuary cults in ancient Palestine, raises the important issue of the difference between ancestor worship (personal, familial relationship) and the cult of the dead (impersonal, non-familial relationship), both of which are considered here. The cult of royal ancestors is not considered because it was independent of beliefs and rituals relating to close kin.

---

[6] Summarised in her 2007 article *Shades of meaning: the significance of manifestations of the dead as evidenced in texts from the Old Kingdom to the Coptic period*.

[7] Mentioned in *Egyptian Archaeology* 24, 2004: 44.

[8] But see Ronika Power's (2012) PhD dissertation: *From the cradle to the grave: child and infant burials in the Egyptian archaeological record*, Macquarie University, Sydney.

It is not possible within the scope of this book to cover every aspect of mortuary cult and ancestor worship, or every cemetery at which these phenomena are evident. Rather, the research presented here is intended as an overview of the evidence for cultic activities and beliefs regarding death and the dead. Despite the apparent wealth of information available from ancient Egypt and the vast amount of literature dedicated to it, our understanding of many aspects or religious life and the ways in which people, from fishermen to pharaohs, dealt with death and its aftermath is still patchy at best. Nor does this volume address the entire chronological spectrum from the Predynastic to the Late Period, but focuses on the Old to New Kingdoms, with particular emphasis on the latter.[9] This is due in part to the nature of the evidence – the sites of Deir el-Medina and Amarna are obvious starting points for discussions of domestic religion, for instance – but it also involves a critique of religious practices and beliefs from textual, iconographical, and archaeological sources over the course of approximately 1500 years: the use of broad brushstrokes in constructing a picture of interaction between the living and the dead over such an expanse of Egyptian history is therefore inevitable.

[9] For the interaction between the living and the dead in the Old and Middle Kingdoms, see the thesis by Julia Troche, Brown University (PhD in process).

Acknowledgements

I will always be deeply grateful to John Baines for supervising my doctorate and the many hours he spent reviewing the thesis on which this book is based. Any remaining errors are entirely my own. The Topographical Bibliography team, Jaromir Malek, Elizabeth Fleming, Alison Hobby, Diana Magee, Cat Warsi and Jenni Navratil have been remarkably supportive through my years as student, colleague, and researcher. I am indebted to Liz Frood, who has been a great source of help and enthusiasm, and to Gay Robins who kindly agreed to examine the thesis and subsequently encouraged me to publish it. I am also extremely grateful to John Taylor for his constructive criticism and willingness to review the book. I would like to express my appreciation to Len Barrett and Richard Carter for their unfailing good humour and witticisms: they are the Sackler Library's Statler and Waldorf.

I was privileged to have been involved in the anthropoid bust volume and would like to express my gratitude to both Jean Lewis Keith and Sylvie Donnat for inviting me to contribute and for sharing their views, even if we did not always agree on certain interpretations. In addition, Sylvie generously gave me a copy of her doctoral thesis as well as a couple of her published articles. Neal Spencer provided detailed information on the ancestor bust discovered at Amara West, and for permission to study and photograph busts in the collections of the British Museum and the Petrie Museum of Egyptian Archaeology I am very grateful to Derek Welsby, Hugh Kilmister and Tracey Golding.

Thanks are due to the Institut Français d'Archéologie Orientale, especially Nadine Cherpion and Laure Pantalacci for granting access to the village of Deir el-Medina. I would like to express my appreciation to the Supreme Council of Antiquities, particularly Janice Kamrin and Sultan M. Eid, for permission to photograph Theban tomb chapel decoration. Thank you to Deborah Sweeney for copies of reviews, Geoffrey Killen for discussions about furniture, and José Galán for information on his work in Theban Tombs 11 and 12 at Dra Abu el-Naga. I am very grateful to Hana Navrátilová for her discussions about New Kingdom graffiti and for access to unpublished articles, to Cynthia May Sheikholeslami for sharing her thoughts on banqueting and festivals, to Eva Hofmann for permission to publish images in the University of Heidelberg archives, and to Amandine Marshall for her correspondence regarding children in ancient Egypt.

For his support during the course of the D.Phil. and beyond I am grateful to Bill Harrington-Stewart. I also need to acknowledge the assistance of Bob Heron, Cat Warsi, and Liz Frood, who read and commented on draft copies, and whose comments and suggestions have assisted in strengthening the text. Clare Litt, Lizzie Holiday and Sam McLeod at Oxbow Books have displayed remarkable patience, as has Gareth Roberts of the Online Egyptological Bibliography, for which I am thankful. Finally, in a study of death, it seems appropriate to remember two people for whom the day of mooring arrived too soon. Firstly my father, Alan Midgley, and secondly Barbara Adams, a great teacher and friend. I hope this volume would have made them both proud.

Timeline[1]

Old Kingdom	**2575–2134**
4th Dynasty	*2575–2465*
5th Dynasty	*2465–2323*
6th Dynasty	*2323–2150*
7th/8th Dynasty	*2150–2134*

First Intermediate Period (9th–11th Dynasties) 2134–2040

Middle Kingdom	**2040–1640**
11th Dynasty	*2040–1991*
12th Dynasty	*1991–1783*
13th Dynasty	*1783–1640*

Second Intermediate Period (15th–17th Dynasties) 1640–1532

New Kingdom	**1550–1070**
18th Dynasty	*1550–1307*
Ahmose	1550–1525
Amenhotep I	1525–1504
Thutmose I	1504–1492
Thutmose II	1492–1479
Thutmose III	1479–1425
Hatshepsut	1473–1458
Amenhotep II	1427–1401
Thutmose IV	1401–1391
Amenhotep III	1391–1353
Amenhotep IV/ Akhenaten	1353–1335
Smenkhkare	1335–1333
Tutankhamun	1333–1323
Ay	1323–1319
Horemheb	1319–1307
19th Dynasty	*1307–1196*
Ramesses I	1307–1306
Sety I	1306–1290
Ramesses II	1290–1224
Merenptah	1224–1214
Sety II	1214–1204

[1] Based on Baines and Malek 1980: 36. Dates are BC unless otherwise stated.

Amenmesse	1204–1198
Twosret	1198–1196
20th Dynasty	*1196–1070*
Sethnakht	1196–1194
Ramesses III	1194–1163
Ramesses IV	1163–1156
Ramesses V	1156–1151
Ramesses VI	1151–1143
Ramesses VII	1143–1136
Ramesses VIII	1136–1131
Ramesses IX	1131–1112
Ramesses X	1112–1100
Ramesses XI	1100–1070

Third Intermediate Period (21st–25th Dynasties)	**1070–712**
Late Period (25th–30th Dynasties)	**715–332**
Greco-Roman Period	**332 BC–AD 395**

Maps

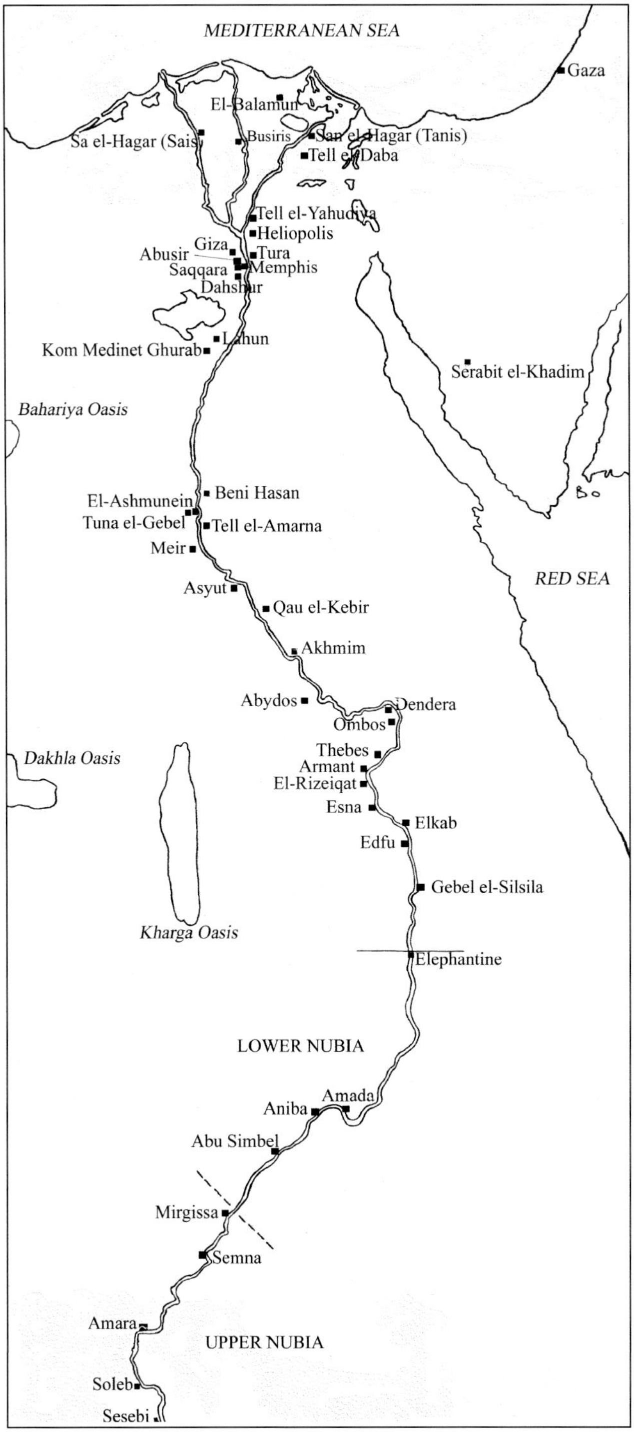

Map 1: Egypt and Nubia.

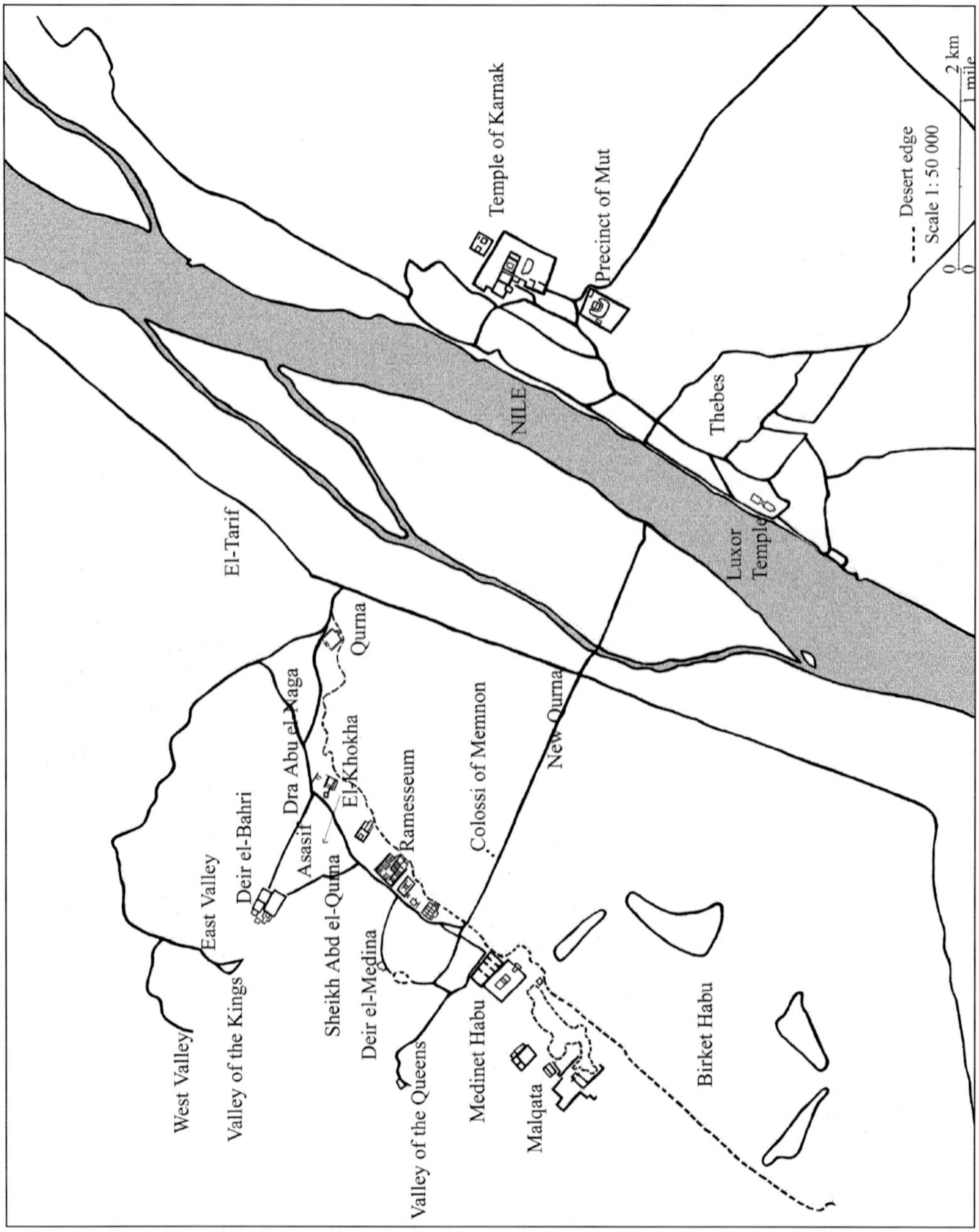

Map 2: Thebes. Based on Baines and Malek 1980.

Chapter 1

The nature of the deceased: constituent parts, character and iconography

The body of a man is very small compared with the spirit that inhabits it.[1]

In order to discuss ancestors, cults, and the relationship between the living and the dead, it is first necessary to consider what and who the dead were in Egyptian thought, and how they differed from the living in iconography and character. The essential elements of the living and the dead are listed in Table 1. Most aspects of the living were maintained beyond the grave, but acquired new meaning and focus in the transformative process from life to death.

Characteristics of and terminology relating to the dead

Death resulted in the fragmentation of the individual person, forcing apart the physical from the spiritual. According to Assmann,[2] a newly deceased person emerged in their various aspects or constituent elements, which took on a life of their own. The most important of these elements were the *ba*, *ka*, *ib*-heart,[3] name, shadow, and *akh*, along with the image/statue (*twt*), mummy (*sꜥḥ*), and corpse (*ẖꜣt*).[4] A unique text in the 18th Dynasty tomb of Amenemhet[5] includes five personifications of destiny, namely fate/destiny (*šꜣii*), lifetime (*ꜥḥꜥw*), birthplace (*msẖnt*),[6] development/fortune (*rnnt*), and 'personal creator god' (*ẖnmw*), as well as physical objects (such as offering stone, stela, tomb), and 'all his manifestations (*ẖprw.f nbw*)'.[7] Magic (*ḥkꜣ*) is another constituent part of the dead referred to alongside the *ba*, *akh* and shadow

1 African oral tradition: Föllmi and Föllmi 2005: 47.

2 2005: 87.

3 For the dead to become an *akh*, his moral character had to be tested, and it was the responsibility of his *ib*-heart to ensure that he was proven free (*šw*) of wrong-doing in the presence of Osiris (Book of the Dead, Spell 125; Faulkner 1985: 29–34).

4 Lloyd 1989: 118; Assmann 2005: 87. For an overview of the *ba*, *ka*, and *akh* see Smith 2009: 4–7.

5 TT 82: Porter and Moss 1960: 163–7; Gardiner and Davies 1915: pls 19, 23.

6 Roth and Roehrig 2002: 136–7.

7 Assmann 2005: 88–9.

Attributes of the living	Additional attributes gained after death	Objects created for the continuation of the dead in the world of the living	Other
Ka (*kꜣ*; vitality)	Corpse (*ḫꜣt*)	Tomb (*is, mꜥḥꜥt, ꜣḫt, mr*)	Heka (*ḥkꜣ*; magic)
Ba (*bꜣ*; movement)	Mummy (*sꜥḥ*)	Statues/statuettes (*twt*)	*Akh* (*ꜣḫ*; powerful state of entire being)
Name (*rn*; individuality)		Stelae (*ꜥḥꜥ, wḏ*)	
ib-heart (emotion, intellect, morality)		Offering tables (*ꜥbꜣ*)	
ḥꜣty-heart (physical organ)		Anthropoid busts (*twt*)	
ḫt-body (physical appearance)		Shabtis (*ušbty*)	
Shadow (*šwt*; movement)			

Table 1: Attributes of the living and the dead.

in the Coffin Texts,[8] and as something that should not be removed from the deceased in the afterlife in the Book of the Dead.[9] The many components of the dead person enabled him to pervade the entire cosmos,[10] and it is often not possible to differentiate between humans and deities in the underworld books because of the manner in which they are mixed together.[11] Equally, the blessed deceased may be identified as Sia, the personification of perception, who is shown on the right hand of Re.[12]

The only physical attribute acquired in death is the mummified corpse, which replaces the *ḫt*-body, and through the embalming process regains some of the deceased individual's physical appearance, with facial features being augmented by the mummy mask. Statues and statuettes, along with depictions on stelae, substituted for the visible form of the deceased (see Chapter 2), while emphasis is placed upon the *ka* and *ba* to replace the living essence and the deceased's ability to move and consume food and drink, capacities that were interrupted by the individual's death. Here I discuss in particular the *ba*, *akh*, and shadow, as these are the elements of the individual that could travel, and thus affect the living, and they are most frequently referred to in funerary literature.[13] John Gee has suggested that the terms *bꜣ*, *ꜣḫ*, and *nṯr* (god) were related

[8] See Etienne 2000. E.g. Coffin Texts Spell 491: de Buck 1956: 69, a; Faulkner 1977: 133; Žabkar 1968: 106, n. 107.

[9] E.g. Spells 32, 149, k1; Allen 1974: 42, 145.

[10] Žabkar 1968: 135, n. 61.

[11] Hornung 2008.

[12] Pyramid Texts 250, §268b: Goebs 2008: 257. See also Coffin Texts, Spells 958 and 1006: de Buck 1961: 176, 222.

[13] Coffin Texts, Spell 488: Faulkner 1977: 132; de Buck 1956: 67, a–b. Book of the Dead, Spell 91: Faulkner 1985: 86; Allen 1974: 75. Compare CT 413 (B2B0): Faulkner 1977: 64; 65, n. 5; de Buck 1953: 241 a–e, 242 a–c.

in the Egyptian mind in a hierarchical way.[14] While 'gods' in the sense of blessed dead are undoubtedly lower on the scale than major deities, to give individual characteristics ranks in this way may not be particularly meaningful; all parts were integral to the survival of the whole being.[15]

Constituent elements of the dead

The ba

The *ba* has been likened by Nadia el-Shohoumi to the modern Egyptian *rūḥ*,[16] and is defined by Žabkar in relation to the deceased (as opposed to the gods or the king) as a representation of an individual, 'the totality of his physical and psychic abilities':[17] personified in the Coffin Texts, it becomes a man's *alter ego*, and by performing physical functions for him, is one of the means by which he continues to live. Žabkar[18] was adamant that '*ba*' could not be translated as 'soul', either internal or external, and he considered the Egyptian concept of man to be *monistic*, not an element or form of manifestation of the man, but the man himself. His views have not been universally accepted, and most scholars still interpret *ba* as 'soul' or part of the spiritual and physical dimensions of an individual.[19] Žabkar[20] also rejected the idea that the *ba* existed during a person's lifetime, instead proposing that man lives in his *ba* after death, rather than possessing it while alive, which leads to a very different translation of certain texts such as the Instructions of Ptahhotep and the Instruction for King Merikare.[21] In support of Žabkar's hypothesis, it seems likely that the Dialogue Between a Man and his *Ba*[22] represents an introspective philosophical debate between a man and his conscience and reflects the beliefs and doubts of the period in which it was written.[23]

That the *ba* embodied the ability of the deceased to move around during the day is indicated by its avian form, initially represented by a jabiru stork,[24] which by the New Kingdom was often replaced by the human-headed falcon (Figure 1). A specific quality of the *ba* was also that it could assume any form it desired[25] as stated, for instance, in the Opening of the Mouth ritual.[26] The capacity of the *ba* to take flight was essential in enabling the deceased to communicate

14 2003: 231. Cf. Smith 2009: 5.
15 Zandee 1960: 19.
16 2004: 232–3. Compare Blackman 1927: 110.
17 1968: 3.
18 1968: 113, 130, 141, 162.
19 E.g. Assmann 2005: 89–90; 1989: 147; Lloyd 1989: 120; Baines 1991: 145; Parkinson 1998: 151.
20 1968: 116–18.
21 Lichtheim 1973: 73, 101, 106; Parkinson 1991: 52–4: 'The wise feeds his *ba* with what endures,/So that it is happy with him on earth'; 'The *ba* comes to the place it knows/ … It comes to those who give it water.'
22 Parkinson 1991: 132–3; Lichtheim 1973: 163–9; Allen 2011.
23 Ouellet 2007: 1441.
24 Janák 2006.
25 E.g. Frood 2007: 147.
26 Otto 1960: II, 194, kk; I, 160.

Figure 1: The tomb owner greets his ba. *The text behind the latter is a spell for 'being transformed into a living* ba'. *Tomb of Inherkhau (TT 359), Deir el-Medina, 20th Dynasty.*

with the gods and the dead,[27] and to ensure the preservation of the body through the provision of sustenance.[28] In the 19th Dynasty tomb of Paser the *ba* is depicted giving the breath of life to the mummified corpse as part of the embalming ritual.[29]

Baw – plural of *ba*[30] – is interpreted by Borghouts as a form of divine retribution documented by the expression *b3w nṯr ḫprw*, 'a manifestation of a god has come about',[31] and the *baw* in this sense may be understood as manifest in the *ba*. Whereas the king's divine status made it possible for him to send his *ba* to places where he was not physically present,[32] when ordinary citizens are said to send their *baw*[33] one may assume that they are doing so from or within the next world. The mobility of the *ba* could create problems for the living, perhaps in terms of some kind of haunting, or the disruption of daily life as indicated in O. IFAO 857, a question

27 E.g. Stewart 1986: pls. 4–6.

28 Cf. Žabkar 1968: 145–6.

29 TT 106; Porter and Moss 1960: 223 F [c]; Davies 1938: 30, fig. 9.

30 See e.g. Gee 2003: 232.

31 1982: 5–6. See also Žabkar 1968: 98, 161: *ba* as a manifestation of power in the Old Kingdom.

32 P. Anastasi II; Borghouts 1982: 13.

33 E.g. CT 99: Gee 2003: 230; de Buck 1938: 94 d.

presented to an oracle: 'is it the manifestation (*b3w*) of Anynakht?',[34] and seems unlikely that a passage on one side of an ostracon apparently concerned with a form of haunting by the *baw* is unrelated to the image of a *ba*-bird on the other side.[35]

Coffin Text spells reveal that the deceased was able to send his *ba* to appear before the living. In some cases rituals involving the burial of figurines were required, so presumably the dead relied on the living for this to be realised: [36]

> *Go forth, go forth, my* ba, *(so that) yonder man (may) see you.*
> *Appear opposite him in every place where he is.*
> *Rise up before him in the form of an* akh.
>
> *Words to be recited over an image of clay...*
> *Fashioned there, (with) the name of the man on it,*
> *and (placed) in the ground, the ground.*

Middle Kingdom parallels to Book of the Dead Spells 92 and 188[37] indicate that the *ba* can appear before someone in human form, and be able to enter his house. Fear that the *ba* may leave the corpse and not return is apparent in Book of the Dead, Spell 89, which specifies that an amulet of gold and precious stones[38] should be placed on the mummy's breast to prevent it from departing. The same concern is shown in the design of several shabtis, which depict the *ba* resting as though partially merged with the deceased.[39]

The Teaching for King Merikare, dated to the Middle Kingdom, suggests that the *ba's* behaviour is to some extent governed by familiarity and necessity: 'The *ba* comes to the place it knows,/ It does not miss its former path,/ No kind of magic holds it back,/ It comes to those who give it water'.[40] The *ba* is also a means by which the deceased could perpetuate his rebirth. David O'Connor proposed that erotic meaning was encoded in tomb decoration for the purpose of ensuring rebirth:[41]

> *deceased Egyptians achieved ... perpetual regeneration and rebirth ... by impregnating their deceased wives who – following paradigms based on solar and other mythology – would conceive, and then give birth to a renewed form of the deceased himself. The maintaining of sexual potency and the achievement of intercourse and orgasm was therefore of great importance to deceased males, and magically effective means of ensuring these had to be supplied.*

The concern of the dead to be able to engage in sexual activity is expressed in mortuary texts, and copulating in the form of one's *ba* (*nk m b3*) is mentioned in both the Coffin Texts and

---

[34] Borghouts 1982: 22.

[35] Cairo CG 25106; Borghouts 1982: 24. See also O. Abd el-Qurna 12202, a text that mentions the *baw* of Amun-Re as a negative force: Borghouts 1982: 9. For the *ba* in relation to Theban Amun-Re theology, see Assmann 1995: 133–55.

[36] CT 103: de Buck 1938: 110, i–l. Cf. Gee 2003: 230; Faulkner 1973: 101; the London Medical Papyrus BM EA 10059, lines 3–5 (Leitz 1999: 57). For the cultic aspect of the *ba* and *ba*-summoning in the New Kingdom, see Kessler 2001.

[37] Allen 1974: 76, 211; cf. Faulkner 1985: 185.

[38] Allen 1974: 75. E.g. BM EA 3361: Ikram and Dodson 1998: pl. xiv.

[39] E.g. Stewart 1995: 23, fig. 20.

[40] Lichtheim 1973: 97, 101.

[41] 1996: 630.

the Book of the Dead.[42] The deceased in *ba* and shadow form had the ability to have sexual intercourse with the living,[43] which seems to have been one of the reasons that they were feared, particularly by pregnant women,[44] presumably because of the risk of miscarriage. According to the Calendar of Good and Bad Days, death by copulation was a possibility on certain dates, though the reason is not specified.[45]

The *ba* as protector of the corpse is illustrated in funerary papyri vignettes, where it is depicted hovering over the mummy, holding the *shen*-symbol of eternity in its talons.[46] Through its falcon-like appearance, the *ba* is reminiscent of Horus and thus, like the *akh*, associated with the sun and renewal. This solar connection is emphasised on the 21st Dynasty coffin of Amenemopet, which bears a depiction of a *ba*-bird with the gilded *tp*-face representative of Re and human limbs holding aloft the horizon.[47] The interior of another 21st Dynasty coffin shows a *ba*-bird with a human head and legs flanked by the inscription 'going forth as a living *ba*'; its position at the base of the coffin meant that the deceased lay in its embrace.[48]

In several Book of the Dead papyri, the *ba* is shown to be present at the weighing of the heart ceremony, where it functioned as a witness for the deceased.[49] Obtaining a successful result enabled the dead to separate into the constituent parts that would allow him to progress into the afterlife: 'Your *ba* to heaven, your corpse to the underworld'.[50] As Assmann states: 'The separation of *ba* and corpse was one of the goals of the transfiguration rituals, and was part of the transformation of the deceased into transfigured ancestral spirits'.[51] The unique painting in the tomb of Nakhtamun[52] may be an illustration of this separation process, the human winged form representing the union of *akh* (in human form) and *ba*. This division also enabled the deceased to be reborn like Re.[53] This involvement of the soul in the circuit of the sun is apparent in the Book of the Night, attested from the 19th Dynasty, where the Western *ba*s are said to tow the sun god into the sky.[54]

---

42 For texts relating to copulation in *ba*-form, see Gee 2003: 233; Žabkar 1968: 101–3, e.g. CT 193 (de Buck 1947: 109 d), CT 503 (Faulkner 1977: 134, 141), CT 96 (de Buck 1938: 78–81, B1L, B1Ca). Other texts relating to the sexual activity of the deceased include CT 576 (Faulkner 1977: 181; de Buck 1956: 191) and Book of the Dead, Spell 175 (Allen 1974: 184).

43 E.g. CT 71: de Buck 1935: 297, T2C d–e; Žabkar 1968: 98.

44 Leitz 1999: 68, pl. 34, lines 4–7.

45 Troy 1989: 136.

46 E.g. Stewart 1986: pl. 15; cf. Faulkner 1985: 90.

47 UC 15703: Stewart 1986: pl. 10. For the face of Re, see for example the eleventh hour of the Book of Gates: Hornung 1999: 76, fig. 40; cf. Ikram and Dodson 1998: 186, fig. 216; Volokhine 2000: 22–3, 75–6. The same motif also occurs on beaded masks covering the faces of mummies (e.g. Liverpool Head no. 19; Gray and Slow 1968: 67, pl. 98).

48 Stewart 1986: pl. 7; Volokhine 2000: 90–1. See also Taylor 1989: 44, fig. 34; Schäfer 1986: 208, fig. 213.

49 E.g. Ani; Russmann 2001: 198, no. 102; Žabkar 1968: 147.

50 Žabkar 1968: 131.

51 2005: 91.

52 TT 341: Davies and Gardiner 1948: pl. xxvi; Porter and Moss 1960: 408 [2].

53 Assmann 2005: 93; cf. Žabkar 1968: 106–12, 151.

54 Hornung 1999: 135; cf. Assmann 2001: 65; Roulin 1998: 1008–9. In the Coffin Texts the close relationship between the sun god and the *ba* is mentioned; the latter is said to be 'with Re daily' (Faulkner 1977: 135; cf. *ibid.*: 136–8).

The deceased could play senet with his *ba*,[55] a game that became linked with the passage of Re through the underworld in the 20th Dynasty. This board game was used as a means of communication between the living and the dead at least from the Old Kingdom.[56] CT 405 states in relation to the deceased:[57]

> *Let him sing, let him dance, and let him receive ornaments,*
> *Let him play senet with those on earth.*
> *It is his voice that is heard but he cannot be seen.*

The phrase 'It is his voice that is heard but he cannot be seen' also occurs in relation to Osiris in the Book of the Dead Spell 1B, a spell for going forth by day or 'causing that the mummy descend to the netherworld on the day of joining the earth' (i.e. on the day of burial).[58]

Although *baw* are often said to be 'living', the 19th Dynasty Book of the Dead of Herunefer refers to 'dead *ba*s (*b3w mwt*)',[59] presumably meaning the *baw* of the wretched or malevolent dead, which in the Books of the Day and Night, Caverns, and Gates, are described as the souls of the enemies of Re and Osiris, 'the damned ones, whose tortured and mutilated corpses, Shadows, and *Ba*s are turned upside down in the Place of Destruction'.[60] *Bas* were unable to speak, instead making a bird-like noise or a sound of distress, as indicated on the cosmological ceiling in the temple of Sety I at Abydos: 'these birds, whose faces are like those of men and whose nature is like that of birds, one of them speaks to the other with words of weeping'.[61] Shadows equally did not have a voice with which they would be able to communicate with the living, producing only a whispering or buzzing sound, or screaming (*sbḥ)* when in pain.[62] The only aspect of the deceased able to communicate directly with the living was the *akh*.

The akh

The *akh* was not so much an element of the deceased as the transfigured deceased in his entirety who had attained the status of an ancestor, was able to communicate with the living, and appeared before them in corporeal form.[63] The meaning of *3ḫ* seems to stem from two roots: the initial essence of 'to shine', and related solar imagery,[64] and the broader notion of what is 'beneficial', 'effective'.[65] Both are relevant to the spirits of the dead, who were intrinsically bound to the solar cycle,[66] and could be efficacious in their communication and arbitration with/for the living.[67]

---

55 E.g. the New Kingdom stela of Wepwawetmose (Vienna no. 55): Piccione 1994: 198.

56 Piccione 1994: 197–8.

57 De Buck 1954: 209–10; Assmann 2005: 213; Piccione 1994: 197.

58 Allen 1974: 6–7.

59 Spell 183: Žabkar 1968: 142.

60 Žabkar 1968: 143; cf. Hornung 1968: 29–30.

61 Žabkar 1968: 147.

62 Amduat, 8th Hour: Zandee 1960: 63; 11th Hour: Hornung and Abt 2007: 349.

63 Spell 64, Book of the Dead: Demarée 1983: 252, n. 295; Friedman 1994: 114; Allen 1974: 59. For the interaction between the *akhu* and the living, see Smith 1989: 124–5.

64 Janák 2006.

65 Friedman 1982: 145–6.

66 The dead shared some of Re's attributes, as indicated in Coffin Texts Spell 44 (Goebs 2008: 201; de Buck 1935: 181g), 'for being transfigured into an *akh* with radiance like Re (*s3ḫ m stt mi rˁ*)'.

67 Goebs 2008: 201.

Coffin Texts Spell 99 indicates that the dead appeared to the living in *akh* form:[68]

Go my ba, in order that that man may see you, as he passes his life (ꜥḥꜥ ḥmsi); (appear) in front of his sight [literally 'face'] in my form and in my true nature as a living akh

This concept is also found in Book of the Dead Spell 64, which states that the *akh* would appear in the shape of a living person:[69]

I have come forth as a powerful[70] *akh*
(but) I am seen in my human form

Statues and other representations of the deceased thus depict them in *akh* (transfigured) form, and the act of 'feeding the *akh*' (*snmt ꜣḫ*) was performed through the medium of the statue.[71] This implies a complex relationship between the *akh* and the *ka*: while both could be present to receive offerings simultaneously, it was the *akh* that the living saw, the *ka* being the invisible force within the image.

As an inducement to continue to provide frequent offerings, essential to both deities and the dead, the living were promised preferential treatment in the afterlife. Passages in the Book of Gates, for instance, indicate that Re will secure protection and *akh*-status for those who present offerings to him during their lifetime, and that after death they will be able to partake of offerings upon earth.[72] Without such divine assistance, one needed identification with a god (particularly Re or Osiris), special knowledge, or the recitation of particular formulae (*sꜣḫw*)[73] by qualified priests in order to become an *akh*.[74]

One of the most important features of the *akh* was its ability to communicate with the living – a feature seemingly not shared by the *ka*, *ba*, or shadow. Thus, when the deceased states:[75] 'I will speak to you, who exist upon earth and who will come to be …',[76] he is probably referring to himself in his *akh*-form. According to the Amduat:[77]

The one who knows this mysterious image will be a well-provisioned akh.
He will always leave and enter the netherworld, and speak to the living.

This spirit in human shape is depicted on *akh iqer en re* stelae (Figure 2), and is probably also represented by anthropoid busts (Chapter 2).[78] It may be significant that the *akhu* shown on

---

68 De Buck 1938: 94, e–f; cf. CT 101, Gee 2002: 85; 2003: 230.

69 Donnat 2003: 38; cf. Friedman 1994: 114; Allen 1974: 59.

70 A translation of 'powerful' for *iqer* is preferred here to the usual interpretation ('effective'), as this better conveys the sense of the *akh's* potency (see Demarée 1983: 195–7).

71 Friedman 1995: 86–90; Demarée 1983: 205.

72 Wente 1984: 167, 170, 172.

73 E.g. O. Turin 57003: McDowell 1999: 160. For transfiguration hymns see Assmann 1986: 998–1006; Assmann 2005: 244.

74 Demarée 1983: 243–4.

75 Frood 2007: 144.

76 Tomb of Nefersekheru at Zawyet el-Sultan: Osing 1992: pl. 35.

77 Lines 297–299; Wente 1982: 166; Hornung and Abt 2007: 424.

78 The role of *akhu* as intermediaries between gods and mortals is alluded to in some *akh iqer* stelae where the deceased is depicted in the presence of a deity, but not in a pose indicative of adoration; see for example Schulman 1986: 325–6.

Figure 2: Typical akh iqer *pose, though the deceased holds an* ankh *rather than a folded cloth. Stela of Panakht. Deir el-Medina, 19th Dynasty. Louvre E 16367.*

stelae[79] sometimes wear unguent cones.[80] Although rock-cut tomb statues are not specifically identified in inscriptions as showing the tomb owner and his family in the form of *akhu*, some of them have cones (Figure 3),[81] suggesting there might be an iconographic link between statues and stelae, particularly at Thebes where the stelae are prevalent.[82]

Despite the power of the *akh*, indicated by their role as the 'bodyguards of Osiris' with the authority to detain *ba*s and shadows,[83] there seems to have been some ambivalence over *akh*-

[79] E.g. Chicago 14649; Schulman 1986: 230, no. A60; Stewart 1976: pl. 36, 2.

[80] See Joan Padgham (2012) *A New Interpretation of the Cone on the Head in New Kingdom Egyptian Tomb Scenes*, Archaeopress, Oxford.

[81] E.g. Neferrenpet, TT 178 and Nefersekheru, TT 296: Hofmann 2004: pl. ix.

[82] Demarée 1983: 279.

[83] Žabkar 1968: 137, n. 75.

status, and it is instructive that the word '*akh*' developed into the Coptic term for 'demon'.[84] The Calendar of Good and Bad Days relates in several cases specifically to the *akhu*.[85] Their negative aspect is suggested in these texts, which give orders to 'appease (*sht*)' and 'pacify (*sḥtp*)' the *akhu*[86] – implying that they can be angered. The texts specifically mention that voice offerings (*prt-ḫrw*) should be presented to these spirits. This offering is made at the time when Osiris is rejuvenated and able to accept offerings,[87] suggesting an association between the risen god and the *akhu*.

A description of the *akh* as a disruptive force is found in the Instruction of Ani:[88]

> *Satisfy the* akh*; do what he desires,*
> *And abstain for him from his abominations,*
> *That you may be safe from his many harms.*
> *Every misfortune is his.*
> *The head of cattle is taken from the field?*
> *It was he who did it (lit. has done the like).*
> *Any damage (to) the threshing floor in the fields?*
> *'It is the* akh*!' they say again.*
> *Uproar in the house? Hearts are discouraged?*
> *All these are his doing.*

A less well-known magical text from Deir el-Medina addressed to a malignant spirit describes the indiscriminate nature of the *akh* as a destructive force:[89]

> *You enter heaven and then you eat all the stars that are in it.*
> *You sit down on the soil and then you dislodge the seed which people have sown in it.*
> *You stretch your hand toward the desert and you kill all the game that is in it.*
> *You are put on the border of the sea and you make all the fish die that are in it.*

The *akhu* collectively acted as a judicial body, particularly in afterlife tribunals,[90] with their primary role being the evaluation of the newly deceased. Mortuary texts, especially the appeals to the living, indicate that they could also judge and punish those still on earth:[91]

> *All who enter my [tomb] in their impurity and who have eaten what an eminent spirit (ꜣḫ iḳr) detests, ... I shall seize his neck like that of a bird, putting fear into him, so that the spirits which are on earth, see it and fear ... an eminent spirit*

In this role, the dead act as moral guides, punishing breaches of rules and reinforcing the social status quo.[92]

---

[84] *iḫy*: Demarée 1983: 194; Koenig 1979: 113–4.

[85] Leitz 1994: 191 n. 77, 231, 233.

[86] Troy 1989: 145.

[87] Leitz 1994: 191.

[88] P. Bulaq IV, 22, 1–3: Quack 1994: 114–7, 182–3, 324–5 (plates); McDowell 1999: 104; Demarée 1983: 269. Quack (1994: 115) translates *akh* as 'demon'.

[89] P. Turin 1995 and 1996, recto 5.8–10: Borghouts 1994: 126; Pleyte and Rossi 1869–75: 124.

[90] Willems 2001: 341–2.

[91] Sixth Dynasty tomb of Khentika: Zandee 1960: 34, 197; Sethe 1906: 260, 12. The dead as judges of both the living and the dead may be related to their association with the sun god (as *ꜣḫw iḳrw n rꜥ*), because Re also acts in a judicial capacity (Zandee 1960: 34; Donnat 2003: 242–50).

[92] Cf. Smith 2008: 192, re. comparable Aboriginal beliefs.

The shadow

The shadow was an essential part of the living person that took on great importance in death, and shared with the *ba* the responsibility of fetching food for the corpse.[93] The *akh* was said to possess a shadow in the Book of Gates: one who offers to them on earth 'is a powerful excellent *akh*, who possesses a shadow',[94] either implying a close association between the two or suggesting that the *akh*, as a transfigured person, was able to retain the shadow he possessed in life.

The shadow has a solar connection, being the image of a person on the ground, the most powerful of divine manifestations.[95] In Amarna beliefs, the shadow was a visible expression of Re/solar energy.[96] It is pictured in Book of the Dead, Spell 92 leaving the tomb and 'going out into the day' in the company of the *ba* (Figure 4).[97] The shadow had a close affinity with the *ba*, and they were judged together in the netherworld.[98] The destruction of the shadow by knives or by being devoured by a demon[99] suggests that the *šwt* was understood as corporeal rather than ethereal, and the fact that the extermination of the shadow leads to the annihilation of the entire being[100] shows how fundamental it was to the continued existence of the deceased. Shadows were considered to be in some way attached to the deceased (even though they were depicted as independent of one another), because they could be 'cut off'.[101]

Book of the Dead Spell 188, a spell for sending forth the soul and going forth by day as a man, states:[102] 'You have blessed me with a (*ba*)-soul and shadow, so that we may be seen yonder.' Coffin Texts Spell 413 is a request for the divinisation of the *ba* and the shadow,[103] again suggesting that these two entities are closely connected in Egyptian thought. The association between the *ba* and the shadow and their relationship with the corpse in turn may partly explain the sexual aspect of the shadow. There are a few texts in which the word *šwt* associated with a god describes the sexual power of that deity.[104] The connection between the shadow and the sexual aspect of the deceased may explain why the shadow is depicted with a penis in some vignettes to the Book of the Dead Spell 92,[105] going forth in the day, when the shadow was free to walk the earth at will before returning to the corpse in the evening.

---

[93] Lloyd 1989: 119; Zandee 1960: 182. See Blackman (1927: 113), El-Shohoumi (2004: 86), and Ogden (2001: 219, 223) for shadow-equivalents and beliefs about shadows in 20th century and modern Egypt and the Greek and Roman worlds.

[94] *m 3ḫ iḳr sḫm šwt*: Wente 1982: 172.

[95] Goyon 2000: 15.

[96] Mantellini 2007: 1239.

[97] Allen 1974: 76; Herbin 2000: 7. E.g. P. Neferubenef, Louvre N 3092: Herbin 2000: 7.

[98] Assmann 2005: 112; Žabkar 1960: 182.

[99] Žabkar 1960: 183.

[100] Žabkar 1960: 20.

[101] E.g. BD 191; Allen 1974: 214.

[102] After Allen 1974: 211.

[103] Faulkner 1977: 64.

[104] Žabkar 1968: 104.

[105] E.g. P. Neferrenpet: Speleers 1917: pl. xxvii.

Figure 3: Rock-cut statues wearing unguent cones. Tomb of Neferrenpet (TT 178), Khokha, 19th Dynasty.

Figure 4: Ba *leaving and returning to the tomb, and shadow with phallus. Tomb of Amennakht (TT 218), Deir el-Medina, Ramesside. Altenmüller 1990: 16, fig. 6. Reproduced with the kind permission of Hartwig Altenmüller.*

The ka

According to Jan Assmann, the fundamental differences between the *ka* and *ba* are that:[106] 'the *ba* belonged to the physical sphere of the deceased, restoring his movement and his ability to take on form, while the *ka* belonged to his social sphere and restored his status, honor and dignity… It was soul, protective spirit, and doppelgänger, all rolled into one'. The importance of progeny is expressed through this element of the individual, since the *ka* was passed on through successive generations.[107] Unlike the *akh*, however, the *ka* was shown as an abstract concept – either the symbol itself (two arms joined in the centre with bent elbows and lower arms apparently upraised, palms facing outwards), or as a person wearing the hieroglyph on his head. While the king's 'double' is regularly depicted,[108] however, the *ka* of elite individuals is not explicitly shown (or at least not captioned) and its presence is suggested in more subtle ways, often as the sign on a standard; between the arms food, lilies and bowls of incense may be piled, as though the *ka* is embracing the offerings (Figure 5). In the early 18th Dynasty tomb of Ahmose son of Ibana at Elkab, the tomb owner is captioned as 'reaching for his *ka*',[109] combining the imagery of his next-worldly self and the nourishment needed to sustain it.

The arms of the *ka* hieroglyph are outstretched in a gesture of embracing, not upraised as it might appear.[110] The gesture is mentioned in the Pyramid Texts:[111] 'Atum put your arms around Pepi Neferkare as *ka*-arms, so that the *ka* of Pepi Neferkare might be in it, firm for the course of eternity. Ho, Atum! May you extend protection over this Pepi Neferkare, and prevent anything bad from happening to it for the course of eternity, like you extended protection over Shu and Tefnut.' According to one myth, Atum created Shu and Tefnut by embracing them and imparting his 'vital force' [*ka*].[112] Embracing as a means of transferring life and protection to the recipient is suggested in the speech of the *ankh*-holding Goddess of the West in the tomb of Amenemhet:[113] 'twice welcome to me in peace, that I may embrace you and enfold you in my arms, and command life [for your …]. Truly I will be a protection for your flesh, and my arms will encircle you for ever and ever.' This imagery is reminiscent of Nut embracing the mummified corpse in coffins.[114] Given that the act of embracing was a way of transmitting *ka* force, it may be significant that during the daily cult ritual, the officiant embraced the statue, entering the shrine and inserting his outstretched arms.[115] Naophorus statues may also be part of this tradition, with the statue-owner shown embracing the cult image of a deity in its shrine,[116] as might the ceremonial garment worn

---

106 2005: 97. He also describes the *ka* as 'the vehicle of vindication that restored the individual's status as a social person' after death (*ibid.*).

107 2005: 44.

108 Greven 1954.

109 West wall; Lorton 1999: 180–1; Porter and Moss 1937: 182 with reference.

110 Assmann 2005: 101; Hornung 1992: 175.

111 PT 600, a spell for the protection of the pyramid of Pepy II: Allen 2005a: 269. See also Lesko 1991: 92; Heiden 2003: 310.

112 Lorton 1999: 182.

113 TT 82: Gardiner and Davies 1915: 48, pl. x.

114 E.g. BM EA 24906, 22nd Dynasty: Taylor 2003: fig. 58. Cf. Sugi 2003 on the theme of embracing and giving life.

115 Lorton 1999: 141.

116 Van Dijk 1993: 125.

Figure 5: Offerings embraced by the ka*-sign. Tomb of Nakhtamun (TT 341), Sheikh Abd el-Qurna, 19th Dynasty. After Davies and Gardiner 1948: pl. xxviii.*

by the *sem*-priest during the Opening of the Mouth ritual[117] (following his overnight stay in the tomb) known as *ḳni*, which is a homophone of a root meaning 'embrace/to embrace'.[118]

Like the *ba* and *akh*, the *ka* could be a negative force. The *ka* of a god, for example, could punish the living, such as the workman Nakhtamun at Deir el-Medina:[119] 'I made for him praises to [Amun's] name … On behalf of the draftsman Nakhtamun, justified, who lay sick unto death, <in> the power of Amun, through his sin. … May your *ka* be kind (*w3ḥ k3.k*), may you forgive, it shall not happen again.' The *ka* of the deceased presumably also needed propitiation, hence offerings were made 'for the *ka* of' a dead person from the Old Kingdom onwards.[120]

Andrew Gordon describes the *ka* as an 'animating life force',[121] an 'impersonal vital energy that makes the world live and function.' One source of this force is food.[122] Living animals, such as the calf whose foreleg is severed and offered to the deceased,[123] or freshly killed ones, particularly bulls (themselves *k3w*), would contain a great deal of [*ḥk3*] energy which could be

117 Scenes 11–19; Assmann 2003a: 56; Fischer-Elfert 1998: 6, 40–3.

118 Faulkner 1962: 279–80.

119 Lichtheim 1976: 106–7, 108.

120 Gordon 1996: 34. In reference to BD 105 (spell for appeasing the *ka* in the necropolis), Janák (2003: 195) rejects the translation of 'appease' or 'propitiate' for *sḥtp*, because he believes that this incorrectly 'presumes a negative position of the *ka*'. He prefers to translate 'to appease by an offering', but the essential meaning remains the same.

121 1996: 35.

122 *k3w*; see also Roth 1992: 126.

123 E.g. the Papyrus of Hunefer: Champdor 1963: 148.

transferred to the living or the dead.[124] If this is the case, it could explain why bulls led for sacrifice in tomb scenes are depicted with a water lily blossom, symbolising life, around their necks;[125] through their death, the tomb owner could experience rebirth. The foreleg was used during the Opening of the Mouth ceremony to revivify the mummiform deceased; it was part of equipment that included feathers, an adze, a finger, and sacred oils, which were all designed to bring about rebirth.[126]

Iconography: Distinguishing the dead from the living

From the Old Kingdom onward, the tomb owner was distinguished by his greater size in proportion to other figures,[127] by facing in a different direction to others, such as offering bearers, and often by some form of barrier.[128] The greater size of the deceased in relation to other people is explicable in terms of the tomb owner's higher rank or importance than those around him,[129] but also the anticipation of gaining physical stature in the afterlife.[130] The 'partition' between figures of the living and the dead may be in the form of an offering table, columns of text, or items held by the deceased, particularly staves. Papyrus kiosks are sometimes used to separate the tomb owner (and his wife) from activities going on around him. In the tomb of Rekhmire,[131] the tomb owner's mother, who predeceased him, is distinguished from the other banquet guests by being seated before her own offering table and served separately, as well as by the *m3ʿ-ḫrw* (*maa-kheru*) epithet.

The use of *maa-kheru* as a designation of the dead is disputed, not least because it appears alongside images of people still alive when the inscription was written.[132] In theory, the epithet *maa-kheru*, 'true of voice', indicated that the person had passed through the judgement process successfully and could become a glorified ancestor and join the other blessed dead who themselves judged the dead in the law courts of the netherworld.[133] According to Thomas Allen,[134] the title 'carries an overtone of magic, for it amounts to an advance verdict of innocence at the judgment of the dead described in Spell 125.' Given the element of propaganda and

---

[124] Gordon 1996: 35.

[125] E.g. Davies and Gardiner 1936: pl. lix.

[126] See Roth 1993.

[127] Kanawati 1981: 216–21.

[128] See Seidelmayer 2001 for a discussion of the iconography of the dead in the Old and Middle Kingdoms.

[129] Kanawati 1981: 222.

[130] Hornung 2008. This idea may be supported by the presence of oversized shirts in 18th Dynasty burials, see e.g. Hayes 1959: 187.

[131] TT 100: Davies 1943: pl. lxvi.

[132] For this reason, Schulman (1984: 179, 181) translated the phrase as '[he] who will be justified'.

[133] Zandee 1960: 40, 273. It is worth noting that the judgement was not religious in the sense of atoning for sins against gods (as found on votive stelae of the New Kingdom, thought to indicate 'personal piety'), but rather secular: the deceased is tested for his moral goodness, to ensure that he has not committed acts against *maat*, i.e. the social order (Allen 1988: 47).

[134] 1974: 3.

self-aggrandisement evident in many Egyptian monuments,[135] it is not surprising that when commissioning inscriptions for their monuments elite individuals emphasised their high moral stature by describing themselves as guaranteed to survive legal processes in the afterlife. The tomb owner and his wife are most commonly captioned *maa-kheru*, as are the deceased depicted on stelae and deceased children shown with their parents. The use of the phrase in association with banquet guests and musicians are sometimes may be intended to indicate the liminal nature of feasts that took place simultaneously in the worlds of the living and the dead (see Chapter 4).

Individuals explicitly identified as deceased are often depicted holding an object, usually a strip of cloth, the stem of a water lily blossom, a sceptre, or less frequently, an *ankh*. None of these items should be considered as objects in their own right; their purpose was to pictorially express the divine status attained by the deceased, and emphasise the powers he possesses as an *akh*. The (fringed) cloth indicates divine perception, the water lily the ability to be reborn and deceased's affinity with the sun god, the *sekhem*-sceptre represents power (Figure 6),[136] and the *ankh* eternal life. Tomb owners (who are predominantly male) often carry a staff in one hand and a folded cloth or sceptre in the other. In her analysis of the iconography of masculinity, Gay Robins notes that:[137] 'The figure of the standing man holding a staff and cloth forms the determinative for the word *sr*, 'official', while as a hieroglyph, the scepter determines the words *sḫm*, 'power', and *ḫrp*, 'to control'. Thus the staff, cloth, and scepter are symbols of authority referring to the elite male's role in the ruling bureaucracy.' A person may also hold, or be presented with, a miniature ship's mast with its sail billowing to show that they possess the breath of life.[138] Often the deceased reaches towards a table of offerings, palm downwards, in a gesture of ownership rather than one of requesting (Figure 7);[139] perhaps to suggest that the individual is supplied with food and does not need to rely on the living to provide it. The symbols and gestures create an image of the blessed dead as equipped (*ꜥpr*) and divine (*nṯr*), thus capable of acting on behalf of (or against) the living.

The depiction of non-royal individuals holding the *ankh* seems to have been introduced in the First Intermediate Period;[140] by the Middle Kingdom stelae were decorated with the symbol, which formed a central feature[141] of the monuments. The stela of Amenyseneb from his tomb[142] at Abydos, for example, is similar in content and style to the 'chapel stela' of Senwosret, which consists of three separate limestone blocks and is decorated with scenes of banquets, fishing and fowling, and the owner's funeral, and could be described as a precursor of New Kingdom tomb

[135] Simpson 1982. The biographical inscription of Nefersekheru in his tomb at Zawyet el-Sultan states with some irony: 'every man boasts about himself in his own writing' (Frood 2007: 146).

[136] It was also considered to be among the components of a deceased individual (Budge 1924: 25–6).

[137] 2008: 211.

[138] *ṯꜣw n ꜥnḫ*: Fischer 1973: 27. E.g. Sennedjem, TT 1: Bovot 2002: 307. See also the image of the *ba* presenting the breath of life to the mummified corpse in the 19th Dynasty tomb of Paser, TT 106 (Davies 1938: 30, fig. 9).

[139] E.g. the Old Kingdom rock-cut bust of Idu; Simpson 1976: pl. xxix.

[140] Fischer 1973: 23; 26 n. 49.

[141] Vienna ÄS 109, a large carved *ankh* surrounded by figures of the deceased (Bröckelmann 2006: 6); Kitchen 1961: pls ii and iii ; Bourriau 1988: 60–3, no. 48; Baines 2009: 21–22, figs 4a, b; Bomann 1991: fig. 84; Cairo CG 20353: Hawass and Garrett 2002: 37.

[142] Or offering chapel according to Bourriau 1988: 63.

Figure 6: Tomb owner holding a staff and sceptre. Tomb of Ramose (TT 55), Sheikh Abd el-Qurna, 18th Dynasty.

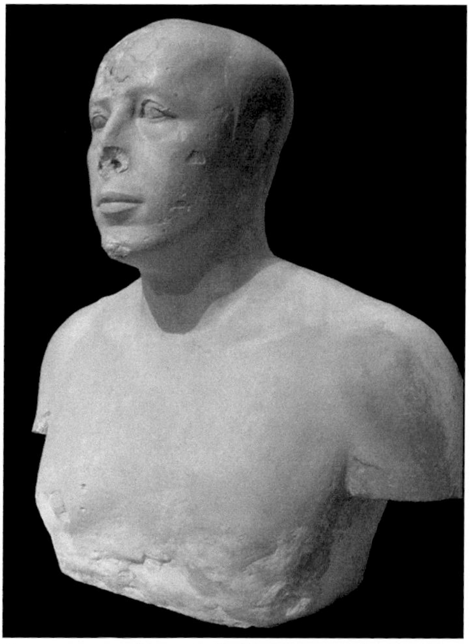

Figure 7: Bust of Ankhhaf, whose separately modelled arms would have been extended, palms upward, as though requesting the presentation of offerings. Plastered and painted limestone. Giza, Eastern Cemetery, tomb G 7510. 4th Dynasty. 50.5 cm high. Museum of Fine Arts, Boston 27.442.

scenes.[143] The shabtis of private individuals from the Middle Kingdom onwards were occasionally represented holding the symbol of life instead of the typical agricultural implements,[144] a trend that continued into the New Kingdom.[145]

The New Kingdom saw the introduction of explicitly labelled *akh iqer* stelae[146] and the occasional representation of the deceased holding an *ankh*[147] in preference to the usual strip of cloth.[148] In his tomb at Deir el-Medina, Inherkhau is shown with an *ankh* suspended from his hand while he is accepting offerings (Figure 8). A New Kingdom stela from Abydos shows a woman offering to a deceased couple who are seated behind an offering table, reaching toward them with one hand and holding an *ankh* in the other, as if she is giving life (although not as explicitly as a deity). There are no texts to identify the woman or the *sem*-priest behind her, though she may be their daughter.[149] An 18th Dynasty stela from Thebes depicts a man receiving an *ankh* from his son and two daughters, while his mother passes an *ankh* to his father.[150] On a wooden painted shabti-box of the 20th Dynasty, the owner is depicted carrying the feather of Maat in one hand and an *ankh* in the other prior to being presented to Osiris.[151] By the 21st Dynasty, non-royals were shown holding *ankhs* on stelae and on the interior decoration of coffins.[152] In three-dimensions, the deceased is sometimes depicted wearing an *ankh* pendant,[153] and private statues incorporating *ankhs* are known from Ptolemaic times.[154]

The New Kingdom saw the introduction of the *ankh* in floral bouquets, carried in procession or offered to the deceased and the gods.[155] The *ankh*-symbol in this period is sometimes associated with the *ba* of the deceased, as exemplified in the head-end of a coffin, where it is held in combination with the feather of Maat,[156] and the ascending *ba/akh* of Nakhtamun (TT 341, Figure 9).[157] The apparent connection between possessing an *ankh* and being a blessed spirit may explain some vignettes from the Book of the Dead where the deceased is shown holding

---

143 Louvre C16-18: Kitchen 1961: 17.

144 Stewart 1995: 39; Peet 1914: pl. 13.3. Renseneb also holds a *hes*-vase, the hieroglyph for 'favour' (Bourriau 1988: 99–100, no. 83).

145 E.g. Berman 1999: 343, 345, nos 256, 257 (18th Dynasty). Berman considers the *ankhs* held by the loops to be 'a holdover from the Amarna period' (*ibid*., 344).

146 Demarée 1983.

147 The much later Liturgy of Opening of the Mouth for Breathing (dating to the 1st century AD) states: 'Maat will be placed on your body, a mirror of gold at your left side, and an *ankh* at your right … You will go forth because of your amulets and achieve a state of blessedness'; Smith 1993: 31.

148 Schulman 1986: 339–340, no. C21 (BM EA 932), an *akh iqer*-style stela dated to the 18th Dynasty.

149 Lacau 1909: pl. xxxv, no. 34.059.

150 Fischer 1973: 25.

151 Botti 1932: pl. 27b.

152 E.g. Saleh and Sourouzian 1987: no. 238.

153 Bovot 2003: 15; Parkinson 1999: 120–1; Fischer 1976: 127. For the *ankh* as an emblem, see Fischer 1972.

154 Fischer 1973: 27, n. 59.

155 Fischer 1973: 25; Polz 1988: fig. 14; JE 34.120 (Catalogue du Musée); Pischikova 1994: 71; Hartwig 2004: 234, fig. 33; cf. Queen Tiye, who holds an *ankh*-shaped bouquet in the tomb of Anen (TT 120), but a plain *ankh* in the tomb of Kheruef (TT 192); Davies 1928–9: fig. 1.

156 Schäfer 1986: 208, fig. 213; Volokhine 2000: 166, fig. 115. See also the 19th/20th Dynasty *ba* pectoral of Sutymose (Bouquillon *et al.* 2005: 16, no. 6, Louvre AF 13043).

157 Davies and Gardiner 1948: pl. xxvi; Smith 1998: 221, fig. 376.

the symbol, presumably having passed the judgement and been transformed into an *akh*[158] or, in the case of Neferrenpet, a god.[159] Other than Fischer's (1973) study of Cairo JE 88876 and related material, little attention seems to have been paid to the appearance of the *ankh*-symbol in non-royal contexts, and the subject would benefit from further research.

In some royal and private imagery, the folded cloth that is often held by the deceased is substituted with an *ankh* or other symbol. The interchange between the cloth and the *ankh* on the *akh iqer* stelae of Panakht and Ptahhesy (Figures 2 and 10) is paralleled by scenes in the tomb of Sety I; priests are shown performing the Opening of the Mouth ritual on two almost identical statues, the only difference between them being the item held in the left hand – a folded cloth in one vignette, and an *ankh* in the other.[160] The significance of the cloth may lie in its word association, *sia* being both the symbol of a strip of material and the name of a deity. Authoritative utterance (*ḥw*) and understanding/perception (*si3*) are attributes of the sun god, personified as divinities, and are intimately associated with him.[161] In the Book of the Night (19th Dynasty onwards), Sia addresses the deceased, blessed and damned, and announces their fate in the afterlife.[162] In the Pyramid Texts Spell 250, the deceased is said to appear as Perception (*si3*) in the sun boat,[163] while Coffin Texts Spell 958 is a text through which the deceased hopes to 'become Sia who belongs to Re',[164] and CT 1006 states:[165] 'Hail to you, Re-Atum in On, for I am Sia who is in the midst of your Eye … I am your image'. The ability of white fringed linen to lighten the darkness of the netherworld is indicated in the Book of the Dead Spell 80:[166] 'I am one who has put on the fringed linen of the Deep, the white (raiment) that illumines one who is before him.' Alternatively, if the cloth is understood as '*s*' the seated deceased could be interpreted as *s-3ḫ* – transfigured,[167] which would accord with the Egyptians' use of rebuses and verbal puns. Kenneth Griffin[168] identifies the cloth as the '*snb*-cloth', a symbol of rebirth.

The water lily, commonly and erroneously referred to as the 'lotus',[169] was identified by the Old Kingdom as the god Nefertum, the 'water lily at the nose of Re'.[170] This identification

158 E.g. Neferubenef (18th Dynasty); in his left hand he carries a *was*-sceptre, implying that he has obtained dominion as well as eternal life; Herbin 2000: 4. See also P. Cairo SR VIII 10247, and P. Cairo SR IV 982 (Niwinski 1989: pl. 44b, pl. 21a) for owners of the Book of the Dead holding *ankhs*.

159 Indicated by the divine beard and royal kilt (Speelers 1917: pl. xxvii).

160 Hornung 1990: 170, pls 130 and 131. Compare an image of the deified prince Ahmose-Sipair wearing a *nemes*-headdress and holding the stem of a water lily blossom in one hand and an *ankh* in the other (Vandersleyen 2005: 94, no. 40, BM EA 932). On another stela the prince is identified as an *akh iqer*, and is depicted with the cloth and lily (*ibid.*, 95, no. 41, Lyon 1969-211).

161 Blackman 1925: 203, n. 5.

162 Hornung 1999: 125.

163 Allen 2005: 42.

164 Faulkner 1973: 90; de Buck 1961: 176–7.

165 Faulkner 1973: 108, de Buck 1961: 222.

166 Allen 174: 70.

167 See Assmann 1986 for a discussion of this term.

168 2007: 142, n. 56, citing Wolfhart 1967: 148–9.

169 Two species of lily were known to and depicted by the ancient Egyptians: *Nymphaea cerulea Savigny* (blue) and *Nymphaea lotus Linnaeus Willdenow* (white: Irvine and Trickett 1953: 363–4). The lotus (*Nelumbo* as opposed to *Nymphaea*) was not present in Egypt in the New Kingdom. *Nelumbo nucifera*, the eastern sacred lotus, was introduced from India in the Persian period (Germer 1985: 39–40; Hepper 2009: 11).

170 PT 249, §266; Szpakowska 2003: 228; Faulkner 1969: 61. Also Allen 2005: 42: 'Unas will appear as

Figure 8: Deceased receiving offerings. Tomb of Inherkhau (TT 359), Deir el-Medina, 20th Dynasty.

Figure 9: The tomb owner ascends from the Hall of Maat as a justified ba/akh. *Blue radiating lines indicate air movement as he flaps his wings. Weighing of the heart scene. Tomb of Nakhtamun (TT 341), Sheikh Abd el-Qurna, 19th Dynasty. © Heidelberger Ramessidenarchiv, 62818. Reproduced with the kind permission of Eva Hofmann.*

Figure 10: Akh *with* ankh. *Stela of Ptahhesy, probably from Thebes, 19th Dynasty. Manchester Museum 1554.*

may explain why the *akhu iqer en Re* were also depicted holding a water lily to their noses,[171] since they adopted some of Re's divine attributes after having successfully passed through the underworld tribunal. Chapter 81a of the Book of the Dead, the spell for being transformed into a water lily states: 'I am this pure (water lily) that ... is at Re's nose', and is illustrated by a vignette showing a man's head rising from an open lily flower.[172] A text relating to the mortuary

Nefertem, as the water-lily at the Sun's nose when he emerges from the Akhet every day, the one at the sight of whom the gods become clean'.

[171] Water lilies could not have been held as depicted because the stems are too weak to support the weight of the flower which consequently hangs down (Ossian 1999: 53). The lily is shown in a more realistic manner in certain tombs, for example User (TT 21): Davies 1913: pl. xxv. It may be significant that Nefertum was also the 'lord of food' (David 1973: 263).

[172] Allen 1974: 70; Schott 1950: 127. Vignette: e.g. P. Ani, BM EA 10470/28: Faulkner 1986: 79; compare the wood and plaster sculpture from the tomb of Tutankhamun (Noblecourt 1963: pl. ii).

cult in the tomb of Menkheperreseneb (TT 112) states that the owner appears as Nefertum, 'as a [water lily] to the nostril of Re. The gods are pure because of seeing him daily'.[173]

It may be suggested, following this brief summary of objects typically held by tomb-owners and other recipients on stelae, wall paintings (and to a lesser extent, statues; Figure 11), that a deeper significance should be sought in these items. They are characteristics literally possessed by the dead, images of which on tomb walls and stelae served to remind the living of the renewed status of the deceased, their relationship with the sun god, and their power.

The malevolent dead

The malevolent dead, usually the *mwt* in contrast to the blessed *ȝḫw*,[174] are characterised in texts such as P. Edwin Smith as those who have died violently or prematurely, as a result of snakebite, crocodile attack, murder or drowning,[175] and who as a result may not have received a proper burial or funerary offerings.[176] Similar malign spirits are attested in ancient Greece,[177] Mesopotamia, and modern African societies.[178] Letters to the dead (see Chapter 2) indicate that the living could be plagued by deceased individuals who have been wronged in some way,[179] though in general the restless dead are mentioned as a collective body.[180] The malevolent dead were said to be responsible for disasters in all forms, from miscarriage and crop failure to disease and premature death.[181]

Means for warding off evil spirits included carving figures of apotropaic knife-wielding demons into headrests (Figure 12),[182] and rituals and incantations (for execration rites see Chapter 2). For example, one of the Bankes' Late Ramesside Papyri (BM EA 75021) seems to refer to the manufacture of a talisman to protect the complainant, the scribe Djehutymose, from the 'eye of a dead one', and O. Gardiner 363, a spell against nightmares, states:[183]

---

173 Davies 1933: 22.

174 Zandee 1960: 35; Ritner 1997: 141. Also Ritner 1993: 137, n. 611; *ibid.*, 141. The *akhu* had the potential for malevolent behaviour, and the deceased required divine protection for his surviving family against both *ȝḫw* and *mwt* as indicated in CT 131 (Faulkner 1973: 113–4).

175 Breasted 1930: 480–1; Ritner 1997: 180–1; Zandee 1960: 236–7.

176 In modern Egypt those who die of unnatural causes (immolation, drowning, scorpion sting) or those far from home, unmourned in a foreign land, are addressed with specific lamentations (Wickett 2010: 81), presumably to aid the passage of the souls to the afterlife and discourage them from returning to harm the living.

177 Especially *daemons, aōroi,* and *biaiothanatoi*: Gordon 1999: 176–7; Anderson 2002: 231.

178 Scurlock 2006: 50; Hackett 1996: 167. Cf. Mesopotamian ghost-induced illnesses from those who died in battle, by murder, from dehydration, drowning, or immolation (Scurlock 2006: 5). In modern Egypt ghosts are believed to remain in the vicinity of graves (including the ancient tombs beneath Qurna houses) and in the desert, and as a result people will not venture into the desert at night, as explained by an inhabitant of el-Gezira, Thebes, to the author in April 2008. Expensive exorcisms by high-ranking religious men are required to remove *afrit/jinn* from houses. See also Blackman 1927: 21; Burnett 2000: 61.

179 E.g. by infidelity; Wente 1990: 216–17.

180 Kousoulis 2007: 1045.

181 CT 140: Willems 2001: 334, 336; de Buck 1935: 173–6; Faulkner 1973: 32–3; see also de Buck 1950.

182 Szpakowska 2003a: 173; Romano 2001: 162–163, no. 74.

183 Demarée 2006: pl. 24, lines 9–10; Ritner 1990: 25–6. As James F. Romano (1982: 75; cf. Hellinckx

Figure 11: Statue of Sennuwy. Found at Kerma, probably originally from the tomb of Djefaihapi at Asyut. Granodiorite. 12th Dynasty. Museum of Fine Arts, Boston 14.720.

Figure 12: Headrest of Qenherkhepeshef, inscribed with a text for 'a good sleep in the West, the necropolis of the righteous (smt n mꜣꜥty)', suggesting that it was intended to protect the owner in the afterlife. Limestone. Deir el-Medina. 19th Dynasty. 18.8 cm high. British Museum, EA 63783. © Trustees of the British Museum.

> *Oh male adversary (ḏꜣy), [female adversary (ḏꜣy.t), male ghost (ꜣḫ), female ghost (ꜣḫ.t)] be far from [me(?)...] oh dead man (mwt), dead woman (mwt.t), without coming (?). He will not go forth with face forward, with limbs as [sound] limbs,*
> *since his heart is destined for the Evening Meal of the one in the act of striking.*
> *NN born of NN has [extracted] your hearts (ib.w), oh dead ones (mwt.w). [He] has taken your hearts (ḥꜣty.w), oh dead men and dead women. To the striker (ꜣw.(t)) he has offered them [for] his sustenance (of) his limbs.*
> *As for you, you will not live; your limbs are [his(?)] offering cakes. You will not escape from the [four Noble Ladies (?)] from the fortress of Horus Imy-Šnw.t.*[184]
>
> *Recite over 4 [ura]ei made of pure [...] clay with flames in their mouths.*
> *One is placed in each corner [of every room/of any bedroom]*
> *in which there is a man or a woman [...] sleeping with a man [or a woman(?)]*

2001: 92) pointed out: 'Like many people, the ancient Egyptians saw the hours between sunset and dawn as the time when they were most susceptible to malevolent forces that would pose little threat to safety during daytime.'

184 'Horus who is in the town of Shenut' was the 'patron of slaughter blocks and braziers who "burns the rebel for all eternity"' (Ritner 1990: 32).

This spell may help to explain the numerous pottery snakes found in domestic contexts throughout Egypt, including Memphis (Kom Rabiʿa) and Amarna.[185] A similar text against night terrors includes an address to *akhu*, the dead, and all their forms:[186]

> *The Book of Driving out Terrors which come in order to descend upon a man in the night: 'Put [your] face backwards, when you raise your head, together with your* ba, *your shapes, your corpses, your magic, together with your shapes, your forms.*
> *Oh male* akhs, *female* akhs, *male dead (mwt), female dead, male adversaries (ḏ3y), female adversaries, in the sky and [on?] the earth:*
> *You shall contemplate and look!*
>
> *Beware of the flame which comes forth from the Two Horizons!'*
> *Words to be said over the image which is [drawn] upon a choice piece of linen, to be placed (on) the throat of a man until he is seen to be quiet.*

The placing of linen on the throat of the victim may be due to the vulnerability of the neck, hence the threat of the 6th Dynasty official Khentika (in *akh* form) to wring the necks of trespassers in his tomb.[187] Some Third Intermediate Period oracular amuletic decrees seem to be intended to prevent visitations by malevolent entities, including the dead, in the night, and to protect against demons identified as 'fighters' and 'wanderers'.[188]

In addition to nightmares, the dead could cause mental illness and emotional disorders, as suggested in P. Edwin Smith, Spell 5:[189]

> *Hysteria, hysteria, you should not acquire this my mind or this my heart for Sekhmet ... any male spirit (3ḫ), any female spirit (3ḫ.t), any male dead, any female dead,*[190] *the form of any animal, one whom the crocodile has acquired or the snake has bitten, one condemned to the knife*[191] *or who has passed away on his bed, [and] the night-demons ...*
>
> *To be recited over Sekhmet, Bastet, Osiris, or Nehebkau. To be written in myrrh on a strip of fine linen, and given to a man at his neck...*

The belief that deceased men and women could be the cause of, or responsible for prolonging, a disease is visible in medical papyri. For instance, the London Medical Papyrus, Incantation 10,[192] a spell against skin disease (*tmyt*), states:

---

185 Giddy 1999: 13–27; Peet and Woolley 1923: 66. Jeffreys suggested that the pottery snakes may be representations of Renenutet (2003: 204), though most do not bear the goddess' characteristic crown; cf. Szkapowska 2003c: 119.

186 P. Leiden I, 348 v. 2; Szpakowska 2003a: 168; 2003c: 121. For a spell against nightmares caused by an unidentified entity, see McDowell 1999: 115, no. 84 (P. Chester Beatty III/'Dream Book' 10688); Gardiner 1935: pls 8, 8a, recto 10, 10–19.

187 Szkapowska 2003c: 120; Zandee 1960: 34, 197; Sethe 1906: 260, 12. A modern parallel may be the belief among Aborigines in Coen, Cape York Peninsula, Australia, that ghosts visit grieving relatives in their sleep and attempt to strangle them (Smith 2008: 191–2). For ghosts haunting houses in ancient Egypt, see Koenig 1979: 116.

188 *Khatyu* and *shemayu*, e.g. 21st Dynasty P. Cleveland 14.723: Meeks 2002: 105; cf. Graves-Brown 2005: 66; Kousoulis 2007: 1044; Bohleke 1997: 158.

189 Allen 2005: 109, v. 2, 2–14.

190 Perhaps 'in' should be inserted here; the text goes on to list people who have died unnaturally.

191 For public executions, see Willems 1990; cf. Assmann 1992.

192 BM EA 10059, Wreszinski Incantation 10.

My incantation is what will save me (rꜣ.<i> šd wi) [from? the] effect of a dead male or female etc. (ḥmt-r) on earth. Men see them, the [pꜥt-]people see them, the ḥnmmt-people of Re see them. This incantation is to be spoken over the clay of a potter...

The dead were also thought to attack pregnant women, or facilitate an enemy's sexual assault on them:[193]

Come out, venomous seed (mtwt) of Horus and Imy-nhd-f, come out to a dead male or female, etc. The name of the enemy, the name of his father, the name of his mother. O Mafdet, open your mouth wide against that enemy, [a dead male] or female etc. Do not allow him to see <even one> opportunity. Words to be spoken over an erect phallus of a donkey of dpt-cake, inscribed with the name of his enemy [...] name of his father, name of his mother...

The word *mtwt* can be translated as 'semen' or 'poison', and is interpreted by Kousoulis as 'toxic matter, injected into the body by magical means possibly analogous to, or associated with, ejaculation by a hostile entity',[194] again showing an association between attacks by the malevolent dead and sexual activity.[195]

Medical texts indicate that the living were afflicted by dead entities through a form of possession (*nsy*), with the dead entering the body, often through the eyes, and causing illness from within by introducing harmful substances into the victim.[196] The Bentresh Stela, which dates to the Late Period, but is fictitiously set in the reign of Ramesses II, states that the *akh* is responsible for attacking individuals: 'when the priest arrived at Bakhtan [near Afghanistan], he found Bentresh like one afflicted by an *akh* (*m sẖr ẖrt ꜣẖ*)'. This spirit was then pacified by a (mortuary) offering.[197] People believed to be possessed by the spirits of the dead or under the influence of gods (possibly actually suffering from epilepsy) were among those prohibited from entering temples,[198] and in P. Chester Beatty VIII, the dead are said to cause illness by having power over (*sẖm m*) the body of their victim.[199]

According to Kousoulis: 'The dead bring about disease because they are a force of chaos, and inherently hostile to mankind'.[200] This chaos, and the animosity that the dead seem to show towards their kin, may be representative of the ambivalent feelings of the living for their ancestors. Haunting in particular can be an expression of socially repressed feelings of anger or guilt toward deceased relations, or be the result of a sense of abandonment felt by the living projected onto figures of dead relatives.[201] Various Egyptian texts, from love songs and votive stelae to funerary laments express this fear of isolation, of being ignored or ostracized by loved

---

193 Leitz 1999: 68, pl. 34, lines 4–7.

194 2007: 1048.

195 See also Koenig 1979: 111–13, n. h.

196 Kousoulis 2007: 1046; Koenig 1979: 106–7, n. a .

197 Broze 1989; Gee 2003: 231; de Buck 1963: 107–9; Ritner 2003: 365. Winifred S. Blackman (1927: 54) noted the persistence of a similar belief: 'one man, a village guard far south in Upper Egypt, had a fish tattooed on the inner side of one arm near the wrist, as a cure for *afrit* [ghost] possession.'

198 Sauneron 1960.

199 Recto 7, 1–3; verso 15, 4: Plater 2001: 99; Gardiner 1935: II, pls 41, 49.

200 2007: 1050.

201 Smith 2008: 194–5; Kübler-Ross 1970: 4.

ones, the gods, or the dead. The resentment aroused by apparent abandonment may have found expression in the perception of negative and disruptive behaviour by spirits of the dead, who were no longer receptive to the needs of those that they had left behind.[202]

Conclusions

The belief that the inexplicable or unexpected is a result of divine or ghostly intervention is a near-universal phenomenon, for example:[203]

> *While the African dead ultimately do control the fertility of the living, the animals and the fields, this is often only in a negative way through their power of disruption ... This power is established retrospectively. You fail to give an offering you owe them, commit incest with a woman too close in kinship and you may get away with it. Suddenly, years later, they pay you back with leprosy, a deformed child, or a dead cow. The dead are above all capricious, which makes them of great explanatory power. They fill the gaps in the process by which the world is made logical.*

While a corpse could not be reanimated, the deceased could be manifest in a form that possessed the power of movement, could be seen or experienced by the living and could communicate with them. The sending of the *ba* or *akh* to the living, often in dreams, is attested in texts and probably in archaeological remains from the Old Kingdom onwards.[204] In the Book of the Dead, Spell 65 states: 'I have gone forth in the form of a living *akh* whom the common folk on earth worship'.[205] The form of this 'living *akh*' in relation to artefacts such as busts and statues is analysed in the next chapter. The above overview of the components of the deceased suggests that the Egyptians viewed their dead as both powerful and vulnerable. This understanding formed the basis of the reciprocal relationship between the living and the dead, and encouraged interaction in a range of locations discussed in Chapter 3.

---

[202] One example of this is 21st Dynasty letter to Ikhtay's coffin, where Butehamun complains that Ikhtay 'has been ungrateful to her brother who fulfilled all her wishes', and has not responded to him when he has appealed to her (Frandsen 1992: 33).

[203] Barley 1997: 92; cf. Borghouts 1982: 14.

[204] Gee 2003: 231.

[205] After Allen 1974: 60.

CHAPTER 2

The cult of the ancestors

The death of an individual is experienced almost universally as a psychological blow to those socially near him and also constitutes a shock to the structure of social relations of which he was a part. This personal and social damage is everywhere responded to with ritual and ceremony which function to relieve the emotional tensions, anxieties, and fears of bereaved individuals and to repair the social gap in the interpersonal network of interlocking obligations and reciprocal activity patterns.[1]

Mortuary cult and society

Mortuary ritual, as opposed to ancestor worship, is not a universal phenomenon.[2] In his discussion of the archaeology of ancestors, Ian Morris distinguishes 'rite-of-passage ceremonies which separate the deceased from the living, producing the archaeological remains of burials which we excavate', which he terms 'ancestor cult', from 'rituals which provide continued access to the deceased in the afterworld', or 'mortuary rituals'.[3] In this chapter I define mortuary cult in Egypt as ritual action in relation to the dead, and look for evidence of this in archaeological remains and textual sources. 'Rite-of-passage ceremonies' are discussed in Chapter 4. Major forms that mortuary ritual took included the deposition of offerings during visits to the necropolis, which could involve petitioning the deceased orally and/or in written form, and meals held in the chapel or courtyard of a tomb during festivals or personal feast days (see Chapter 3).

The creation and utilisation of monuments specifically for the benefit of the deceased, or for the living in relation to them (those that facilitated contact with dead relatives and friends), could also be considered part of mortuary cult, albeit in a limited sense if the artefacts were produced during the owner's lifetime in anticipation of his death. Relevant monuments include offering tables, stelae, and anthropoid or 'ancestor' busts. Objects, even those discovered in situ, provide only a certain amount of information about mortuary cults. As is the case for votive offerings, artefactual remains of ancestor cults are not representative of a complete ritual, but the surviving parts of an act of worship.[4]

---

1 Kennedy 1978: 224.

2 Steadman *et al.* 1996; Harrington forthcoming.

3 1991: 150, following Max Gluckman 1937.

4 Pinch 1993: 339.

The establishment of mortuary cult seems to stem from two basic concepts: need to mark the individual as distinct from society,[5] and the legitimation of rights and social identity by association with the past. Such concepts are explicit in Egyptian sources, as in the Harper's Song from the tomb of Neferhotep: 'This land that has not its opponent, all our kin rest in it since the time of first antiquity'.[6] Ancestor cults and their related rituals are developments connected with sedentary, as opposed to nomadic, lifestyles. Prior to modern government intervention, for example, the Mbeere of Kenya were highly mobile and disposed of their dead by leaving corpses to decompose in the wilderness; 'weakly corporate descent groups made for a weak relationship between lineages and territories, and thus militated against the development of ancestral shrines as centres for sacrifice and collective observance'.[7] In 'delayed-return' societies[8] such as Egypt, where social continuity is of greater concern than in hunter-gatherer ('immediate-return') systems, ancestor cults and mortuary rituals form a type of 'cultural cement'[9] that assists in holding society together. This aspect of ancestor worship, as a focus for social cohesion, led to its prohibition in Mao's China because it was perceived as a threat to the authority of the government.[10] This is in complete contrast to ancient Egypt, where didactic texts such as the Instruction of Ani suggest that reverence towards and cultic activity for predecessors was officially sanctioned and encouraged.

In Egypt, elite couples seem to have faced considerable pressure to conform to the expected pattern of family life and provide for their own afterlife and the continuity of the community by having children, through adoption if necessary.[11] Eldest sons were expected to perform important roles in transforming their deceased parents into blessed ancestors: through the actions of their children, parents were reborn and able to provide protection and guidance to their kin. This principle was also followed in Mesopotamia: an Ugaritic text known as 'The Duties of an Ideal Son' emphasises the need for a descendant to protect the honour of his father while he lives and erect stelae or statues to preserve his memory after death.[12] Emphasis is often placed on the veneration of parents, as opposed to dead kin in general,[13] as well as the reciprocal relationship between parents and children.[14] When the dead eventually faded from social consciousness, typically after a couple of generations,[15] individuals became assimilated

[5] Chapman 1994: 44.

[6] TT 50; Lichtheim 1945: 197; Osing 1992a: 16. Cf. e.g. the admonitions in the Tale of Sinuhe against dying or being buried abroad (Lichtheim 1973: 229–30).

[7] Glazier 1984: 133.

[8] Woodburn 1982: 205–7.

[9] Watson 1988: 7.

[10] Whyte 1988: 293. Cf. Bloch-Smith 1992b: 222.

[11] E.g. O. Berlin 10627; Wente 1990: 149, no. 206: 'As for him who has no children, he adopts an orphan instead [to] bring him up'. This may also have been the case in non-elite communities, but perhaps with different emphasis. See also Eyre 1992.

[12] Lewis 1989: 53–5.

[13] 'Libate for your father and mother, who are resting in the [necropolis]' (Instruction of Ani: Lichthiem 1976: 137); 'May ... the children of your house offer libations to you at the door of your tomb' (Tomb of Meryre at Amarna: Murnane 1995: 161; Davies 1903: 53, pl. xxxix).

[14] 'May you be a protection for your children, forever and ever' (TT 82; Assmann 2005: 219). See also *ibid.*, 451, n. 36.

[15] McDowell 1992: 107; Baines 1991: 147.

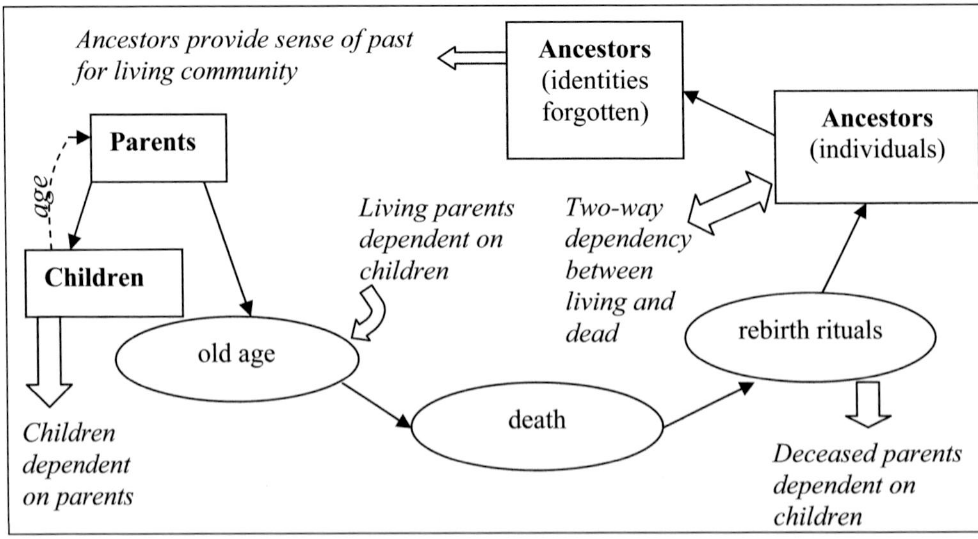

Figure 13: Social cohesion through generations: dependence and reciprocity.

into the general community of ancestors who existed in a state of 'collective immortality'[16] that provided a backcloth onto which views of the past could be projected (Figure 13).

The prominence of personal piety during the New Kingdom[17] appears to have coincided with a change in the status of ancestors. Objects specific to mortuary cult, such as *akh iqer* stelae, anthropoid busts, and bust amulets, were widespread during the period but ceased to be produced by the end of the 20th Dynasty.[18] At Deir el-Medina, a movement away from ancestors and towards the gods may have been partly due to the apparent relocation of the villagers from the tomb-surrounded settlement to the temple of Medinet Habu as a result of political and social upheaval.[19] A measured shift towards interacting with gods rather than with previous generations is paralleled in other cultures, including those of the European Neolithic.[20]

Political and economic changes influenced religious development, as is evident in the aftermath of the Amarna period, when the difference in the choice of motifs for tomb decoration is striking, exhibiting a gradual transference of emphasis from familial relationships and work life to interaction with deities and existence in the afterlife.[21] The legacy of Amarna also saw the disappearance of the informal banquet scene and other festive images from tombs. Strudwick states that although the Festival of the Wadi continued, it 'seems not to have been

[16] Mbiti 1969: 26, 84.

[17] E.g. Baines 1991: 179–86; Szpakowska 2003a: 134; Assmann 2002: 229–46; Pinch 1993: 349; Luiselli 2009.

[18] Demarée 1983: 283.

[19] McDowell 1994: 57; Černý 1973: 277–8; Wente 1990: 171. The resettlement of the villagers at Medinet Habu has, however, been challenged by Demarée (2007) and Weiss (2009: 194).

[20] Parker Pearson 1993: 226. Spiegel 1956: 202–3.

[21] Cf. Strudwick 1994: 330; Assmann 1992: 155.

worth a formal place in the new decorative layouts'.[22] Withdrawal of the early 18th Dynasty-style banquet scene from standard tomb decoration may have resulted from the manner in which banqueting became associated with Akhenaten and his family on household stelae and in the mortuary sphere,[23] as well as the reduction of constraints in tomb decoration that permitted the use of extensive religious imagery in the wake of the Amarna period.[24]

Recognition of the finite duration of mortuary cults is expressed in the Egyptians' preparation for the hereafter in the form of tomb scenes with depictions of offerings that perhaps could be relied upon should people fail to visit the tomb, as well as appeals to the living (Figure 14), including any strangers who passed by.[25] It would seem that ancestor stelae (and probably busts too) commemorate and were intended as an interface with those within living memory, not members of generations long past.[26] John Baines and Peter Lacovara note that: 'In principle, funeral rituals and the mortuary cult, rather than the tomb, were crucial to continued existence', yet 'whatever the kinship context, the Egyptian dilemma of succeeding generations vying for position in the next world ... is symptomatic of how almost all the more remote deceased must fade from awareness, and from the responsibility of the living, if the burden of the dead is not to become intolerable.'[27] This abandoning of the ancestors after a few generations is paralleled in many societies, including the Nubians in the 1960's prior to the obliteration of their land by the Aswan High Dam.[28] It may explain, for instance, why seven anthropoid busts were discovered in the 'great pit' at Deir el-Medina, having apparently been discarded.[29]

The existence and character of social aspects of mortuary cult, for example the identities of those who participated in it and how they did so, the involvement of women and children, the attendance of neighbours and friends at the funerary and other commemorative meals or festivals in the presence of the dead, are matters of conjecture because evidence is sparse. The issue of non-elite practices is also a problem; in Egypt as in Iron Age Levantine society (1200–586 BC) and many others, the number of burials cannot be correlated with the estimated population.[30] Most individuals were presumably either buried in a manner that left little archaeological trace or were subject to informal disposal.[31] Although it is not possible to reconstruct mortuary rituals or cults of the majority of ancient Egyptians, this does not necessarily mean that most of the population was excluded from any knowledge, understanding, or participation in ritual activity concerning the dead.[32] Work at the non-elite South Tombs Cemetery at Amarna has indicated that while the burials themselves were simple, with no evidence of mummification, mortuary cultic activity is suggested by the presence of ceramic vessels and stelae.[33] Stevens

---

22 1994: 324.

23 E.g. the tomb of Huya at Amarna; Davies 1905: pls iv, vi.

24 John Baines, personal communication; Strudwick 1994: 330.

25 E.g. Kitchen 1993: 256, 269; 2000: 14, 147.

26 Demarée 1983: 282.

27 Baines and Lacovara 2002: 16, 27; cf. Meskell 2002: 203–4, 206.

28 Kennedy 1978: 232.

29 Keith-Bennett 1981: 47; Pinch 1983: 411. Cf. Jeffreys 2003: 204; Stevens 2006: 327.

30 Bloch-Smith 1992a: 22; Baines and Lacovara 2002: 13–14, with references.

31 Parker Pearson 1999: 5.

32 Eyre 2002: 49.

33 Kemp 2007: 31, 33; Stevens 2006: 294; 2009b: 16.

Figure 14: Stela of Ankhren with an appeal to the living in the section below the offering scene: 'O you who are living on earth, all scribes, all lector priests, and every waab*-priest who will read [out?] this stela, as you desire that your local gods favour you, say ... 'an offering which the king gives ... for the* ka *of ... Ankhren, justified". Probably from Abydos. Limestone. 12th Dynasty? The Queen's College 1113 (on loan to the Ashmolean Museum). Photograph by the author, used with the kind permission of Linda Irving-Bell of The Queen's College, Oxford.*

notes that most burials probably contained at least one pottery vessel, 'reinforcing the focus on sustaining the deceased in the afterlife at the time of burial',[34] if not afterwards.

Lists of absences from work by the Deir el-Medina artisans indicate that it was standard practice to take time off for personal festivals and family sickness, as well as mourning and caring for the dead. In a single list, libating, mourning, and embalming/wrapping corpses accounted for seventeen days' absence, and 'offering to' or 'burying the god' for a further nine days.[35] The involvement of women and children is suggested, at least in part, by tomb scenes and funerary stelae, though the male-oriented focus of most mortuary monuments means that the information that can be gathered is limited.[36] However, as Geraldine Pinch points out:[37]

> *Since most women were not in state employment, their time may have been more flexible than that of their male relatives. Women probably performed religious duties on behalf of their families, in the home, at family and community shrines, and on visits to state temples ... The votive material from Deir el-Bahri is particularly important as evidence for women's participation in religion because it includes objects which not only depict women but which were presumably commissioned by them. Several stelae and textiles show a woman as the principal donor making the sacrifice to the deity, while men take the passive secondary role usually allotted to women.*

The ritual feasting at funerals and in the ongoing cult of the dead was socially significant.[38] Christopher Eyre observes that: 'it is likely that continued mortuary and ancestor cult provided the typical framework within which 'private' meat consumption took place',[39] although there could have been equally important occasions where meat was eaten of which nothing is known. The butchery and processing of animals, particularly cattle, valued for their labour and milk as well as meat and fat, is depicted in tomb scenes as a group activity. The subsequent distribution of meat would relate to the social status of those present at the meal through the differing quality and quantity shared among individuals.[40] There remains the issue of the expense involved in slaughtering cattle;[41] it seems unlikely that bovids were sacrificed for every funeral, festival, and offering ceremony, as is implied by the decoration on tomb walls.[42] Perhaps, as with the Nuer of Sudan, less costly animals or birds, such as goats or geese,[43] or even vegetables[44] were substituted: 'what remains constant is the meaning of sacrifice'.[45]

---

[34] 2009b: 17.

[35] O. BM EA 5634: Kitchen 2000: 361–7, no. 229/A15; Janssen 1980: 138–41, 149.

[36] For women's votive stelae, see Robins 1997.

[37] 1993: 343.

[38] See Chapter 4; cf. the ritual of Amenhotep I, where meat offerings were associated with Horus and Seth (McDowell 1999: 94).

[39] 2002: 200.

[40] Eyre 2002: 201, 203.

[41] For their cost in the New Kingdom, see Černý 1954: 908, 912; Janssen 1975: 172–7; table xv, 173.

[42] Although forelegs of cattle have been found in burials as offerings to the dead, for example the Middle Kingdom tomb of Wah at Thebes (Lilyquist 2003: 11).

[43] Metcalf 1981: 563; cf. Mbiti 1969: 150.

[44] Evans-Pritchard 1956: 202–3.

[45] Metcalf 1981: 564. Cf. Barley 1997: 77–8, on 'cheating' the dead by offering partial sacrifices.

Evidence for mortuary cult

Letters to the dead

Letters to the dead apparently formed an irregular part of the mortuary cult as most of those known were the result of unforeseen or unusual circumstances, but they are worth reviewing here because of the information they provide on interaction between the living and the dead that is not present in other sources. The letters have been discussed by numerous scholars,[46] though few have considered the significance of their comparative scarcity: to date only sixteen definite examples and eight less certain ones have been discovered.[47] One might expect a larger number, given the longevity of the practice and the evident tradition of visiting tombs to request assistance or intervention. There are several possible reasons for the shortage of these documents, perhaps the most obvious being fragility, along with illicit or careless excavations: thirteen of the twenty–four examples are unprovenanced, and only one is known to have come from Deir el-Medina (the letter to Ikhtay's coffin),[48] which is striking given the amount of inscribed material recovered from the site. In some cases, a document's affiliation to the corpus has not been recognised.[49] By analogy with invocation offerings[50] and appeals for the dead to listen and respond,[51] it seems likely that the general content of the letters was presented aloud prior to deposition.[52] In the words of Sylvie Donnat:[53] 'the letter to the dead itself is not only a written text. It is a ritual performance.' The expectation that the dead would react to appeals from the living in return for offerings is stated, for example, in the 18th Dynasty tomb of Paheri at Elkab:[54]

> *I will not fail to respond.*
> *The deceased is a father*
> *for him who acts for him;*
> *He does not ignore the one who libates for him.*
> *It is good that you should hear.*

and in the 19th Dynasty tomb of Paser at Saqqara:[55]

> *May you incriminate (your enemies) and heed the petitions*
> *of the children and the servants of your house.*
> *... When you are called, may you come immediately,*
> *May you visit your house on earth.*

---

46 E.g. Gardiner and Sethe 1928; Gunn 1930; Simpson 1981: 173–9; Quirke 1988: 106–7; Donnat 2003, with references.

47 Donnat 2003: 395–588.

48 O. Louvre Inv. 698; Sweeney 2006a: 157; Frandsen 1992.

49 E.g. Buchberger 1991; Donnat 2007a: 136–41.

50 *prt-ḫrw*: Donnat 2002: 222; Demarée 1983: 222, n. 141.

51 E.g. the Cairo bowl and Louvre Ostracon 698: Gardiner and Sethe 1928: 7; Frandsen 1992: 34, cf. Wente 1990: 219; see also model ears and ear stelae from Deir el-Medina and Deir el-Bahri: Sadek 1987: 245; Parkinson 1999: 66–7; Bruyère 1925: 204, fig. 94; Morgan 2004; Pinch 1993: 246–53. Keith (2011: 86) suggests that the prominent ears of some anthropoid busts are related to their function in hearing prayers and petitions.

52 Baines 1987: 87; Baines and Lacovara 2002: 22; cf. Haring 2003: 154.

53 2007: 6.

54 EK 3; Tylor 1895, pl. xvi, lines 51–2; cf. Lichtheim 1976: 20.

55 Assmann 2005: 220, 451 n. 36; Martin 1985: pl. 10.

Geraldine Pinch argues that, since rates of literacy were low, many uninscribed bowls may have been dedicated with similar verbalised petitions to the deceased, and that 'appeals to the dead are most likely to have been made at periods when access to the higher supernatural powers inhabiting state-run temples was particularly limited'.[56] On the Hu Bowl dating to the First Intermediate Period, the voice offering is specifically mentioned in regard to the deceased: 'One makes invocation offerings (*prt-ḫrw*) to an *akh* in return for interceding (*sbi ḥr*) on behalf of the survivor!'[57] It is possible that petitions found *in situ* remained unfulfilled: if the subject of a complaint was not resolved, petitioners may have returned to the tomb and repeated their requests for assistance; should this fail, they had the option of taking their complaints elsewhere.[58] If, however, the petitioners received resolutions to their problems, the letters might have been removed and destroyed because they had served their purpose, and could then have been replaced with offerings in gratitude to the dead. As Donnat points out, the inclusion of the term *prt-ḫrw* in the letters served to remind the dead of the ritual performances done by the living on their behalf,[59] invocation offerings being a central part of the mortuary cult.

The living anticipated assistance from the dead, but the act of writing to them or making oral requests in their presence may also have helped to alleviate the sensations of loss, guilt, or anger often associated with bereavement.[60] Writing to or about the deceased is even now recommended by psychiatrists as a means of coming to terms with death,[61] and writing letters to the dead and Islamic saints is still practised in Egypt.[62] Another means of contacting those in the next world both in Egypt and in Mesopotamia was through dreams.[63] Here too, the dead could pose difficulties for those on earth, as indicated in the late Old Kingdom or First Intermediate Period Papyrus Naga ed-Deir N 3737, in which a man named Heni states that one of his father's servants, Seni, is visiting him in his sleep, perhaps because he was murdered:[64] 'He should be guarded until he has ceased to visit me ... once and for all.'

A hieratic letter inscribed on the back of a First Intermediate Period stela includes a request from the author to his deceased wife:[65] 'Please become a spirit for me [before] my eyes so that I may see you in a dream fighting on my behalf'. In return, he promises to 'deposit offerings for you [as soon as] the sun has risen and outfit your offering slab for you'. This is the only example where potential action following a successful outcome is mentioned.[66] The Ramesside

---

56 2003: 445.

57 After Demarée 1983: 214; Gardiner and Sethe 1928: 5. See also Murnane 1995: 131, 180. For the oral dimension of letters to the dead, see Donnat 2003: 151.

58 Baines 1987: 87.

59 2007b: 6.

60 E.g. Lloyd 1989: 122–3; Abu-Lughod 1986: 197; Hammond 1978: 399.

61 Davies 1994: 36–8; Butler and Hope 2007: 305.

62 E.g. el-Leithy 2004; Sattin 2000: 91; Reeves 1995.

63 Thomsen 2001: 87–8. In the Greco-Roman world, 'visitors sometimes slept on or near ... tombs to communicate with the dead through dreams, although the dead could visit the living in dreams spontaneously': Ogden 2001: xvii, 11–12, 75–6; cf. Ray 1999: 241–7; Szpakowska 2003b. This phenomenon is known from the Thutmose IV Dream Stela, and may have much earlier precedents in Egypt (Szpakowska 2003a: 135, and Chapter 3; *ibid.*: 142–151, on incubation). For incubation in temples see Frood 2007: 229–30; Pinch 1993: 223.

64 Parkinson 1991: 143–5; Wente 1990: 213; cf. Simpson 1966: 41.

65 Simpson 1966: 45; Wente 1990: 215; cf. Parkinson 1991: 142.

66 McDonald 2005.

Dream Book (Papyrus Chester Beatty III) indicates the importance of dreams in everyday life, including those involving the ancestors:[67] 'If a man sees in a dream nomads: Good, (it means that) the love of his ancestor [literally 'dead father'] will come into his presence.' The Dream Book also shows that dreams were a means through which the dead could make demands upon the living: 'If a man sees himself in a dream placing his face against the floor: BAD, (it means that) something will be required from him by the ones who are yonder', and 'If a man sees in a dream one of his [...] being removed: BAD, (it means) a message (*wpwt*) concerning him by those who are yonder.'[68] The association between anthropoid busts and headrests also suggests that the ancestors could be contacted in dreams.[69]

The magical character of some letters to the dead may be suggested by the way they were written in a spiral.[70] Thus the linear texts of the Qau, Cairo, and Hu Bowls can be compared with the spiral texts of the Louvre and Berlin Bowls.[71] The latter's ink inscription is an appeal by a husband to his deceased wife, whom he suspects is involved in disrupting family life: 'If it is the case that these injuries are being inflicted with your knowledge, see, the house is held by your children, and yet misery is renewed'.[72] The text is divided into two separate lines, both of which start at the same point in relation to the seated figure in the centre[73] that evidently represents the wife, whose name is in line with the figure and who is thus surrounded by the inscription.[74] Details of relationships and issues that would be informative for the modern reader are not supplied in the letters to the dead because prior knowledge of the situation and characters involved is assumed: the texts were not intended for an audience. Several were written because of grievances regarding inheritance.[75] Others are requests for children, including the related inscribed female figurines of the Middle Kingdom,[76] which according to Pinch 'were offered to the dead, rather than to a deity'.[77] The remainder of the letters refer to being in some way plagued by the malevolent dead (see Chapter 1).[78] For example, in the 19th Dynasty letter to the *akhet iqer*[79] Ankhiry, her

---

67 Recto 6, 24: Szpakowska 2003a: 125; Gardiner 1935a.

68 Recto 9, 14, recto 7, 10: Szpakowska 2003a: 125.

69 Hellinckx 2001: 92–3. For the association between headrests, dreams, and the ancestors of the Ngoni in Malawi, see Dewey 1999: 208.

70 Donnat 2002: 217.

71 Dated to 6th–11th Dynasty, 12th Dynasty, First Intermediate Period, First Intermediate Period–Middle Kingdom, and 12th Dynasty respectively: Donnat 2003: pls xvi–xx, xxiv–xxix.

72 Wente 1990: 214; cf. Gardiner and Sethe 1928: 7.

73 Gardiner and Sethe 1928: pls v, va.

74 Coffin Text Spells 758–760 describe the 'Roads of Mehen', on which the deceased travel on an inward spiral towards a figure of Re in the centre. Piccione 1990: 44–7, 50–1; Ritner 1993: 143; de Buck 1956: CT 758 VI: 386. This may be relevant to the spiral letters since the blessed dead were strongly associated with the sun god: e.g. Demarée 1983: 252, 284; Assmann 1983. For parallels of the close relationship between the sun god and the dead in Mesopotamia, see Lewis 1989: 38–9.

75 Qau bowl, Cairo linen; Gardiner and Sethe 1928: 1, 3–4; Wente 1990: 211–12.

76 Donnat 2003: 571–6; Gardiner 1930: 21.

77 1993: 224.

78 Cairo bowl, Leiden Papyrus, Berlin bowl, Hu bowl, Papyrus Naga ed-Deir N 3500; Gardiner and Sethe 1928: 5, 7, 8–9; Wente 1990: 215, 218–9.

79 The feminine form of *akh iqer* is inconsistently used on objects relating to the death and afterlife existence of women. Kathryn Cooney (2008) and Heather Lee McCarthy (2002) have convincingly argued that rather than scribal errors, the use of masculine suffixes and iconography (red skin tone, for example)

widowed husband claims that she is disregarding how well he has treated her, and accuses her of haunting him.[80]

In some cultures infertility is thought to be caused by the dead;[81] if this belief was held in Egypt, it could explain why requests for children were made to them. The notion that dead were able to litigate with others in the afterlife is clear from the letters and from mortuary texts;[82] that they could also be involved in the judgement of the living or intervene in their destiny is apparent both in the letters and in tomb inscriptions.[83] Jan Assmann states that the desire of the dead to return home 'was connected [to] the age-old concept of the ancestral spirit as protector of his family, a concept that lay at the heart of the Letters to the Dead'.[84] The fact that several letters to the dead were written on bowls similar to those broken in execration rites, and rituals of transference through breakage, suggests that such divergent uses of the vessels may have been linked in Egyptian thought: the bowls would then be both a medium for presenting offerings and a means of keeping the dead and the living apart.

Breaking the red pots and associated rituals

'Breaking the red pots (*sḏ dšrwt*)' was a form of execration ceremony performed during offering rituals for the dead that involved bowls similar to those bearing letters to the dead, and was another act intended to overcome threatening influences.[85] Jacobus van Dijk remarks:[86]

> *It seems likely that the destruction of figurines or pottery vases inscribed with the names of enemies and the breaking of the red jars at the end of the offering-ritual are variants of one and the same ritual aimed at the destruction of evil forces lurking beyond the borders of the cosmos. Although the ritual may be described in a technical sense as an act of sympathetic magic it is more likely to be interpreted as a rite of reassurance, enacted to reassure and thereby protect the participants of the ritual when they approach the dangerous borderline between the ordered world and the domain of the powers of chaos.*

In this context, it may be relevant that most execration finds derive from cemeteries, suggesting that the rituals were mainly concerned with dead rather than living enemies, as is further intimated by the fact that the expression *ꜣḫ iḳr* occurs in Old Kingdom execration texts[87] as well as in addresses to the living inscribed on tomb walls.

Breaking, like burning, was a means of transferring the essence of substances and objects from the world of the living to that of the dead.[88] Just as food and incense were burned for the benefit

---

for females was a means of ensuring that they could be reborn in a similar manner to their male kin. This inequality stems from the concept of women as vessels in which the child developed – only men and gods were able to create new life (*ibid.*).

80 Wente 1990: 216–17.

81 Steadman *et al.* 1996: 66.

82 O'Donoghue 1999: 99–101; Zandee 1960: 39, 266; Smith 1993: 33. For the *akhu* as a collective, judgemental body, see e.g. Willems 2001: 341–2.

83 Zandee 1960: 264–5; Willems 1990: 27, 34–5; Assmann 1992: 152–3; Silverman 2000: 10–11.

84 2005: 220.

85 Willems 1990: 352. Cf. Ritner 1993: 144–7, 159, 174; Polz 1993: 237, pl. 44b.

86 1986: 1393.

87 Demarée 1983: 218.

88 Chung 2000: 134; cf. Walter *et al.* 2004: 153; Parker Pearson 1993: 204.

of the deceased, so the breaking of wine vessels, as depicted for example in the tomb of Shuroy at Dra Abu el-Naga (TT 13) and the Saqqara tomb of Horemheb,[89] was probably symbolic of transference. This scene seems to show that the smashing of vessels during funerary/mortuary rites followed a specific pattern, coinciding with the slaughter of a sacrificial ox,[90] the burning of incense, and the presentation of burnt offerings. The wine vessels are replaced by cuts of meat, vegetables, and bowls of incense, with the pots broken in sacrifice substituted by parts of the slaughtered bovid.[91] Interestingly, the pots are smashed not by priests, but by ordinary citizens; soldiers, overseers, gardeners, and mourners (Figure 15).[92]

The ritual of breaking ceramics in funerary or mortuary contexts is first attested in the Old Kingdom.[93] According to Pinch, the rite of breaking pots during funerals 'may sometimes have been [performed] to drive away the dead themselves, rather than to destroy evil forces'.[94] The idea that ceramics could repel the dead was found in nineteenth century African-American burial customs, where broken pots were placed on graves to prevent the dead from returning, the bowl being used as a means of containing the soul.[95] Pot-breaking has a range of meanings in different cultures. In China, for example, a bowl is broken by the chief mourner to signal the end of formal mourning, but bowls may also be broken to signify that offerings can no longer be made to parents, or to allow or prevent the deceased from drinking in the afterlife,[96] whereas for the Abaluyia of Kenya, smashing a pot before burial symbolises the loss caused by death.[97] Nigel Barley remarks:[98]

> *The irreversibility of a broken vessel offers a way of speaking of the irreversibility of human time, the change from living to dead. The ritual smashing of pottery creates a clean break between the two. ... So around the world, death ceremonies often involve the smashing of pots, just as the ceremonies of marriage and life involve their creation.*

---

89 Martin 1989: 100–103. See also the relief from the tomb of Ptahemhat at Saqqara (Wildung 1996: 35, fig. 27). A similar scene was probably included in the extensively damaged tomb of Sennedjem and Senqed at Akhmim (Ockinga 1997: pls 55, 58, 60, 62). Borchardt (1929: pl. 1) illustrates other examples, including a female mourner (captioned 'the servant Ta ... men') breaking pots in TT 44 (Amenemheb, Ramesside). Van Dijk (1993: 179–82) lists all known pot-breaking scenes. See also Zivie (1976: pl. viii) and Berlandini (1977: pl. iv) for scenes of pot breaking from the tombs of Khaemwaset and Piay at Saqqara.

90 Van Dijk 1993: 187. Janssen (1975: 172) notes that only one text (O. Berlin 1268, vs. 6) mentions a bull (*kꜣ*); in most cases the general term for cattle (*iḥ*) is used or simply a determinative that leaves the exact reading in doubt.

91 For non-Egyptian examples of sacrifice as substitution, see e.g. Bloch and Parry 1982: 8; Becker 1973: 99. For bovids as substitutes for the *ka* of the deceased, see Eyre 2002: 161 and BD 105 (Lichtheim 1976: 123; Eyre 2002: 159).

92 Van Dijk 1993: 182–3.

93 Pyramid Texts Spell 244; Faulkner 1969: 58. However, the ritual 'killing' and burial of flint knives is known from the Predynastic Period (Stevenson 2009b).

94 2003: 446.

95 Parker Pearson 1999: 10.

96 Naquin 1988: 43, 57.

97 Mbiti 1969: 154.

98 1997: 178.

The act of breaking or burying objects that were deemed to have been polluted by death or the corpse itself[99] is part of the process of separating the dead from the world of living and is common in many cultures.[100] At Tell el-Daba, offering deposits in the vicinity of tombs consisted of everyday vessels that had been intentionally destroyed prior to deposition,[101] suggesting perhaps that the pottery utilised during a cultic meal was in some way polluted and could no longer be used by the living, or that sustenance had been offered to the dead by means of breaking the vessels. Evidence of the practice of smashing pottery following funerary meals was found in 17th Dynasty tombs at Dra Abu el-Naga, where sherds had been gathered and placed into storage jars before final deposition near the burial chamber, or ritually 'killed' by knocking holes into or near the base.[102] Evidence of breaking pots and 'cult ceramics' in the vicinity of tombs in the 18th Dynasty was discovered in enclosures K 91.5 and K 91.7 at the same site.[103] The early 18th Dynasty tomb of Djehuty (TT 11) at Dra Abu el-Naga has a pit in the courtyard containing deliberately broken vessels and floral bouquets,[104] and pottery jars used in funerary offerings at the South Tombs cemetery at Amarna also bear 'killing holes' on the shoulders and bases.[105]

Fear of malevolent spirits of the dead was expressed in several ways. Execration texts, which are attested from the Old Kingdom to the Late Period,[106] usually identify the individual(s) to be cursed in inscriptions on figurines and ceramic vessels, which were then broken, burned,[107] or buried, thus symbolically annihilating the enemy, who is often termed *mwt* or *mwt.t* 'dead man/woman'. The relative rarity of execration material may be a result of the use of wax, wood, or other perishable substances which leave little or no archaeological trace[108] or were completely destroyed during the rituals.[109]

Coffin Texts Spell 103 seems to show the deceased summoning his *ba* and *akh* in order to haunt a living enemy, whereas CT Spell 37 contains ideas relating to the destruction of living enemies, to be accomplished by the burial of wax figures in the 'place of Osiris', presumably the necropolis.[110] Some wax figurines have survived, including a Late Period example moulded around a rolled papyrus curse,[111] and other figures of the deceased, including shabtis, could

---

99 Allen 2003; cf. Parker Pearson 1993: 207; Ritner 1993: 153; Kennedy 1978: 130; Watson 1982: 168.

100 Parker Pearson 1993: 203–4; see also Scurlock 2002: 4 (quoting Feuchtwang 1974: 120); Woodburn 1982: 204; Thompson 1988: 81; Grinsell 1960, 1975.

101 Müller 1998: 798.

102 Seiler 2005: pl. 4b. A similar practice was carried out in the cemetery at Sparta in the late Hellenistic period. Vessels were pierced at the base so that they could not be reused, and were therefore permanent gifts to the dead. Evidence for the ceremonial breakage and burial of vessels was also found in the cemetery, as well as sherds from drinking cups used by relatives during the funeral banquet (Tsouli 2010).

103 Seiler 1995: 187, 191.

104 Lopez-Grande and Torrado de Gregorio 2008.

105 Stevens 2009b: 58–9.

106 Ritner 1993: 137. E.g. Old Kingdom (Quack 2002); Middle Kingdom (Abdalla 1992: 93); early 18th Dynasty (Fuscaldo 2003); see also Posener 1958, 1987.

107 As perhaps at Amarna: Stevens 2003: 160. It may be significant that 'pieces of wax-like substances' were found in residential areas of this site: *ibid.*: 159; 2006: 212.

108 Van Dijk 1986: 1390; Raven 1983. Compare Mesopotamian rituals: Thomsen 2001: 38, 49, 51, 80.

109 Quack 2002: 155.

110 de Buck 1935: 156 h, 157 a–d; Willems 2001: 310, 318.

111 BM EA 37918: Ogden 1999: 71–79, fig. 5; Faraone 1991: 204–5; Raven 1983: 12.

Figure 15: Breaking of the red pots. Tomb of Amenemheb (TT 44), Sheikh Abd el-Qurna. Ramesside. © Eva Hofmann/Ägyptologisches Institut Heidelberg, 48098. Reproduced with the kind permission of Eva Hofmann.

also become the focus of execration rituals.[112] The concern over the wrath of the deceased may sometimes explain the widespread deliberate damage sustained by figures of individuals on tomb walls,[113] mummified remains,[114] and statues.

Statues

The mortuary cult centred on the presentation of food offerings, libations and incense to statues and images of the deceased in the tomb chapel (or stelae), and thereby to the deceased person himself (Figure 16).[115] The importance of statuary in ancestral cults is alluded to in tomb inscriptions, such as that of Amenemhet (TT 82), dating to the reign of Thutmose III: 'May your name endure inside your mansion, may your images (*twtw.k*) be in their chapels; may your *ba* be living, your corpse [established] in your tomb of the necropolis, [your name being established] and lasting in the mouth(s) of your children forever.'[116] The inscription on the seated statue of Mose and his wife at Saqqara states: 'May [Ptah-Sokar-Osiris] grant a good remembrance before the sun disc enduring in the mouth of the living; and provisions and food

112 See e.g. Assmann 2005: 435, n. 83.

113 E.g. Ockinga 1997: 57–9; Baines 1991: 140–1, 151–2.

114 As indicated in the Tomb Robbery Papyri (Peet 1930: 39, 49, 62), specifically P. Leopold Amherst: Capart *et al*. 1936.

115 Baines and Lacovara 2002: 11.

116 Manuelian 1999: 288.

Figure 16: View of the statue, offering table and false door of Akhmeretnisut in the inner room of his chapel at Giza. Cemetery G 2100, tomb G 2184. 5th/6th Dynasty. © Museum of Fine Arts, Boston, A675_NS.

offerings daily before my statue, [my] name abiding eternally, engraved forever.'[117] The word *twt* seems to describe all anthropoid representations, including 'ancestor' busts,[118] implying that no distinction of overall category was made among different three-dimensional depictions of the deceased, perhaps because of their shared attributes, in the same way that votive and funerary stelae were both termed *wḏ*.[119]

The deceased could be manifest in the form of the tomb statue through his *ka*-force: 'The deified man is [re]incarnated and thus rendered cultically accessible through animating his statue with his *ka*. If his *ka* cannot resort to a statue, the dead man does not live an earthly life of the kind implied by the concept of *ka*'.[120] According to David O'Connor, the power gained through receipt of cult offerings was then transferred to two-dimensional representations of the deceased, because reliefs of the tomb owner were thought of as being the same entity, or the 'alter ego', of three-dimensional figures.[121] The tomb statue could only contain part of the deceased's essence because all of his two- and three-dimensional representations would be ritually active to some degree,[122] although the *ka* was apparently divisible without diminishment.[123] By dividing his presence between the objects that represented him,[124] including all those subject to the Opening of the Mouth ritual, the deceased could theoretically ensure a constant source of nourishment.

The responsibilities of and payment for funerary priests began during the lifetime of their employers, as did the tomb cult itself in the Middle Kingdom,[125] and it can be assumed that similar arrangements continued into the New Kingdom, with the erection of tomb and temple statues.[126] Thus the mortuary monuments of the elite functioned in a similar way to the mortuary temples of kings, such as that of Sety I at Abydos: 'When the temple was completed before the king's death, the chief god, until that king's death, was the deified, living king, anticipating his ultimate ancestral form; he was, for a time, performing the ritual for his own anticipated ancestral form.'[127] Another comparable example is the Syro-Hittite stela of Kuttamuwa from a house in Zincirli, Turkey, on which the owner states that he oversaw the production of the stela and established a feast in the chamber where it was located.[128]

Temple statues of individuals that were dedicated to gods, such as that of Ptah commissioned by the vizier Paser at Memphis, were created for the immediate benefit of the living official

---

[117] *Temp.* Ramesses II: Kitchen 2000: 305, no. 192/1.

[118] For the rarer feminine *rpwt*, see Eaton-Krauss 1984: 84–5. For an ancestor bust that refers to 'this image' (*twt*), see for example the diorite bust of Ramesses-Smanakht: Habachi 1974: 139–42, 144–7.

[119] Demarée 1982: 106.

[120] Finnestad 1978: 134. According to Lorton (1999: 143), the vital force (*ka*) present in the statue is sustained by cult offerings (*kaw*).

[121] O'Connor 1996: 624; cf. Assmann 2005: 215.

[122] Lorton 1999: 182, n. 75; 134, n. 14.

[123] Lorton 1999: 183.

[124] Finnestad 1978: 118.

[125] Russo 2007: 208; see e.g. the stela of Wepwawetaa, overseer of priests, *temp.* Amenemhet II (Munich Gl.WAF 35): Eyre 2002: 198; Sethe 1928: 74, 21–3. For royal cult statues, see Sweeney 2001: 99, cf. Frood 2007: 213–6.

[126] Bolshakov 1991. E.g. the statue of Huti from the temple of Amun at Karnak: Kitchen 2000: 96, no. 88/3; for temple statues in the New Kingdom see Kjølby 2007, 2009; Otto 1948. Cf. Wente 1982: 175.

[127] David 1973: 150.

[128] Struble 2010.

and his perpetual benefit after death.[129] Other statue inscriptions show that it was not the tomb owner directly but his statue that received the bouquet of Amun, a scene sometimes depicted in Theban tombs in connection with the banquet: 'Receive bouquets which come forth from the (divine) presence, from the Temple of Amun in Karnak, you being in favour and you receiving food offerings, your body having scented incense …'[130] This text is inscribed on the pair statue of Amenemope and his wife, suggesting that the seated tomb owner and his spouse shown in banquet scenes could be understood as statues (animated by *ka*-force), around which the banquets centred.[131] A similar request is found on the Ramesside statue of Panehsy:[132]

> *O my likeness, may you be firm for my name,*
> *the favourite of everyone,*
> *so that ⌈people⌉ will stretch out their hands to ⌈you⌉, bearing splendid bouquets,*
> *that you may be given libations and incense,*
> *as the remainder of your lord,*
> *and then my* ba *will come fluttering,*
> *so that he may receive offerings ⌈with you⌉*

The inscriptions on this statue also indicate that it was not only a long-term medium through which the deceased could benefit from contact with the living, but also a dwelling place for the soul:[133]

> *O my statue, you are before the lords of the sacred land;*
> *place yourself as the memory of my name in the domain of the lords of Tawer,*
> *for you are here for me as an abode (?); you are my true body;*
> *for the* ka *of ... Panehsy, true of voice.*

The fundamental functions of a mortuary statue were to 'receive life (*r šsp ʿnḫ*)',[134] and to present the 'true form' of the deceased.[135] The statue was rendered able to receive life and sustenance through the Opening of the Mouth ritual,[136] the text of which, particularly Scene 71,[137] indicates the function of the statue and the importance of the provision of offerings for the deceased:

> *I have provided the* akhu *with their images (ḏbꜣ.n.i ꜣḫw m sšmw.sn),*
> *(And) many thousands of prt-ḫrw offerings of cattle as a perfect action (ỉrt nfr).*

---

[129] Cairo CG 630: Kitchen 2000: 10, no. 3/5.

[130] Berlin 6910: Kitchen 1993: 316, no. 4.

[131] See Chapter 4. For group statues see Rzepka 1995; Hema 2005.

[132] Frood 2007: 169. Right side of BM EA 1377: Bierbrier 1982: 22, pls 49–51; Kitchen 2000: 93, no. 87/1; van Dijk 1993: 122–3.

[133] Frood 2007: 170. The idea of the soul inhabiting and being in some way sheltered by the statue in a tomb or temple is also known from Mesopotamia: Scurlock 2002: 1–2.

[134] 19th Dynasty statue of Iuny from Asyut: MMA 33.2.1; Kitchen 1993: 288–9.

[135] E.g. the inscription in the Horus niche in the tomb of Nefersekheru at Zawyet el-Sultan: 'All you people who will come … may you care for my statue in my august tomb, my lifelike image – its form is truly my appearance.' Osing 1992b: 75, pl. 43; Assmann 2005: 256.

[136] Eaton-Krauss 1984: 75–6; Roth 1992: 146–7; Otto 1960: 2–4; cf. Pahl 1986. The vignette illustrating Spell 23 in the Book of the Dead of Neferrenpet (Milde 1991: 223) shows the deceased seated; the man performing the Opening of the Mouth ritual for him holds a chisel in one hand and an *ankh* in the other, thus illustrating the desired effect of the ritual.

[137] Otto 1960: II, 193–4, cc–kk; I, 159–60; see also Assmann 2005: 327.

> *The one who is in the horizon rejoices over N. I have fashioned*[138] *him.*
> *He is coming and making his divine forms (ḫprw.f nṯryw). I have placed him among the justified.*
> *He will come because of the creation (of) his images (iw pr.f ḥr irt sšmw.f).*[139]
> *His mouth is opened. He is provided for in accordance with Maat.*
> *His name will be established for ever. He will be an* akh iqer *in the netherworld/necropolis,*
> *Hearing the invocations of the one who is his dependant, and protecting the body/flesh of one who libates for him (sḏm.f nis wnn m mrw.f mꜥk.f ḥꜥ n sti n.s mw).*
> *He has power over bread. He has power over beer.*
> *He goes forth as a living* ba, *making his manifestations according to his heart's desire in any place where his* ka *is.*[140]

This scene is followed by no. 73, which depicts priests carrying the statue into the tomb or shrine.[141] Roth interprets this ceremony as a means by which the reborn deceased was enabled to eat both real and symbolic food, through a performance evoking stages of childhood development – from cutting the umbilical cord to physical independence.[142] This interpretation accords with Finnestad's comment that: 'It is the basic idea of being animated that lies behind all the rites involving the statue; they all presuppose a conception of life.'[143] The use of a foreleg from a living or recently slaughtered bovid as a symbolic adze to strike open the mouth of the mummy or statue[144] was intended to suffuse the inanimate deceased with the essence of life. Perhaps, as Gordon and Schwabe point out, *wḥm ꜥnḫ*, in which *wḥm* is written with a bull's leg, should be understood as 'rebirth' in the sense of being endowed with new life,[145] so that the standard translation 'repeating life' does not convey its full meaning. The violence inherent in the slaughter and butchery required in order to present the foreleg and heart was a necessary stage in transferring life and health from one being to another:[146] sacrifice, even if only symbolic, was essential to revitalise the deceased. The Egyptians were not alone in believing that bovids contain a potent source of vitality; for example, the Bara of Madagascar slaughter cattle at funerals 'so that the living can protect themselves by absorbing the force of life inherent in beef.'[147]

The consecrated status of the statue is indicated by the use of milk to purify the paths along which the statues were dragged prior to the Opening of the Mouth ceremony at the tomb entrance, as is stated in an inscription in the tomb of Nakhtamun.[148] Marianne Eaton-Krauss

---

[138] *ms*: see Roth 1992: 146–47. In Mesopotamia a special verb meaning 'to give birth' was used for statues, rather than 'to make' (Roth 1993: 77).

[139] I.e. the deceased is able to respond to the voice and partake of offerings through the medium of the statue.

[140] I.e. the deceased travels everywhere by means of his *ka*; compare, for example, the 19th Dynasty stela of Huy (*temp.* Sety I; Turin 1609/N.50069): Kitchen 1993: 330, no. 4.

[141] Otto 1960: I, fig. 1.

[142] Roth 1992: 147. Such a connection is denied by Lorton 1999: 165, and Quack 2006: 149–50.

[143] 1978: 124.

[144] E.g. scenes 23–25, 43–45, and scene 46 in the tomb of Rekhmire (TT 100), illustrated by Otto 1960: I, fig. 1.

[145] 1998: 468–9.

[146] Lorton 1999: 165; Gordon and Schwabe 1998: 466, 468.

[147] Metcalf and Huntington 1991: 126–7; see also Metcalf 1981: 563; Welsby and Anderson 2004: 70, 75, cat. 275–80.

[148] TT 341; Kitchen 2000: 262.

Figure 17: Statues and stela in courtyard. Tomb of Amenemopet (TT 41). Sheikh Abd el-Qurna. 19th Dynasty. © Eva Hofmann/Ägyptologisches Institut Heidelberg, 18719. Reproduced with the kind permission of Eva Hofmann.

suggests that the Opening of the Mouth was carried out in the workshop,[149] because the statue was offered incense during transportation to the tomb. While some form or part of the ritual may have taken place at the workshop, it seems more likely that its main stages were performed in the tomb and that the fumigation with incense, like the pouring of milk,[150] and the use of milk in the ritual,[151] was intended to purify the statue rather than feed it.[152] That the statue was unable to receive offerings without the performance of rituals is suggested by the fact that the *ka* had to be summoned to meals.[153] The texts of the daily temple ritual also imply that the presence of the recipient (deity or *ka*) in cult statues was dependent on the ritual actions of others; awakening at dawn, for example, 'can only occur in response to the performance of the cult.'[154] The association between *ka* in the sense of living spirit and *kaw*[155] is made explicit in tomb scenes where the tomb owner is depicted seated before a table on which the food offerings are contained within the arms of an outsize *ka*-hieroglyph.[156] Statues could be located in the tomb interior, in the forecourt (Figure 17), or in a chapel within the court that may have been the locus

[149] 1984: 75–6. See also Finnestad 1978: 119; Lorton 1999: 153. In contrast, Stevens (2006: 327–8) suggests that workshops at Amarna were not the location for such 'activation rituals'.

[150] Kitchen 2000: 261–2.

[151] Blackman 1924: 55.

[152] For a discussion of the Opening of the Mouth ceremony and the transference of the deceased's essence into the statue, see Chapter 4. The reason milk was used as a purifying substance is not clear, but may be related to its colour, since white was indicative of cleanliness, and its association with the cow goddess Hathor.

[153] E.g. Assmann 2005: 337–8. Here one may compare Mesopotamian offering rituals, particularly the 'liturgy of nocturnal sacrifices' and *kispu* texts (Lewis 1989: 2, 7, 12).

[154] Lorton 1999: 139; see further Heiden 2003.

[155] Food offerings; Gordon 1996: 33–5; Lorton 1999: 143.

[156] Termed by Davies a symbolic '*sekhet-hotep*' table (1933: 59). See also Muhammed 1966: 105–6.

of mortuary cult.[157] Some statues were set up in mud-brick tomb superstructures, as with the sculpture of Senimenu with Princess Neferure and his wife or mother[158] and the contemporary structure above the Sheikh Abd el-Qurna tomb of Senenmut.[159]

Discussions of statues rarely address the experience of seeing them in their original settings: the combination of darkness, lamp/torchlight, and shadows would have created an atmosphere in which they took on a significance that they do not possess either in daylight or in a museum environment. The three-dimensional image of the deceased was the focal point for most major tombs, as indicated at Thebes by their location within shrines; anyone approaching them was obliged to walk to the back of the tomb, which would be in near-darkness, illuminated chiefly by lamps,[160] as suggested by the stela text in Paheri's tomb: 'A torch will be burned for you in the night, until sunlight rises on your breast'.[161] Such a passage may allude to ritual vigils as well as to the regular mortuary cult. A similar text is found in the tomb of Amenemhet: 'A light for the use of every day, illuminating the road of darkness for the scribe who reckons the grain, the steward Amenemhet, everywhere that he goes.'[162] The importance of light to the dead (on a daily basis as well as during festivals), particularly its protective qualities as the eye of Re, is reflected in the tombs of Amenemhet (TT 82), Menkheperreseneb (TT 112) and Senemioh.[163] Spell 80 of the Book of the Dead is intended to give the deceased the ability to banish darkness: 'making transformation into a god, causing the darkness to be light.[164] The effect of such an environment on ancient visitors who subscribed to the underlying belief system is very difficult to reconstruct, but was presumably far more involving than modern viewers can comprehend.

A scene in the 4th Dynasty tomb of Debehni at Giza shows the end of the funeral procession, and the presentation of offerings to a statue of the deceased with *s3ḫw* recitations[165] and performances associated with the funerary meal, prior to the deposition of the statue in the tomb.[166] That similar rituals may have taken place in the New Kingdom is suggested by fragments from the 19th Dynasty tomb chapel of Horemheb at Saqqara.[167]

In periods after the Middle Kingdom, temple statues of individuals became a greater focal point for mortuary ritual,[168] so that the dead participated more directly in the cult of the gods

157 TT 15 (*temp.* Ahmose/Amenhotep I): Kampp 1996: 195–6, figs 96–8; see further Davies 1925.

158 TT 252; Kampp 1996: 527–8, fig. 424.

159 TT 71; Kampp 1996: 301, fig. 186. For a similar mud-brick structure above the tomb of Paser (TT 106), see Seyfried 1990: pl. 60.

160 TT 276 of Amenemipet; *temp.* Thutmose III/Amenhotep II, for example, has lamp niches on either side of the entrance to the longitudinal hall: Kampp 1996: 574, fig. 443; Hermann 1940: pl. 12a. Cf. El-Shohoumi (2004: 201–2, 69–70) for modern rituals involving light for the soul of the dead in mortuary and domestic contexts.

161 Assmann 2005: 258; Tylor 1895: pl. xvi, line 18.

162 Gardiner and Davies 1915: 97.

163 TT 127: Gardiner and Davies 1915: 98, 106.

164 Amenemhet, TT 82; south wall of the burial chamber: Gardiner and Davies 1915: 104; Allen 1974: 70.

165 Assmann 1990, with references.

166 Eyre 2002: 55; Hassan 1943: 176, fig. 122.

167 Kitchen 2000: 132, no. 107/1; see also Assmann 2005: 320.

168 Bourriau 1991: 15; Baines and Lacovara 2002: 21; Verbovsek 2004.

as well as being members of the temple community.[169] Pinch comments[170] that the intermediary statues at Deir el-Bahri provided a 'counterpart in the official [Hathor] cult for the role of the dead in popular religion', a role that the 'bald' statues may also have performed in the temple or chapels during the 19th Dynasty at Deir el-Medina.[171] On an 18th Dynasty intermediary statue from the Hathor temple at Deir el-Bahri, the inscription states that in return for reciting the offering formula, the male owner would grant women happiness and a good husband.[172] Another, commissioned by the Royal Butler Tjau, states:[173]

> *I am the [musician?] [...] of Hathor, who listens to the petitions (sḏm spr) of every young girl who weeps and who trusts in Hathor. Place perfumed oil upon my forehead, and beer for my mouth, bread and beer from what you offer, place offerings in front of (me); then I shall speak to Hathor, (for) she has listened to what is repeated.*

The best known intermediary is the 18th Dynasty official Amenhotep son of Hapu,[174] who had at least ten statues in the temple of Amun[175] at Karnak, as well as his own Theban mortuary temple.[176] The opportunity for privileged individuals to commission such sculptures was provided by the king,[177] as stated on one of Amenhotep's statues: 'Give me an offering and pour a libation for me, because I am an intermediary nominated by the king to hear the requests of the supplicant'.[178] The statues enabled the elite to 'achieve moral stature in this world and the next by interceding on behalf of their social inferiors',[179] and the extent of their popularity is indicated by the amount of wear their inscriptions sustained.[180]

In the 19th Dynasty, a new intermediary statue type appeared,[181] through which people could address their concerns to deities.[182] The dedicatees were termed 'the bald one (*pꜣ is*)',[183] and

---

169 Simpson 1982: 267.

170 1993: 347.

171 Clère 1995: 135.

172 Robins 1995: 104–5, no. 63; Pinch 1993: 335. Cf. the intermediary statue of Neferhotep who also appeals specifically to women: Clère 1995: 110–11, text D, lines 4–7.

173 Pinch 1993: 331, pl. 40. See also the statue of Amenemonet (*temp.* Ramesses II) from Deir el-Bahri: Clère 1995: 90–1, lines 3–4; Frood 2007: 191.

174 Also known as Huy; Wildung 1977b.

175 Teeter 1995: 232; Parkinson 1999: 136–7, no. 51; Saleh and Sourouzian 1987: nos 148–9. Amenhotep son of Hapu is depicted in the tomb of Inherkhau (TT 359, 20th Dynasty) being worshipped alongside deceased monarchs (McDowell 1992: 97, 100), which may indicate that he was appealed to in tombs as well as temples. For the worship of royal ancestors and the association between figures of deceased kings and the Feast of the Wadi, see Redford 1986: 45–56.

176 Robichon and Varille 1936. The mortuary cult of Amenhotep son of Hapu was established at least three years prior to his death according to Bolshakov 1991: 216.

177 Eyre 1987: 198.

178 Statue from the vicinity of the tenth pylon: Wildung 1977a: 88; see also Otto 1948: 462.

179 Baines 1991: 183.

180 Wildung 1977a: 88.

181 Franke 1988; Clère 1995; cf. the statue of Peraha (BM EA 501); Russmann 2001: 187–8, no. 95. Intercessory stelae are also attested, for example BM EA 706 from the Middle Kingdom temple at Deir el-Bahri: Kitchen 1993: 267–9.

182 Baines 1991: 183.

183 Clère 1995: 49, fig. 20. Not all men captioned *is* were depicted bald, however; see e.g. the statue of

most such statues depict them crouching or sitting with their hands cupped before their mouths in anticipation of receiving offerings, essentially a development of the block statue form.[184] A combination of statue and stelae, the 'healing statue', attested from the reign of Ramesses III and set up in the outer parts of temples, had a dual function: water poured over the monument became imbued with potency absorbed from the inscribed spells, producing a medicinal drink for the sick, while also providing the statue's owner with a liquid offering.[185]

Statues located in tomb forecourts partook in New Kingdom religious developments and in the greater integration of deities and the divinised deceased into mortuary architecture.[186] In principle, New Kingdom tombs contained at least one statue of the owner,[187] not all necessarily of stone; sufficient wooden examples exist[188] to suggest that our picture of life-size statue placement in and around tombs may well be incomplete; as Baines points out,[189] 'Our image of Egypt is probably over-dominated by stone, which survives well in an archaeological record from which much else disappears or is recycled.' The 19th Dynasty saw the introduction of statues of deities in private tombs,[190] commonly either Osiris[191] or a triad of Osiris, Isis, and Horus. Where statues of gods are present, they are often more prominent than those of the deceased. For example, in the tomb of Nefersekheru (TT 296), the rock-cut standing statue of Osiris dominates the entrance, while in the slightly later tomb of Tjay (TT 23), the divine triad essentially replaces the tomb owner and his family in the furthermost niche.[192] In the forecourt of the Ramesside tomb of Piay from the reign of Ramesses II there is a niche containing an engaged statue of Hathor in bovine form wearing a *menat*-necklace, probably preceded by a small figure of the king, of which only traces remain.[193] Similar statues are found in the roughly contemporary tomb of Meryptah opposite a statue of Osiris,[194] and in the tombs of Netjerymes at Saqqara and Qen at Deir el-Medina.[195]

Penshen'abu (*temp.* Sety I?); Clère 1995: 116, line 4; pl. xiv.

184 Clère 1995: 11, pl. 1; 80, pl. 3; 82, figs 28, 29; 93, pl. 6.

185 Ritner 1993: 107. See also the statues of Didia (*temp.* Thutmose III), and Neferrenpet (18th–19th Dynasties), and Paser (18th Dynasty) with integral basins for libations or other offerings: El-Damaty 1990: 5, pl. 5, figs a, b; Frood 2007: 133–6; Clère 1995: pl. xxix; Jørgensen 1998: 20–1.

186 After Kampp 1996: 75, table 54; *ibid.*: 495; see Seyfried 1990: pl. 59 for the forecourt statues of Paser (TT 106).

187 For examples of New Kingdom small-scale wooden statuary, see e.g. Kitchen 2000: 464 (Berlin 6909), 477–8 (Leiden D. 19), 498 (Turin 3048), 548 (Leiden D. 29). A list of statue endowments from Abydos dating to the reign of Ramesses II mentions a copper statue (Kitchen 2000: 325, no. 205/12), and TT 329 (Mose) also contains a reference to copper images (Kitchen 2000: 504); any such pieces are likely to have been melted down for reuse.

188 For the cost of wooden statues, see Janssen 1975: 246–8.

189 2007: 264.

190 Hofmann 1995: 275; Frood 2007: 173.

191 Kampp 1996: 566, fig. 460. See Strudwick (1994: 326) for a discussion of the depiction of Osiris in 18th and 19th Dynasty tombs.

192 Kampp 1996: 208, fig. 109.

193 TT 263; Kampp 1996: 541.

194 TT 387; Kampp 1996: 603, fig. 498. For the symbolism of the 'cow and mountain' motif, see Pinch 1993: 347; see also Exell 2004: 53–7; Blumenthal 2000: 44–8.

195 TT 4; Zivie 2003: 74–6, 80, fig. 4; 82, fig. 6; Zivie 2002: 30–1. See also the stela of Khabekhnet, *temp.* Ramesses II, BM EA 555: Bierbrier and Parkinson 1993: pls 30, 31 (fig. 2); and the relief of Ramose

From the prominence of statues of the deceased together with his family in Old Kingdom tombs,[196] to the statues of deities in 19th Dynasty tombs, there was a gradual decline in the salience of the individual within mortuary structures. The emphasis of mortuary decoration shifted towards the relationship between the deceased and the gods, becoming separated from the family and 'daily life' themes prominent in the Middle Kingdom and 18th Dynasty as part of wider developments in religious display. To what extent these changes affected the relationship between the living and the dead is not clear. However, it seems likely that regular interaction with the ancestors in tombs and temples continued as before. This interpretation is supported by the proliferation of cultic emplacements and equipment from sites such as Deir el-Medina.

Anthropoid or 'ancestor' busts

Anthropoid busts,[197] along with other images of the ancestors including those on stelae, provided a means by which the lower or non-elite could access the divine without recourse to intervention by royalty or priests. Use of dead kin as intercessors between the living and the gods may have had an impact on social relations and raised the profile of a family's predecessors to the level of those elite individuals who could afford to erect intermediary statues of themselves during their lifetimes in temples as objects of future cult practices and worship.[198] The manipulation of the power inherent in direct access to deities was expressed in the Maya Late Classic period by the inclusion of ancestral shrines only within elite residences.[199]

In considering African ancestral figures, particularly those of the Yoruba, Rosalind Hackett[200] notes that with the addition of specific substances the figures are believed to become the essence of the deceased individuals whom they represent and are accordingly given their names. Presumably, as with Egyptian busts, the names are not written on the figures themselves. Hackett goes on to state:[201]

> *... instead of asking why Africans fail to distinguish adequately between people and objects, we might reverse the question and ask why we make such a dubious distinction. The answer lies partly in the realization that thingness and personhood are culturally constructed. Western tendencies towards commodification in the modern world obscure the memory of the divine power medieval Christians attributed to the relics of saints.*

---

from Deir el-Medina, Louvre E 16276: Barbotin 2002: 229, no. 184. For the development of the motif of Hathor and the king, see Pinch 1993: 180–1.

196 E.g. Kendall 1981: 104.

197 The term 'anthropoid bust' was introduced by Jean Keith (2011: 2) as a purely descriptive idiom, because she considers the busts to have various functions rather than simply representing ancestors. I prefer a typological distinction, with amulets, 'house busts', and 'tomb busts' (larger than house busts, and with distinguishing features such as striped wigs), forming clear categories. While some may have had secondary uses, I think the majority depict ancestors, and thus use the expressions 'anthropoid' and 'ancestor' busts interchangeably.

198 E.g. Pinch 1993: pl. 40.

199 Dornan 2004: 32.

200 1996: 48.

201 1996: 49.

The bust as a representation of the deceased may thus be seen as an extension of the individual: not merely a temporary receptacle for the spirit, but an entity imbued with life and a part of the family.[202] Such an interpretation may explain the lack of names on busts, which has led many scholars to consider them as representative of generic rather than specific ancestors.[203] This view is exemplified by Lynn Meskell:[204]

> *If ... ancestor stelae ... suggest a penchant for the specificities of memory and remembered individuals, it might be said that ancestor busts reveal a certain willingness to suppress memory, to be comprehensive or more encompassing. There is a subtle difference here. Ancestor stelae embody the identity of the individual and similarly act as a conduit for communication between worlds and persons, living and dead, whereas ancestor busts blended the anthropomorphic qualities of the individual with the statue-like qualities of the divine and tended to be more anonymous and less focussed upon named individuals ... Their lack of specificity might also designate them as objects of forgetting, material places where fixed memory was deemed unnecessary.*

The idea that the busts were intended to be 'objects of forgetting' does not fit well with the material culture of a community like Deir el-Medina, where other artefacts such as stelae seem to emphasize the importance of remembering. If the busts were meant to represent the collective, distant dead, why were they not mass produced or identical in appearance?[205] If they were not representative of close kin, what was their function in the household? Other than as malign entities, the collective dead did not appear to interact with the living, and therefore the reciprocal basis for interrelations was not applicable: if they did not act as the focus of a mortuary cult, what was the purpose of these busts?

The objection that they do not represent individuals because they are not inscribed may be answered in part by their placement in inscribed niches.[206] For example, Bruyère found a small bust and an offering table along with limestone plinth or lintel for a niche inscribed with the name Horinefer in house S.O. III.[207] Niche inscriptions would have obviated the need for an object placed within it to be provided with a dedication of its own. In addition, some busts may have stood on inscribed plinths, as suggested by the few that have bases.[208] A bust was found in a house at Amarna in association with a mud-brick altar-like emplacement, though the exact find spot of the sculpture was not recorded.[209]

---

202 Cf. Meskell 2004: 61.

203 E.g. Keith 2011: 87, with references. For the limited spread of writing and literacy in Egypt see Baines 2007: 33–178.

204 2004: 73–5.

205 Moulds indicate that amuletic busts could have been produced in quantity, but relatively few have been discovered to date. Equally a greater uniformity among Deir el-Medina busts might be expected: Keith (2011: 36) notes that 'no two [busts] are alike'.

206 Statues may likewise be identified by adjacent inscriptions in tombs or shrines, presumably as was the case with BM EA 36, an 18th Dynasty limestone pair statue from a tomb (James and Davies 1983: 37, fig. 43); two wooden statuettes of the 18th and 19th Dynasties, BM EA 32772 and 2319 (Russmann 2001: 182–5); and the possible *akh iqer* statuette from a house at Amarna (Cairo JE 53249: Russmann 1990: 120, fig. 56).

207 1939: 320, fig. 190; Journal no. 27.2.35, p. 10, ms-2004-0156-020 (www.ifao.egnet/bases/archives/bruyere).

208 E.g. Berlin 17826: Keith-Bennett 1983: 68, fig. 11.

209 House Q.46.9: Borchardt and Ricke 1980: 37, plan 7.

Previous research

For some decades following Bruyère's (1939) publication of his Deir el-Medina excavations, anthropoid busts were not the subject of much research, and scholars[210] confined themselves to noting that these objects were part of an ancestor cult. Jean Keith's 1981 article marked the first step in further analysis.[211] Only five among 188 known busts bear inscriptions, and at least two of these were probably later additions to the sculptures. Because of their anonymity and general uniformity of appearance, they were considered to represent the generic dead rather than deceased individuals. Bothmer[212] suggested that the busts represented Hathor and Ptah on the basis of iconographic similarities, while Bruyère,[213] who discovered 75 busts at Deir el-Medina, concluded that they were statues of household gods, and termed them '*bustes de laraires*' – ancestral household gods whose role was the care of living descendants, from the Latin *lares familiares*.[214] Bruyère[215] suggested that wooden labels may have been hung from some busts to identify them individually, but Keith has rejected this idea. Neither she nor Sylvie Donnat is convinced that all anthropoid busts represent ancestors, and they have therefore sought to find alternative explanations for the busts' forms.[216]

Keith takes three inscribed busts from the corpus and attributes different functions to each of them:

DMC 1	*nbt-pr ẖ3nsr m3ʿ-ḫrw* [*m*] *ḥtp Mistress of the House Khanser, justified, in/at peace*
CG 1172	*ỉr n nbt-pr t3ntbḥdt Made by*[217]*/for the Mistress of the House Tanetbehedet*
DMB 1	*ḥwt-ḥr nb*(*t*)*-ḥtp.t wr*(*t*) *wsr*(*t*) *m ỉwnw Hathor-Nebethetepet,*[218] *the Great One, Powerful in Heliopolis*

According to Keith, the epithet *m3ʿ-ḫrw* marks Khanser as an ancestor, while its absence on the Tanetbehedet bust is interpreted as identifying the sculpture as a votive offering presented to a living individual; the 'Hathor bust' is considered from its inscription alone to be an example of the worship of the deity in a house shrine.[219] Such a division may not be particularly helpful in understanding the corpus as a whole, and presenting a sculpture associated with the dead to a living person as a religious offering seems implausible. Donnat, translating *ỉr n* as 'made by', states that the inscription on CG 1172 implies that people named on busts are not those represented by them; but if *ỉr n* is understood as 'made for',

---

210 E.g. Vandier d'Abbadie 1946; Keith 1981; Kaiser 1990; Bomann 1991: 69, 74; Friedman 1994: 14–17; *id.*: 1985; Meskell 2002: 111, 120–1; Stevens 2003: 164–5; Ogden 2001: 219.

211 For an overview of ancestor busts, see Exell 2008.

212 1987: 29; cf. Keith 2011: 78.

213 1939: 168.

214 See e.g. Laing 1921: 137.

215 1939: 173.

216 In Keith 2011.

217 In the sense of 'on behalf of' (Faulkner 1962: 27), or 'commissioned by'.

218 Donnat translates 'Mistress of Peace' (in Keith 2011: 95; cf. Keith 2011: 69–70). Pinch's translation 'Mistress of the Vulva' (1993: 219) would be pertinent if the busts were involved in birth-related rituals (for a photograph of the bust, see Kaiser 1990: pl. 61, 2). An alternative interpretation was provided by Vandier (1958: 82, no. vii), who considered the bust to be dedicated to 'Hathor-Nébet-Hétépet, la Puissante dans Heliopolis.' The style of incised inscription on the bust is similar to one found on the Ramesside statue of a priest (Turin 3036), dedicated to Hathor-Nebethetepet, Mistress of Byblos (Vandier 1956: 82, no. viii, pl. 4).

219 Keith 2011: 88.

Tanetbehedet becomes the dedicatee rather than the dedicator. Part of Donnat's reasoning rests on her interpretation that at least some Deir el-Medina busts symbolize domestic deities, particularly Ipet Taweret;[220] she also supports Bothmer's assertion that double busts represent Hathor and Ptah.[221] Double busts were not discovered by Möller or Bruyère during their excavations at Deir el-Medina,[222] although this does not prove that none originated from there. The sculptors of double busts distinguished genders by depicting the female with a tripartite wig and the male with a shaven head or tight-fitting cap,[223] and as in the case of Louvre E 14702, a beard.[224] No distinguishing feature links these busts iconographically to two- or three-dimensional figures of deities.[225] While I would agree that the 'Hathor bust' described above may have been inscribed as a votive offering to the goddess following its previous function as an ancestor bust, it is also possible that Hathor was invoked on behalf of the deceased person represented by the sculpture.

Provenance and description

Aside from Deir el-Medina, bust findspots include Sesebi, Elephantine, Karnak temple, Abydos,[226] Amara West,[227] Amarna,[228] Sedment,[229] Gurob,[230] Saqqara,[231] Mit Rahina,[232] and Medinet el-Faiyum.[233] Most, however, are unprovenanced. The busts show regional variations, but consist essentially of a human head, either without hair[234] or wearing a tripartite wig, on an armless torso that usually widens towards the base. Some busts were decorated with broad collars and pendant water lily buds and flowers. It is possible that they could have been adorned with garlands of this type during festivals or as part of offering ceremonies: requests for garlands of fresh flowers in texts on New Kingdom statuary[235] suggest that bouquets may have been presented to images of the deceased.[236] The busts range in size from 2cm to 70cm,

---

220 See Bomann 1991: 69–70.

221 1987: 29.

222 Keith-Bennett 1981: 46.

223 E.g. JE 87846, BM EA 49735, Cairo 62371: Keith-Bennett 1981: 70, figs 15–17; Kaiser 1990: pl. 62, 1–3.

224 Kaiser 1990, pl. 62, 4.

225 Cf. Bruyère 1939: 171–2, n. 3.

226 Kaiser *et al.* 1990: pl. 43b.

227 Spencer 2010.

228 Romano 1999: 282; Stevens 2006: 294.

229 Keith-Bennett 1981: 46; Kaiser 1990: 274–6.

230 Thomas 1981: II pl. 55, nos 711 and 712.

231 Raven 2001: 20, no. 6; pl. 14. Late 18th Dynasty unfinished male bust found on a ledge in Chamber G in the tomb of Maya and Meryt.

232 Memphis: Giddy 1999: 48–9, pls. 14, 82; the bust was found within the debris of a house.

233 UC 16550; Harrington 2005: 73, fig. 2.

234 Or with a tight-fitting cap, e.g. Brooklyn Museum 53.246: Kaiser 1990: pl. 61, fig. 3.

235 Clère 1995: 90–91, text G, line 6 (Ameneminet); 106–7, n. f (Bahy). Flowers carved from thin slices of limestone were found in association with busts at Deir el-Medina: Sadek 1987: 77–8; Bruyère 1939: 210–11, 322–3.

236 E.g. Munich statue of Bakenkhonsu (*temp.* Ramesses II), and inscriptions on one of Roma's statues and on the east massif of the Eighth Pylon at Karnak temple (late 19th Dynasty); Frood 2007: 40, 50, 56, 58.

Figure 18: Anthropoid bust, painted limestone, probably from Thebes, 18th–19th Dynasty. Petrie Museum of Egyptian Archaeology, UC 16551.

Figure 19: Anthropoid bust, faience, probably from Thebes, 18th–19th Dynasty. Petrie Museum of Egyptian Archaeology, UC 16553.

and are produced from a variety of materials including limestone, sandstone, granite, faience, and wood (Figures 18 and 19).[237]

The composition of the scene on a stela in the British Museum,[238] one of three depicting anthropoid busts,[239] is similar to contemporaneous stelae that show the dedicator in the lower register worshipping a deity in the upper register.[240] A kneeling figure, identifiable as female by her clothing, is depicted worshipping the three main types of bust: bare-headed with a beard;[241] male with cap (or shaven head);[242] and female(?) with tripartite wig and collar.[243] This generality

[237] Bruyère 1939: 168. Bruyère mentions clay busts but Keith (2011: 29) contests this.

[238] BM EA 270; Budge 1909: 246, no. 912; Keith-Bennett 1981: 62; Bierbrier 1982: 95, fig. 68; Bierbrier and Parkinson 1993: 18, pls 54–5; Meskell 2004: 71, fig. 3.2; Pinch 1994: 148, fig. 79; Harrington, in Keith 2011.

[239] The other two are the stela of Henut (Vandier d'Abbadie 1946: 135), and an unpublished stela with relief busts – Egyptian Museum Cairo, temporary register no. 29/3 (Keith 2011: 74, 318).

[240] E.g. Rigault 2002: 151, no. 94; Zibelius-Chen 2002: 233, no. 189.

[241] E.g. Louvre E 14702, UC 16553 and 2400; Kaiser 1990: pl. 62, fig. 4; Keith Bennett 1981: 64–5, figs. 1 and 2.

[242] E.g. Brooklyn 53.246, BM EA 49735; Kaiser 1990: pl. 61, fig. 3; Keith Bennett 1981: 70, fig. 17.

[243] E.g. BM EA 61083; MMA 26.7.1024; Meskell 2004: 75, fig. 3.3; Kaiser 1990: pl. 63, fig. 5.

might be intended to convey the notion that the woman is addressing all ancestors, male and female. The busts in the upper register are three-dimensional and were individually carved and secured with plaster into recesses around 9mm deep, coated with a further wash of plaster, and then painted.[244] The stela was roughly shaped at the back for placement in a niche, probably in the wall of a house.[245]

At least nine Theban tombs include representations of bust-like objects. The problem of distinguishing busts from masks in such cases is compounded by the fact that the objects are not captioned. Two tombs that show anthropoid busts are those of Irinefer and Horemheb;[246] the former depicts a bust on a plinth in the context of Book of the Dead Spell 151, and the latter shows two bearded busts carried in procession to the tomb. Horemheb's offering bearers also carry a bust-like sculpture with a lappet wig, collar, and divine beard,[247] which is likely to be a mummy mask of the type without cutaway areas for the shoulders that was produced during the mid-18th Dynasty.[248] The 'busts' shown in the tomb of Neferhotep may be a later example of the same style of representation,[249] and the fact that they wear unguent cones, which are otherwise unknown on busts or images of them, makes their identification as anthropoid busts unlikely.

Dating and origins

The earliest known depiction of anthropoid busts is the 11th Dynasty sarcophagus of ʿAshyt from Deir el-Bahri.[250] Two busts are shown on either side of a headrest, facing outwards as though protecting it. The text accompanying the image is a request for a voice offering and a list of seven sacred oils and eye paint; it does not refer to the busts directly. The oils relate to Spell 934 in the Coffin Texts that states in reference to the headrest:

> *O Osiris, this N, your head is supported so that you may live, your* ba *may live, and you may be a god (wsir N pn ṯs n.k tp.k ʿnḫ.k ʿnḫ b3.k wnn.k m nṯr)*[251]

According to de Buck,[252] Spell 934 'may belong to two [headrests] in the frieze of objects, or to two large [busts] with the identical legend: *rdit n.f tp.f ʿnḫ.f* [giving his head to him so that he may live]'. This is fundamentally important to the understanding of the origin, iconography and function of the busts: they are the heads of the blessed deceased in the form of the living, supported and thereby divine.[253] Book of the Dead Spell 151, the spell for the secret/mysterious

244 Harrington in Keith 2011: 324; Keith 2011: 72–3. Compositions like this are rare; on comparable stelae, such as those of Ptah from Deir el-Medina and Memphis (UC14545: Stewart 1976: 36, pl. 29.2; Cairo JE 45555: Schulman 1981: 165) the three-dimensional figures do not appear to be carved independently of the stone.

245 Cf. Bruyère 1930: 10; Meskell 2004: 70. For niches and 'cultic cupboards' in Amarna houses, see Stevens 2003: 150–4.

246 TT 290: Harrington in Keith 2011: 90, fig. 9; TT 78: Brack and Brack 1980: pl. 61c.

247 Brack and Brack 1980: pl. 17a.

248 Ikram and Dodson 1998: 170, pl. 198. Cf. the mask in the workshop scene in the tomb chapel of Ipuy; black indicates the negative space where the mask fitted onto the mummy: Andreu 2002c: 31, fig. 13.

249 TT 49 (*temp.* Ay?): Davies 1933: 44, pl. xxv.

250 Keith 2011: 74–5; Harrington in Keith 2011: 89.

251 De Buck 1961: 136, col. 1, lines 44–6; Faulkner 1978: 69, n. 17; cf. Thompson 1998: 233, 237.

252 1961: 136, n. 1.

253 According to Hellinckx (2001: 92), the head alone could represent the deceased in general.

head (*r n tp št3*) may be a development of CT 934, as it also connects the divine status of the deceased with the head: 'I have caused you to be a god … your head will never be taken away'.[254]

Despite Florence Friedman's suggestion that anthropoid busts developed from Eighteenth Dynasty stelephorous statues,[255] it is more likely that the statues and the busts were produced contemporaneously in a context of increased emphasis both on solar-related ideology[256] and on the mortuary cult of deceased individuals.[257] By the Nineteenth Dynasty stelephorous statues were rarely incorporated into the external structure of tombs,[258] but anthropoid busts continued to be produced and placed within tombs, houses, chapels, and temples.[259]

Gender and stage of life

I have proposed elsewhere that the busts show the dead as idealized, so that they represent the *akh* in human form.[260] If this is correct, it would suggest that the majority of busts represent female ancestors, with males being identified as bare-headed, wearing a close-fitting cap, or with a short wig, as exemplified by the wooden bust from Sedment.[261] Some anthropoid busts have beards, almost all of which are of the standard straight or cropped type worn by the living, not the curled style indicative of gods and the blessed dead.[262] This is consistent with Spell 64 of the Book of the Dead, which states that the *akh* will appear in human form.[263] Examples of busts with divine beards include the two shown being carried on the shoulders of offering bearers in the Theban tomb of Horemheb (see above), and a single bust carried in procession in the tomb of Menkheperreseneb,[264] but these are large in comparison to the offering bearers and therefore are likely to be specifically 'tomb busts'. Three busts bearing platform crowns may be identified as female by this headdress alone.[265]

Skin colour is not a reliable indicator of gender.[266] The use of red or yellow, both solar hues and thus appropriate for the blessed or deified dead, may have been arbitrary, as perhaps

254 Faulkner 1985: 145; Allen 1974: 148, b, c. The link between the head and divinity is noted by Assmann (2005: 107–8), who states that according to mortuary liturgy the mummy mask was 'the "head of a god", a head that enabled the deceased to see and act as a god.' Late Period sarcophagus texts also mention gods named 'lords of the living heads (or, heads of the living)' (*ibid.*: 88).

255 1985: 94.

256 Assmann 1983; 1995.

257 Demarée 1983: 249, n. 282.

258 See Kampp 1996.

259 E.g. the tomb of Amenmose, TT 373 (*temp.* Ramesses II): Habachi 1976: 84–6.

260 Harrington 2005. See also Friedman 1985: 85.

261 UC 16554: Keith 2011: 295–7.

262 Of almost 200 busts, only one bears tripartite wig and a tapering beard that may have curled at the end (BM EA 58783; Keith 2011: 328–9) in the style of P. Neferrenpet, indicating the individual's divinity. Although the blessed dead are said to become gods in mortuary texts, they are rarely explicitly depicted in this form. Perhaps the almost equally rare polos/ platform crown was the female equivalent.

263 Demarée 1983: 252, n. 295; Friedman 1994: 114; Allen 1974: 59. Cf. PT 260, §318–9: Faulkner 1969: 69.

264 TT 79: Guksch 1995: pl. 43a.

265 Keith 2011: 53; see e.g. Bruyère 1939: pl. xxi, 1.

266 See e.g. Pinch 1983: 410; Keith 2011: 84–5. Robins (2007: 211) notes that skin colour in ancient Egypt is largely symbolic, even though it is not always clear what the difference signified.

in the case of the three-bust stela discussed above, on which both three-dimensional figures represent men, but one face is painted red and the other yellow. It is equally possible that the choice of red/brown paint for the representation of deceased females was a means of expressing their transfigured state in the same manner that shabtis and anthropoid coffins belonging to women could possess red or golden faces – colours traditionally associated with men and the gods respectively.[267] For example, the bust of Khanser[268] has a red face but was inscribed with the name and titles of the deceased woman that it presumably represents.

Location

Jean Keith[269] is dismissive of the view that the majority of busts at Deir el-Medina originally derived from domestic contexts, but the fact that most of those found during excavations were discovered in houses[270] suggests that many of the unprovenanced examples may also have come from dwellings. This is supported by the recent discovery of a sandstone bust *in situ* on a brick and sandstone pedestal in a house at Amara West,[271] and the bust from a domestic context at Memphis.[272]

Some niches for busts, stelae, or statuettes of deities bear traces of having been surrounded by lintels and door jambs.[273] The niches may have possessed wooden doors,[274] in effect transforming them into miniature shrines. Just as temple doorways were appropriate places to direct petitions to the gods,[275] the jambs and lintel of domestic shrines may have enhanced their effectiveness and assisted in ensuring that petitions were heard, as well as secluding the busts when they were not being addressed. In addition to the eleven busts discovered in domestic contexts at Deir el-Medina, a further five were found in the domestic rubble of the South Kom, and eight in the 'great pit'.[276]

While the three-dimensionality and free-standing form of most busts would have facilitated their removal from niches for cleaning, garlanding, or during a festival, it seems unlikely that they were carried around during processions or moved from the house to a tomb or temple, as suggested by Lynn Meskell.[277] Statues in tomb courtyards and other images may have sufficed during festivals, and findspots such as the vicinity of the Hathor temple at Deir el-Medina do not necessarily support the proposal that busts were transported as part of rituals.[278] If domestic busts represented recently deceased members of the household, and their function was intimately connected with the house, no reason to move them beyond its confines is apparent.

267 Cooney 2008: 6–7.
268 Keith 2011: 68–9.
269 1981: 48.
270 Three-quarters of provenanced examples: Keith 2011: 15.
271 No. F4182, Building 3, room 26, 20th Dynasty, *temp.* Ramesses III (Neal Spencer, personal communication, August 2010).
272 Kom Rabi'a, EES 47/EAO 4: Giddy 1999: 49, pls 14, 82.
273 Bruyère 1926: 194, fig. 86. All four jambs illustrated are inscribed with requests for offerings for the *ka* of an individual. The figures of a woman and child are both captioned as deceased (*mꜣꜥ ḫrw*).
274 Bruyère 1926: 196, fig. 87; Friedman 1985: 83.
275 Galán 2003: 224–5.
276 Bruyère 1930: 11; Keith 2011: 14.
277 2002: 111.
278 Morris 2002: 267.

Function

I would argue that the busts performed several functions as ancestors, not as deities or votive objects. The largest, including the Gallatin bust and those of Paendjerty and Mutemonet,[279] bear striated wigs, a feature that is primarily associated with the dead – as on shabtis, anthropoid coffins, and mummy masks – or with deities. Striated wigs on taller examples seem to mark a clear distinction between 'domestic' busts and those intended solely for the tomb, and are perhaps indicative of their different roles.

Long, non-striated tripartite wigs, such as those on the busts, were traditionally part of the iconography of women, both during life and in depictions of the afterlife. It is possible that the majority of busts depict women, complementing the *ꜣḫ iḳr n rꜥ* stelae, on which the dedicatee was usually male.[280] The principal basis for this proposal is the role of women in domestic and religious life at sites such as Deir el-Medina.[281] Women are also shown making offerings to anthropoid busts on two stelae.[282] These may be set within the house, in keeping with the instruction in the calendar of lucky and unlucky days:[283] 'II *prt*, day 7. … Make *prt-ḫrw* offerings to the *ꜣḫw* in your house, make *ꜥꜣbt* offerings to the gods'.[284] This suggestion is further supported by the fact, noted above, that on double busts men are distinguished by having beards and shaven heads, whereas women wear tripartite wigs.[285] It is also worth noting that of the inscribed busts, two are dedicated to women and one to a goddess.[286]

Tomb inscriptions suggest that one of the roles of the dead was to act as the guardian of his family:[287]

> *May you open the mound in the realm of the dead so as to see your house of the living again. May you hear the sound of song and music in your (dwelling?) house in this land. May you be a protection for your children, forever and ever.*[288]

> *May he again see his house of the living, so as to be a protection to his children daily, forever and ever.*[289]

---

[279] Habachi 1976: 84–6.

[280] See Demarée 1983.

[281] Cf. Pinch 1993: 343.

[282] Stela of Henut from Abydos: Vandier d'Abbadie 1946: 135; BM EA 270 from Deir el-Medina: Bierbrier and Parkinson 1993: 18, pls. 54–55; Harrington, in Keith 2011: 321–3. Women also provided for and consulted the ancestors in ancient Palestine: Bloch-Smith 1992b: 219. Women are sometimes shown worshipping ancestors on *akh iqer* stelae; see for example Philadelphia E 13598 (Schulman 1986: 333–4).

[283] P. Sallier IV: Demarée 1983: 272; Friedman 1985: 96.

[284] Leitz 1994: 470: see also 191; II pl. 20, lines 1–2 (text C recto xx); 191, n. 77.

[285] Although traces of red paint have been found on the male side of double busts (see Keith 2011), the colour on the female side is either not recorded or no longer apparent.

[286] The Hathor inscription (see above) and the text and figure on the 'Harer bust' (Keith 2011: 356, 360) were probably later additions. See also Keith 2011: 79. Anthropoid amulets also support the case for gender distinctions between larger busts: if the gender of busts was irrelevant, why would it be marked on such small-scale objects?

[287] Assmann 2005: 219, 216.

[288] TT 82, Amenemhet; *temp.* Thutmose III (Porter and Moss 1960: 163–7).

[289] TT 83, Ametju, called Ahmose; *temp.* Thutmose III (Porter and Moss 1960: 167).

Equally, the principal role of busts in the home was perhaps to maintain the wellbeing and protection of the inhabitants. They provided an immediate medium for communication with deceased family members, particularly in cases of potential crisis, such as sickness and childbirth, and an alternative to domestic deities such as Bes and Taweret.[290] Moreover, women, being in the vicinity of the house far more than men,[291] might appeal to female ancestors more than to deceased male members of the family, particularly in matters of birth, menstrual problems,[292] and the welfare of children.

The protective properties of busts are suggested by their production in amuletic form;[293] such amulets were presumably made to be worn in life[294] and are usually unprovenanced, but some were taken to the grave.[295] The amulets may have had apotropaic qualities: the ambivalent nature of the *akhu* meant that they could be responsible for various forms of illness, and in tombs bust amulets may have been used to protect the recently deceased from attack by the spirits of the malevolent dead, in the same manner as magical bricks.[296] The protection against the dead provided by amulets is a very widespread phenomenon;[297] and anthropoid bust amulets were probably considered to have apotropaic properties. These busts were produced in a variety of materials, including gold,[298] and would have been worn for protection against malign influence.

Stelae

Stelae, along with false doors and busts, provided an interface for two-way communication between the living and the dead: 'The stela was the point to which offerings could be brought and contact established between living and deceased relatives through prayers and supplications.'[299] The vast majority of provenanced ancestor stelae (that is, *ꜣḫ ỉḳr n rꜥ* stelae) to which such dedications would have been made were found in chapels and houses at Deir el-Medina. Demarée points out that the concentration of stelae at this site is a result of the specialised nature of the

---

290 Cf. Bomann 1991: 70.

291 This interpretation is based on working practices at Deir el-Medina: in other, less specialised, communities the balance may well have been different, and ancestor worship may have taken slightly different forms. See Olyan 2010 for a cautionary note about gender-based assumptions in relation to domestic religious practices.

292 Wilfong 1999; Frandsen 2007.

293 Blue faience: UC 2400, 2401a, 2401b (Petrie 1914: pl. xxix, 159 e, f, g; Petrie 1894: pl. xvii, 277; Keith-Bennett 1981: 64, figs 1, 2); BM EA 6555 (Keith-Bennett 1981: 53); Cincinnati Art Museum 1924.349, tomb D229 at Abydos, 21st Dynasty (Markoe 1996: 147, j); red faience: MMA 26.7.1024 (Keith-Bennett 1981: 53); carnelian: BM EA 26554, Cairo JE 25868 (Keith-Bennett 1981: 52); fourteen gold, bald male: BM EA 65574 (Andrews 1994: 20, fig. 15b; Keith-Bennett 1981: 52–3); moulds: Petrie 1894: pl. xvii, 278; Stevens in Keith 2011: 250.

294 As suggested by those found in houses, as at Amarna for example: Stevens in Keith 2011: 261, 268.

295 E.g. Markoe 1996: 147, j.

296 BD 151: Régen 2010: 268.

297 E.g. Hildburgh 1951: 231.

298 Andrews 1992: 20, fig. 15b.

299 Demarée 1983: 286; also Assmann 2005: 210. In Chinese ancestor worship a similar function is fulfilled by wooden tablets, which replaced earlier busts of wood or clay. See e.g. Hammond 1978: 329; Naquin 1988: 45; Hozumi 1901: 13–4.

village, and that 'we might well expect similar objects from other settlement areas to be of poorer quality and uninscribed.'[300]

The location of tomb stelae is indicative of the role that they played in the mortuary cult. For instance, many were situated in forecourts and were therefore easily accessible to visitors intending to enter the tomb or to feast or make offerings outside it. The tomb of Maya at Saqqara incorporated a small purpose-built chapel against its exterior wall that housed such a stela, which depicts Maya before Osiris as well as a lector priest performing the offering ritual before the tomb owner and his wife.[301] The general importance of stelae is indicated by O. Petrie 21, which suggests that the placing of such objects in houses (and perhaps tombs) conferred ownership of the building to the person who commissioned the stela.[302] A 'monumental ostracon' of Pakhemeset, dating to the reign of Twosret, includes an admonition against removing a stela from an unspecified place:[303]

> *Amun said when he appeared: 'As for the vizier who sh⌈all remove/overturn this stela from its place:⌉*
> *He shall not be sated with mꜣꜥt; he shall not follow Amun in any of his festivals.'*

If the stela and statue could serve as a medium for two-way communication between the living and the dead, this suggests that when ceremonial banquets were held in the courtyard, the dead would be accessible and able to partake in them. Shafts located below or adjacent to stelae (including false doors) or statues may have provided the route by which the deceased tomb owner could be present when offerings were placed before them.[304] False doors, with their central depictions of the tomb owner seated before a pile of offerings often accompanied by his spouse, show the ideal situation created by communication with the living. The stela is frequently surrounded by images of offering bearers,[305] who bring sustenance in perpetuity as well as indicating the purpose of the false door as a place where offerings were to be presented.[306] The close proximity of stelae to burial shafts may have aided the deceased in gaining access to offerings, or facilitated 'coming at the voice' in response to *prt-ḫrw* offerings, the importance of which is summarised in the appeal to the living in Paheri's tomb at Elkab,[307] and mentioned in tombs at Amarna.[308]

---

300 Demarée 1983: 279–281.

301 Martin 1991: 175, fig. 111.

302 Demarée 1982: 104.

303 Kitchen 1982: 359, 5–6. Translation modified from Morschauser 1991: 192. The warning against moving a stela, decree, or statue became more common in the late New Kingdom (*ibid.*: 193). Similar admonitions may be found on statues, such as a block statue of Ptahmose from Saqqara, although the consequences of moving them are not specified (Kitchen 2000: 301, no. 190/1). See Scurlock (2002: 3) for a Mesopotamian grave inscription warning against the removal of funerary furniture.

304 E.g. TT 11, TT 53, TT 257, TT 288, TT 343, TT 412; Kampp 1996: 191, fig. 93; 259, fig. 151; 527, fig. 431; 561, fig. 454; 583; 614, fig. 509.

305 E.g. Nakht (TT 52); Shedid and Seidel 1996: 42.

306 See e.g. Hermann 1940: 18–19.

307 EK 3: Tylor 1895: pl. xvi, lines 40–44; Lichtheim 1976: 20.

308 E.g. in the tombs of Huya (no. 1) and Pentu (no. 7) at Amarna: Sandman 1938: 34; Murnane 1995: 131, 180.

Offering tables and libation basins

Most offering tables are inscribed with standard offering formulae for the *ka* of the deceased.[309] Some tables from Deir el-Medina, such as the libation basin and offering table of Iyneferet, mention the blessed dead and thus relate specifically to their cult.[310] One example, a libation basin dedicated to the *akh iqer en re* Nebamun, was discovered in the first room of house S.E. VII.[311] Most offering tables and libation basins dedicated to the *akhu* were found in domestic areas of the settlement.[312] Of the nine offering tables from the site, all of which probably date to the 19th Dynasty, three were discovered in houses, others were found in the debris near houses or offering chapels, and one was uncovered in the debris from a tomb.[313] The offering tables may have been used in conjunction with stelae,[314] anthropoid busts, statues[315] or statuettes to contact and propitiate the dead in domestic contexts.[316]

The life-giving properties of offerings are expressed on a fragment of wall relief from a Memphite tomb, showing a man and woman receiving liquid that pours from the channel of the offering table into a receptacle;[317] columns and statues may indicate that the offerings were being received in the courtyard of the tomb. Similar rituals are referred to at Amarna, for example in the tomb of Meryre: 'May [the king] grant that the children of your house offer libations to you at the door of your tomb.'[318] In the tomb of Piay at Sheikh Abd el-Qurna, an inscription states: 'There is made for you a great oblation at the door of your tomb. Your soul (*ba*) comes forth at the voice of your spirit (*ka*) to receive the things set out for it, according to every word [...]. You hear the petitions (uttered) by your children, at the door of your abode'.[319] The desire for daily offerings is stated explicitly on the offering table of Pay and Meryre: 'may [the gods] grant

---

309 E.g. Bruyère 1925: pl. XII; for typology, see Hölzl 2001: 68–9 and fig. 6.

310 Kitchen 2000: 500; Demarée 1983: 287.

311 Demarée 2002: 140, no. 83; Bruyère 1939: 166, fig. 63.

312 Demarée 1983: 287.

313 Demarée 1983: 145–53.

314 Demarée 1983: 287–8. See e.g. Kampp (1996: 416, fig. 307; TT 125, *temp.* Hatshepsut) for an example of an offering table set up before a stela. For comparable Middle Kingdom examples see Parkinson 1999: 163, no. 75; Abdalla 1992: 94 (offering tables before false doors).

315 E.g. the 19th Dynasty shrine stela with associated offering table of Menmaatre-emheb from Abydos (Reeves 1988: 157, no. 108). For Middle Kingdom examples where the offering table and statue are integrated, see e.g. El-Damaty 1990: pl. 3, figs c and d; cf. Leospo 1996: 84. For New Kingdom examples, see e.g. Martin 1989: pl. 154; Russmann 2001: 136–8, no. 55.

316 Friedman 1985: 84–6. For offering tables and basins in domestic contexts at Amarna, see Stevens (2003: 156–7, 160), who also suggests that mats 'may have provided an affordable and accessible means of delineating a sacred, relatively clean space within a domestic setting' for those who were unable to obtain more permanent cultic emplacements (*ibid.*: 161).

317 UC 408; Hofmann 1995: 276, fig. 2; Uphill 1962: 162–3; Hölzl 2001: 61, fig 3; Martin 1987: 24, pl. 18 (no. 51).

318 Murnane 1995: 161; Davies 1903: 53, pl. xxxix.

319 TT 263: *temp.* Ramesses II. Kitchen 2000: 277, no. 71/1. Compare also the tomb of Piay (TT 263; said by mourners): 'water is poured out on the earth for you at the door of your tomb', and the tomb of Ramose (TT 212; addressed to Re): 'may you give me a place in the necropolis before the Lords of Truth; [grant] to (me) that (I) may ⌈drink⌉ water, with baskets of flowers at the door of my tomb' (both *temp.* Ramesses II; Kitchen 2000: 454, no. 255/1; 421 no. 245/2).

that water be poured out for me upon the offering (slab) at the door of my tomb daily'.[320] At least one offering table was discovered *in situ* in the courtyard of a tomb at Deir el-Medina,[321] and a libation table, basin, and platform probably for offerings were found in Burial Chamber F in the Memphite tomb of Horemheb,[322] which was presumably still accessible following the burial, or used for secondary interment. An example of a portable altar made from poorly fired pottery was found in the area in front of the tomb of Sennedjem and Senqed at Awlad Azzaz near Akhmim.[323] Pottery offering tables were also discovered in graves in Cemetery Y at Diospolis Parva dating from the Middle Kingdom to the New Kingdom.[324]

Most offering tables have been separated from their original context, but requests, such as that inscribed on a scarab of Apy from Amarna, suggest that the majority of offerings were to be deposited around the tomb: 'May I receive the pouring of water for me, (and) a libation of wine and milk on the offering table of my tomb.'[325] However, a 19th Dynasty letter regarding a 'house sitting' mentions three offering tables as part of the household contents along with two pieces of *iḳr*-furniture,[326] possibly part of a cultic emplacement.

Banquet scenes and archaeological evidence

Banquet scenes provide an insight into an idealised setting for communication between the living and the dead. The scenes are differentiated from other depictions of family groups and offering bearers by the presence of 'servants' and gestures shared between participants, such as women passing mandrake fruits or 'guests' assisting those who have overindulged. In Chapter 4 I discuss the banquet scene in detail and attempt to establish whether archaeological traces of such feasting can be found in the necropolis. Little relevant material has a known provenance, so that much of the evidence must be gathered tentatively from artefacts in museums. An exception is the 18th Dynasty tomb of Tjanuni, where fragments of pottery, reed mats, and other debris associated with feasting were recovered in the forecourt.[327] Together with depictions in tombs, this find and museum materials provide enough evidence to suggest that the banquets depicted in funerary/mortuary contexts signify actual or desired events.

---

320 *Temp.* Ramesses II: Kitchen 2000: 441.

321 Kitchen 1993: 312–13.

322 Martin 1989: 149, pl. 163.

323 Ockinga 1997: 5, pl. 5.

324 Bourriau 2009: 67, 71–75, 79–89.

325 Murnane 1995: 128.

326 O. Cairo 25670; Murnane 1995: 128; Wente 1990: 138, no. 170.

327 TT 74, *temp.* Thutmose IV; Brack and Brack 1977: 60; Hartwig 2004: 12–13, 43–5; cf. Quirke 1986: 80–81; Ockinga 1997: 4.

Conclusions

K. Maurer Trinkhaus (1984: 674) notes:

> *The remains of mortuary ritual are of particular significance to archaeology. As social ritual, mortuary practices are structured by social relations ... The key to archaeological inference from mortuary remains to social behaviour ... lies in establishing reliable links between ritual and its remains ... Archaeological remains are usually an incomplete source of information, since social structure is reflected in mortuary ritual which is only partly composed of disposal of the body. Associated ritual behaviors also contain social information but are not always reflected in recoverable mortuary remains. Elaboration and form of mortuary remains are therefore an incomplete indication of elaboration and form of mortuary ritual.*

It seems that mortuary cult in New Kingdom Egypt was carried out mostly in the home and in the vicinity of the tomb,[328] and was based largely on the principal of reciprocity. At the most basic level, the deceased protected the living in the house, in exchange for which the living provided for the deceased in the tomb. The Book of Gates and the Amduat along with other less specialised mortuary texts indicate that offering to the gods (particularly Re) and the deceased would ensure protection and blessed status in the afterlife;[329] in this sense mortuary ritual could be seen as an act of self-preservation. The veneration of ancestors and the rituals associated with it would have assisted in social cohesion, providing a sense of belonging to a tangible past and a social order. Ancestors are particularly important to small-scale societies – including artificially created ones like Deir el-Medina – because they are the source of traditions within the group.[330] The communal aspect of ancestor worship and of religion in general is suggested by stelae and tomb scenes depicting groups of people, including children, bringing offerings to the deceased and the gods. This is particularly marked on Middle Kingdom stelae, where images of the gods are rarely present and the emphasis is therefore on family relations.[331]

Many different media were used for communicating with the deceased. These included durable physical objects such as stelae, busts, offering tables, and statues. The statue was the vessel in which the *ka* took up its abode to receive offerings, and as such it needed to be prepared for its role in providing sustenance for the deceased, in the same way that the *ba* could act as a conduit for the transfer of food from the living to the dead.[332] Finnestad noted that: 'The primary function of all accessible statues was to serve as a link between the living and the dead ... Through acts directed towards it, contact is attained with the divine being.'[333] Busts in domestic shrines may have fulfilled a similar purpose on a more intimate level, perhaps performing a role parallel to household deities.

Among shorter-term means of contact were letters to the dead, while ephemeral encounters could be through dreams or intoxication (for which, see Chapter 4). Letters to the dead again exemplify the reciprocal character of the relationship between the living and the dead, with several referring to the breakdown of this relationship. Fear of the dead was probably a motivating

---

328 But also took place in chapels and temples to some extent; see Chapter 3.

329 Wente 1982: 162, 167, 170–2, 174.

330 See Lau 2002: 281, 298.

331 E.g. Bourriau 1988: 30, fig. 20.

332 E.g. the papyrus of Nebqed: Snape 2011: 199; Naville 1886: iv.

333 1978: 122.

factor in the maintenance of mortuary cults, as well as in the execration rituals performed in the necropolis.

Mortuary cult in its various forms was a way of bridging the gap between the living and the dead, a means of providing solace and of keeping the deceased's memory alive. The tomb and domestic shrines with their associated ancestor cults provided focal points for the living to mourn, to gather for festive occasions, and to request help. According to James Watson,[334] writing of the Chinese cult of the dead: 'That which is merely repeated is not necessarily ritual. Rather rituals are repeated because they are expected to have transformative powers. Rituals change people and things; the ritual process is active, not merely passive'. Mortuary rituals were performed in order to transform and renew the deceased and ensure their perpetuation in the afterlife, thereby guaranteeing their presence when they were requested to assist their descendants in the world of the living. As a result of the shallow genealogical depth of Egyptian ancestral memory, it is probably that such rituals were only maintained for a generation or two before being abandoned.

[334] 1988: 4.

CHAPTER 3

Places of interaction with the dead

> *The dead ... were multi-locational and could be thought of as residing in cult temples and in areas of houses set aside for ancestor cults as well as in cemeteries; while many activities other than funerals took place in cemeteries, such as processional visits by the chief deities of the local temple. Ideally we need to look at the religious life of a community as a whole, whether it took place in houses, in temples and shrines, in cemeteries, or in relation to features of the landscape.*[1]

In keeping with Geraldine Pinch's statement quoted above, this 'multi-locational' aspect of the deceased will be considered in this chapter. A comparative table of evidence for cultic activity in houses, tombs, chapels and temples is provided in Table 2, and these sites are discussed below in order of the probable frequency of interaction between the living and the dead.

Houses

The layout of houses needs to be addressed because this influences – or perhaps to a lesser extent is influenced by – the location and nature of cultic installations. Wall decoration, along with architectural features such as niches, false doors, '*lits clos*,' and lustration slabs, can all be related to cultic practices. Movable objects including offering tables, pottery, votives, and to a lesser extent statues and statuettes, are discussed in Chapters 2 and 4 and are therefore covered in less depth here.

Construction and layout (including doorways and false doors)

Kate Spence suggests that dwellings at Amarna consisted of three storeys in accord with her interpretation of the representation of a house in the tomb of Djehutynefer.[2] On the basis of archaeological evidence and models, it seems more likely that houses were normally two storeys

[1] Pinch 2003: 444.

[2] 2004: 140–4. TT 104; Davies 1929: figs 1a–b.

	House	Tomb	Chapel	Temple
Ancestor Busts	✓	✓	✓	✓
Statues	fragments at Amarna	✓	?	✓
Statuettes	✓ (gods and ancestors)	✓	?	?
Libation basin	✓	✓	✓	
Offering table	✓	✓	✓	
Niches	✓	✓	✓	?
Lintels	✓	✓	✓	
Other	*lits clos*, false doors	false doors	inscribed seats, (column bases with concealed names)	
Ceramics	✓	✓	✓	
Amulets	✓	✓		
Flowers	✓	✓		
Mats	✓	✓		
Stelae	✓	✓	✓	?
Votives	✓	female figures, letters to the dead	?	✓
Charred earth, oven	(✓)	✓	✓	
Water supply	✓	✓	✓	
Buried deposit	jewellery, infants	bowls, garlands, execration figures		✓
Textual references	Instruction of Ani, Calendar of Good and Bad Days	Appeals to the Living, letters to the dead	?	inscriptions on intermediary statues

Table 2: Evidence of cultic activity at Thebes and Amarna.

high,[3] with the second floor having a partially open plan or large vents[4] to encourage airflow through the building. In order to incorporate the different sections of Djehutynefer's home into one composition, the artist varied the scale from room to room, so that people and equipment

[3] *Contra* Arnold 2003: 112: i.e. basement, ground floor, first floor and roof space. A plain door without a cornice depicted on the right hand side of Amenmose's house (Strudwick and Strudwick 1996: 82) probably led to the basement area, and the small windows at the base of the Louvre house model (E 5357) may also be associated with rooms below ground level. This model was dated to the New Kingdom by Desroches-Noblecourt (1938: 19) and Gordon (1982: 34), though Ricke (1966: 122–3) considered it to be Greco-Roman. The remains of a two-storey New Kingdom house are preserved at el-Lisht (Arnold 2003: 112). For discussions of second storeys, see Kemp 1977: 125; *id.*: 1986: 21–5; Shaw 1992: 165; Koltsida 2007: 123ff.

[4] Petrie's (1907: 16) '*mulqafs*'; as illustrated in P. Nakht – BM EA 10471/2 (Russmann 2001: 196, no. 100), and TT 90 (Nebamun): Freed 1981: 9, fig. 10.

are shown at several scales,[5] a fact that is not taken into account in Spence's interpretation. A reconstruction of Djehutynefer's house as a two-storey building places granaries and ovens on the roof. Although the location of ovens on the roof may appear potentially unsafe,[6] Barry Kemp found evidence of ovens on the second floor of houses within the workmen's village at Amarna.[7] Meskell[8] proposes that in light of the layout of the settlement at Deir el-Medina, with tightly packed houses divided by small alleyways, contiguous roofing may have provided a means of moving around the village, as well as reducing inside temperatures by minimising the surface area exposed to the sun.

Nigel and Helen Strudwick suggest that the two rows of windows depicted on the house of Amenmose in TT 254 'may be an attempt to show two storeys, but could also depict windows from another side of the house on the side visible to the viewer.'[9] The manner in which the windows are depicted in Djehutynefer's house – framed panels alternating with solid blocks of colour – seems to support the latter interpretation.[10] In a market scene in the tomb of Wensu that shows the delivery of fish to Theban houses,[11] windows and doorways are depicted, along with some apparently internal structures such as a column, painted pillars and an entablature – perhaps visible through the windows (or depicted because they were known features of those houses) rather than being located on walls facing the street. The column shown above the doorway to the house of Nebamun surrounded by a yellow lintel is probably not indicative of a second floor but rather the central support of a window.[12]

Door lintels are generally painted red with the internal void or door coloured yellow.[13] This is true of external doorways and of internal emplacements, including stone lined niches and entablatures.[14] This colour scheme may be associated with divine or solar imagery and signify a protected or ritually important space. The utilisation of specific shapes, materials,

---

5 Despite the draftsman's squared grid, which is still visible; Endruweit 1998: 393, fig. 109.

6 Most ovens were constructed on the ground level, e.g. Bruyère 1939: pl. vii.

7 1987: 26; 29, fig. 2. Roofs at Amarna were constructed with tamarisk poles, acacia beams, and a layer of thick marl mud. Mixed with the rubble from the collapse of this roof type, a second roof of mud and reeds was found in Gate Street 8, along with fragments of a cylindrical oven and an ashy layer that the excavator concluded had derived from a concentration of ash on the roof associated with the slow-burning oven (Kemp 1987: 25–6).

8 2000b: 263; 2002: 40.

9 1997: 40. They note (p. 41) that depictions of houses in Theban tombs are 'relatively rare', 19 being listed in Porter and Moss 1960: 465.

10 Endruweit 1998: 393, fig. 109. Cf. the ostracon bearing an illustrated commission for windows: Andreu 1997: 154, fig. 71. Window grilles from Amarna and Deir el-Medina of the type illustrated in TT 254: Peet and Woolley 1923: pl. VI, no. 4; Bruyère 1939: 309, fig. 180. Fragments of a wooden window frame and pivoting shutter were recovered from Gate Street 8 at Amarna (Kemp 1987: 26).

11 TT A4: Manniche 1988: pl. 8.

12 TT 90: Freed 1981: 9, fig. 10. Cf. similar window design in the cabin of a boat depicted in TT 217 [Ipuy]: Davies 1927: pl. 30. Comparable wooden papyriform columns were used as supports for floor lamps, e.g. Kha's from TT 8 at Deir el-Medina (Manuelian 1982: 65, fig. 28; JE 38642).

13 E.g. TT A4: Manniche 1988: 65. For depictions of yellow-painted doors with stylised wood grain, see e.g. TT 181 (Nebamun and Ipuky: Taylor 2000: 33 – tomb door), and TT 277 (Amenemopet: Goyon 2000: 25 – tomb door).

14 TT 104: Endruweit 1998: 393, fig. 109.

and colours as visual markers of sacred areas in many cultures is noted by Amos Rapoport:[15] 'The boundaries around [cognitive] domains ... are usually marked or indicated in some way to remind people within a specific cultural context of the situation and hence how to act appropriately; the marking is thus a mnemonic.' The doorway of the house depicted in the tomb of Amenmose is unusual because it bears an inscription.[16] Although the lintels of many elite houses were probably inscribed,[17] the text itself is not shown in other depictions of houses. The text comprises standard offering formulae to Amun-Re, Hathor, Mut and Khonsu(?), requesting a voice offering for the *ka* of the tomb/house owner. The mention of the *ka* and the use of the protective colour red around doorways[18] suggests that the house could be accessible to the tomb owner after his death as well as during life. Strudwick and Strudwick take this idea further by linking the 'compressed shrine', composed of a framed stela and statue niche, in the tomb of Amenmose with the house entrance depicted adjacent to it:[19]

> *...the feet of the woman outside the house are hidden by the ramp leading to the door possibly signifying that Amenmose and his son [are] in a different sphere of activity from Amenmose's wife. Following this line of thought, the 'compressed shrine' is outside Amenmose's house and by passing through the frame into the tomb chapel he passes through the doorway and into his house. Thus the tomb chapel and Amenmose's house are one and the same.*

Alfred Hermann recognised the link between false doors in tombs and in houses, both being places where food was provided for the *ka* of the dead.[20] Bruyère found false doors in the main room of Deir el-Medina houses,[21] remains of which may still be seen in the village today (Figure 20). A striking feature of these false doors is the use of red paint around the frame and yellow for the internal panel, a combination also seen on niches,[22] tomb doorways,[23] and house entrances.[24] A low platform for the deposition of offerings was found by Bruyère in front of some false doors at Deir el-Medina.[25] In house S.O. V, room 3, a painted terracotta offering stand was found before a false door, which depicted in a central panel the house owner, Khabekhnet, praising a cartouche of Ahmose-Nefertari.[26]

---

15 1994: 493, 483.

16 TT 254: Strudwick and Strudwick 1996: 82, pls 21c, xxxi; *id.*: 1997: 46.

17 For the texts of inscribed limestone fittings from Deir el Medina, see Kitchen 2000: 414, 415, 418, 434, 442, 488, 490, 546. See also Budka 2001.

18 Meskell 2002: 119. Koenig (1979: 117) states that the red paint was intended to prevent the malevolent dead or demons from entering a room.

19 1997: 44–5, fig. 5.

20 1940: 19.

21 1930: 275. See also Weiss 2011: 198–200.

22 E.g. houses N.49.18, M.50.16 and O.48.17 at Amarna: Peet and Woolley 1923: 10, 19, 28. Red niches were also noted at the site by Frankfort and Pendlebury (1933: 38).

23 E.g. Book of the Dead of Neferubenef, P. Louvre N 3092: Herbin 2000: 7.

24 TT 90: Freed 1981: 9, fig. 10. This is an inversion of the normal tomb door colour, having a yellow frame with a red door, as depicted in the Book of the Dead of Maiherperi, Cairo CG 24095 (18th Dynasty; Saleh and Sourouzian 1987: no. 142), and in the tomb of Nebenmaat (TT 219; Ramesside: Goyon 2000: 24).

25 1939: 261; for example in house N.E. XV.

26 Bruyère 1939: 326–9, figs 196, 197, 200.

Figure 20: False door with yellow central panel and red surround. House S.O. V, Deir el-Medina, 19th Dynasty.

Timothy Kendall[27] notes in the representation of Djehutynefer's house 'an elegant portal adorned with a decorative lattice work lintel'. The entablature he describes is unlikely to be a doorway (for the living at least), particularly as it is depicted on a low platform (Figure 21). The illustration is more likely to be of a *lit clos*-type structure or an elaborate false door of the type found in tombs, providing another means of entry by the deceased into the house.[28] In contrast, the location of the entablature/false door depicted on the stela in the tomb of Ani at Amarna dedicated by Anymen may be deliberately ambiguous, in accordance with Any's desire to receive offerings 'at every shrine of [his].'[29]

The comparatively small dimensions of most houses, as well as the considerable number of occupants,[30] must have encouraged a multifunctional use of space, particularly in the first two rooms, the 'loggia' and 'central' or 'divan' rooms. Meskell[31] argues that houses at Deir el-Medina were divided into 'men's space' and 'women's space', perhaps influenced by similar arrangements in societies such as Classical Greece.[32] The situation at the village, with men

[27] 1982: 26.

[28] A 19th Dynasty ostracon probably from Deir el-Medina bears a sketch of a similar entablature (Fitzwilliam EGA 4298.1943: Burn 2002: 171, no. 115).

[29] Davies 1908: 10, pl. xxii; 17, pl. ix.

[30] Meskell 2002: 94; Strudwick 1995: 100.

[31] 2004: 68. Also 1998a; 1999: 102; 2002: 114, 116–7.

[32] E.g. Walker 1983: 87, fig. 6.2.

Figure 21: House of Djehutynefer as depicted in his tomb (TT 104). After Davies 1929: fig. 1.

being absent for several days at a time, would make such a gendered division unlikely. As Aikaterini Koltsida notes,[33] Meskell seems to contradict herself by initially stating that painted decoration and niches in the second room indicate 'male space', then describing the first room, often with similar decoration, as 'female space'.[34] Koltsida[35] believes that female aspects of domestic architecture have come to be overemphasized, overcompensating for the omission of women in older studies. However, in an environment principally inhabited by women for much of the time, it does not seem unreasonable to suggest that they may have been involved in embellishing the houses that they lived and worked in.[36]

33 2007: 142.

34 Certain elements referred to by Meskell as indicating male elite status have been questioned; for example, her claim that columns were 'often made from exotic imported wood' (1998: 229; 2002: 117, citing Crocker 1985: 58) is refuted by Sweeney (2006a: 156): at Deir el-Medina local palm trunks were used (Bruyère 1939: 69–70, 291).

35 2007: 142.

36 Koltsida (2007: 142) refers to modern Nubian society as a parallel in which women frequently decorate

Other than the divan, which may simply be a bed and seat[37] rather than 'the central focus within the elite male sphere',[38] the other criteria used to establish the second room of Deir el-Medina houses as 'male space' are ancestor busts, libation basins and offering tables. These objects have also been found in the first room. Even if we discount the suggestion that the majority of anthropoid busts represent females (see Chapter 2), libation basins, offering tables, and *akh iqer* stelae were not dedicated exclusively to men.[39]

In long-established communities, ownership of a house in many societies brings with it a responsibility to associated ancestors: in essence the ancestors become part of the inheritance.[40] This was the case in Late Bronze–Early Iron Age Syria, where the 'one in possession of the main house, and thus responsible for the ancestral cult, is the link between the generations'.[41] A similar arrangement is suggested in the 6th Dynasty Cairo Linen letter to the dead:[42] 'Recall what you said to [my] son Iy; 'They are the houses of the ancestors that need to be sustained ... It is a son's house and then (his) son's house.' May your son maintain your house just as you maintained your father's house.' Perhaps by disinheriting her ungrateful children in her will, Naunakht[43] was doing more than just depriving them of financial resources – she was also cutting them off from the home of their ancestors and thus their place in the social fabric. The strong link between the dead and the house is indicated in inscriptions such as that from TT 32:[44] 'May you enter your house of the living, rejoicing and jubilating', and in the passage of TT 82, where the tomb owner is described as going forth 'to see his house of the living.'

Wall decoration

Painting

Painted ornamentation may have been a fairly common feature of many houses from the Middle Kingdom.[45] In relation to the decoration of state buildings, Baines notes:[46]

---

their houses; Kemp (1979: 53), however, states that 'one cannot doubt that [mural decoration of houses at Deir el-Medina and Amarna] was executed by male artists.'

[37] Meskell (1998a: 225) notes that ceramic female figurines recline on beds that do not possess legs, and suggests that 'this is probably because of the clay medium rather than any specific symbolism.' It would seem likely that the 'divan' is represented in these cases, given the general similarity in shape, and their presence in houses where birth is likely to have taken place. A figurine from House N.49.21 at Amarna not only has painted webbing but individual legs (Capel 1996: 67; Peet and Woolley 1923: pl. xii, fig. 5), indicating that the clay medium was not always an issue in figurine manufacture.

[38] Meskell 1998a: 230, 233.

[39] E.g. Bruyère 1939: 310, fig. 181; 318, fig. 187.

[40] Cátedra 1992: 88.

[41] Van der Toorn 1995: 40.

[42] CG 25975; Wente 1990: 211.

[43] Černý 1945: 32; pl. viii, 4, lines 7–8. See further Janssen and Pestman 1968. Hittite law also permitted women, specifically widows, to disinherit their children (Bryce 2002: 119).

[44] TT 32: Assmann 2005: 220. TT 82: Porter and Moss 1960: 164. Compare Book of the Dead Spell 132, 'for causing a man to turn around in order to see his house on earth' (Allen 1974: 108; Faulkner 1985: 121, 124, P. Nebamun BM EA 9964/20).

[45] E.g. at Lahun: Gallorini 1998: 46. O'Connor (1997: 399) noted that centrally located wall paintings in houses at this site 'may well represent the performance of an ancestor (not a divine) cult'.

[46] 2007: 271–2.

> *The effect of Egyptian monuments with their originally white stone surfaces, covered in white gypsum plaster and painted in a range of strong, generally bright colours, and containing statuary and other objects of rich stones, much of it also painted, must have been overwhelmingly brilliant, especially in comparison with the drab mud brick and mud plaster of most structures. Only occasional fragments of relief, as well as some modern coloured reconstructions, give any sense of that appearance. In temples and palaces, these colours were integral to a world that aspired toward and in part recreated the divine, as temple texts make clear.*

Presumably this also applies to domestic rooms where cultic activities took place. Reconstructions in Peet and Woolley,[47] suggest that the main rooms (of large houses at Amarna at least) were brightly painted over plastered and whitewashed walls. Whitewash itself may have had the practical function of increasing the visibility of common household pests, such as scorpions.[48] Several houses at Deir el-Medina and Amarna contained painted figures or scenes (Table 3), mostly associated with fertility and birth, although a few also contained images related to domestic cults in the form of false door panels.[49]

In discussing the decoration on '*lits clos*', Toivari-Viitala comments:[50]

> *With a strong cultural bias for procreation combined with a low fertility and a high mortality rate, it is reasonable to assume that the birth of a child resulted in a display of joy and pride. Public display is too daring a term to be used here, but the wall paintings in the front rooms may perhaps be interpreted to some degree along such lines.*

If a child died in infancy, it may explain why some paintings were deliberately plastered over;[51] the protective and celebratory images would be inappropriate and a reminder of the loss. This explanation also fits with Kemp's conclusion[52] that the paintings and 'birth bower' ostraca are 'essentially prophylactic, illustrating either a successful termination to childbirth and its ensuing period of uncleanliness or the deities who would ensure this (Bes and Thoëris)'. Stevens asserts that the paintings in the Workmen's Village at Amarna were covered as a result of changing socio-political priorities, which led to their being seen as unsuitable for their locations.[53] This seems less likely, particularly given the comparatively short occupation of the site. Peet and Woolley,[54] in contrast, believed that the paintings were covered with whitewash and plaster because the villagers became too poor to have them renewed or replaced.

The function of the *lit clos*, discussed below, is unclear, but the other architectural features and paintings in the first room indicate that the presence and accessibility of dead members of the family was desired and encouraged. This need probably resulted from fear: the dead were thought to be a serious threat to mothers and their unborn children.[55] The imagery in the *lits*

---

47 1923: pls iv, ix, xv.

48 Bruyère 1939: 55.

49 Peet and Woolley 1923: 19.

50 2001: 177.

51 E.g. Kemp 2009: 18.

52 1979: 53.

53 2006: 300.

54 1923: 59.

55 Leitz 1999: 68–70.

House no.	Room	Description	Associated material	References
Deir el-Medina				
S.E. 1		Woman breast-feeding, with three attendants		Bruyère 1923; Brunner-Traut 1953: 15, fig. 5 [reconstruction]; Meskell 2002: 114
C. 7	First	Female kneeling before a stool, facing child on *lit clos*		Bruyère 1939: 311, fig. 182; Meskell 2002: 114
N.O. 12	First	Female (?) on papyrus skiff on *lit clos*	*Niches laraires* above *lit clos*	Bruyère 1939: 286, fig. 157; Meskell 2002: 114
S.E. 8	First	Female pipe player on *lit clos*		Bruyère 1939: 273, fig. 145; Meskell 2002: 115
S.O. 5		Khabekhnet praising cartouche of Ahmose-Nefertari	Polychrome false door	Bruyère 1939: 326–7, figs 196, 197
S.E. 7		Wall painting	False door	Meskell 2004: 69
N.E. 10	First	Winged Bes on *lit clos*		Bruyère 1939: 255, 257, figs. 131, 133
N.E. 13	First	Dancing Bes on *lit clos*		Bruyère 1939: 259, fig. 136
C. 5	First	Dancing Bes and palimpsest of young boy dancing	*Niche laraire*	Bruyère 1939: 305, fig. 172
S.O. 6	First	Dancing Bes figure in white paint on *lit clos*	Next to a large cupboard	Bruyère 1939: 330, fig. 202
Amarna				
Main Street House 3		Group of dancing Bes figures and Taweret in outline		Kemp 1979: 48, fig. 1, pl. vii; Peet and Woolley 1923: 75, pl. xviii, fig. 3
Long Wall Street House 10	First	Line of women and children advancing right	Offering table base? Described as a 'square bin'	Kemp 1979: 49, fig. 2, pl. viii; Peet and Woolley 1923: 84
Workmen's Village house		Dancing Bes figures, brightly coloured		Kemp 2009: 18
Long Wall Street House 7	First	Offering tables, lotus leaves	Double manger or bin. Jar stand	Kemp 1979: 52; Peet and Woolley 1923: 83
Houses 9 and 10 Main Street	2nd floor?	Painted fragments		Peet and Woolley 1923: 59, 80–81
House K.50.1 (Nakht)	Central room	Akhenaten worshipping cartouches of Aten – possibly a false door		Peet and Woolley 1923: 6
House M.50.16	Third room	False door. Central panel: seated couple with attendant		Peet and Woolley 1923: 19
Trial house near et-Til; House P.47.5; House N.49.18	First	Garlands of lotuses, cornflowers & poppies, bird scenes		Peet and Woolley 1923: 44

Table 3: Location and content of wall-paintings at Deir el-Medina and Amarna.

clos decoration is strongly suggestive of a focus on birth in this room,[56] and the ancestors may have been invoked to provide protection for infants and expectant mothers from malevolent gods or spirits, with busts and stelae providing points of contact.

Wall hangings

Few wall hangings have survived, although there are sufficient examples to indicate that they may have been an affordable means of decorating houses and incorporating images of the ancestors into the domestic environment.[57] Painted linen 'funerary' cloths have been found draped over coffins at Deir el-Medina[58] and several votive textiles were discovered at Deir el-Bahri in rubbish mounds and in the Eleventh Dynasty temple.[59] According to Geraldine Pinch,[60] most of the Deir el-Medina cloths are similar to the common type of funerary stela on which the deceased is shown with a table of offerings or with relatives presenting offerings. She comments that it is therefore possible that other kinds of tomb stelae could have their counterparts on linen; reproductions of *akh iqer* stelae scenes or other images of the deceased may have been painted onto material that was then used to decorate house walls. At least one example of such a cloth dedicated to Taweret was found in a Deir el-Medina house, and another which may have derived from the same house was discovered in an apparently unrelated tomb,[61] suggesting that some house textiles may have been divorced from their primary contexts in antiquity.

Lits clos

These mud-brick emplacements with a short flight of steps leading to a platform, with or without enclosing walls, have remained problematic since their discovery by Bruyère at Deir el-Medina (Figures 22 and 23). They are divided into three main types, and seem to date chiefly to the 19th and 20th Dynasties.[62] The most basic form is a mud-brick platform with three steps leading to it; the second type has a low enclosure wall with a central opening, and the third has a higher surrounding wall topped with a cornice. Comparable structures at Amarna have been labelled as household altars, and several scholars[63] have suggested that this was the function of those at Deir el-Medina. Not all houses possessed such a structure, and it may be the case that, like the garden shrines at Amarna,[64] the features could have been shared with members of the community beyond the immediate household. Bruyère stated in his publications that headrests were found on *lits clos*,[65] but an examination of his notebooks has revealed this to

---

56 Bruyère 1923. Since regeneration involved rebirth, the placement of objects such as *akh iqer* stelae and anthropoid busts in a room associated with new life may have also indirectly benefited the deceased.

57 E.g. plain geometric designs (Victoria and Albert T 251–1921: Wenzel 1998: 403); and offering scenes (Rigault 2002a: 145, 288, nos 88 and 232).

58 Simpson 1987: 46–7; Hayes 1959: 320, fig. 202.

59 Pinch 1993: 102–34, pls 15, 16, 18, 21–6.

60 1993: 130.

61 Pinch 1993: 130; Anthes 1943: pl. 18a.

62 Bruyère 1939: 57, fig. 18; 61.

63 E.g. Koltsida 2007: 23–4; Kleinke 2006; Weiss 2009: 208. The plan of *lits clos* alone would seem to suggest their sacred function, compared with libation basins, offering tables, and shrines, for example.

64 Stevens 2003: 88.

65 E.g. 1939: 59.

Figure 22: Lits clos. Houses N.E. XIII (right) and N.E. XII (left) Deir el-Medina, 19th Dynasty.

be questionable.[66] The decoration on *lits clos* relates specifically to fertility and birth,[67] but this need not imply that activities related to this (sexual intercourse, childbirth and postpartum care) occurred there.

Against my conclusion in an article published in 2005, I am no longer convinced that *lits clos* functioned as beds during pregnancy, birth, or postnatal care. Barry Kemp suggested on the basis of painted plaster fragments at Amarna that childbirth took place on house roofs.[68] This would be possible if, as Toivari-Viitala proposes, the 'birthing' beds illustrated on ostraca could be dismantled for carriage and storage.[69] Folding beds, such as the one found in Tutankhamun's tomb,[70] would also have facilitated this. It is worth noting that two 'women's beds' are mentioned in a list along with birth amulets (*s3w msw*).[71] 'Birth-bower' ostraca[72] may well depict temporary structures erected on rooftops to protect mother and child from the heat of the sun. There are sufficient textual references to beds as well as physical examples[73] for

---

[66] Jean L. Keith, personal communication.

[67] Bruyère 1939: 57–9. See also Bruyère 1923, although his reconstruction of the fresco as a religious scene featuring Hathor and Horus rather than a mortal mother and child is questionable. The painting was more plausibly restored by Brunner-Traut (1955: 15, fig. 5).

[68] 1986: 25.

[69] 2001: 178.

[70] Carter 1972: 198; Desroches-Noblecourt 1963: 184–5, figs 107a, b; cf. the model from an 18th Dynasty Gebelein tomb: Hayes 1959: 203, fig. 118.

[71] O. Gardiner 9; Toivari-Viitala 2001: 178.

[72] Vandier D'Abbadie 1937: pls xlix–liv, lvii; Brunner-Traut 1955.

[73] *Contra* Meskell 2002: 121. Figurines (e.g. UC 16601; Meskell 2002: 75, fig. 3.7; Peet and Woolley 1923: pl. xxiii, fig. 5, 22/72; pl.xii, fig. 5; Hayes 1959: 202–3) indicate the structure of beds with criss-crossed webbing held by a wooden frame. P. DM 3 deals with a commissioned bed complete with webbing (Wente 1990: 140, no. 178), and an ostracon (Louvre E 17169) lists household items including two beds,

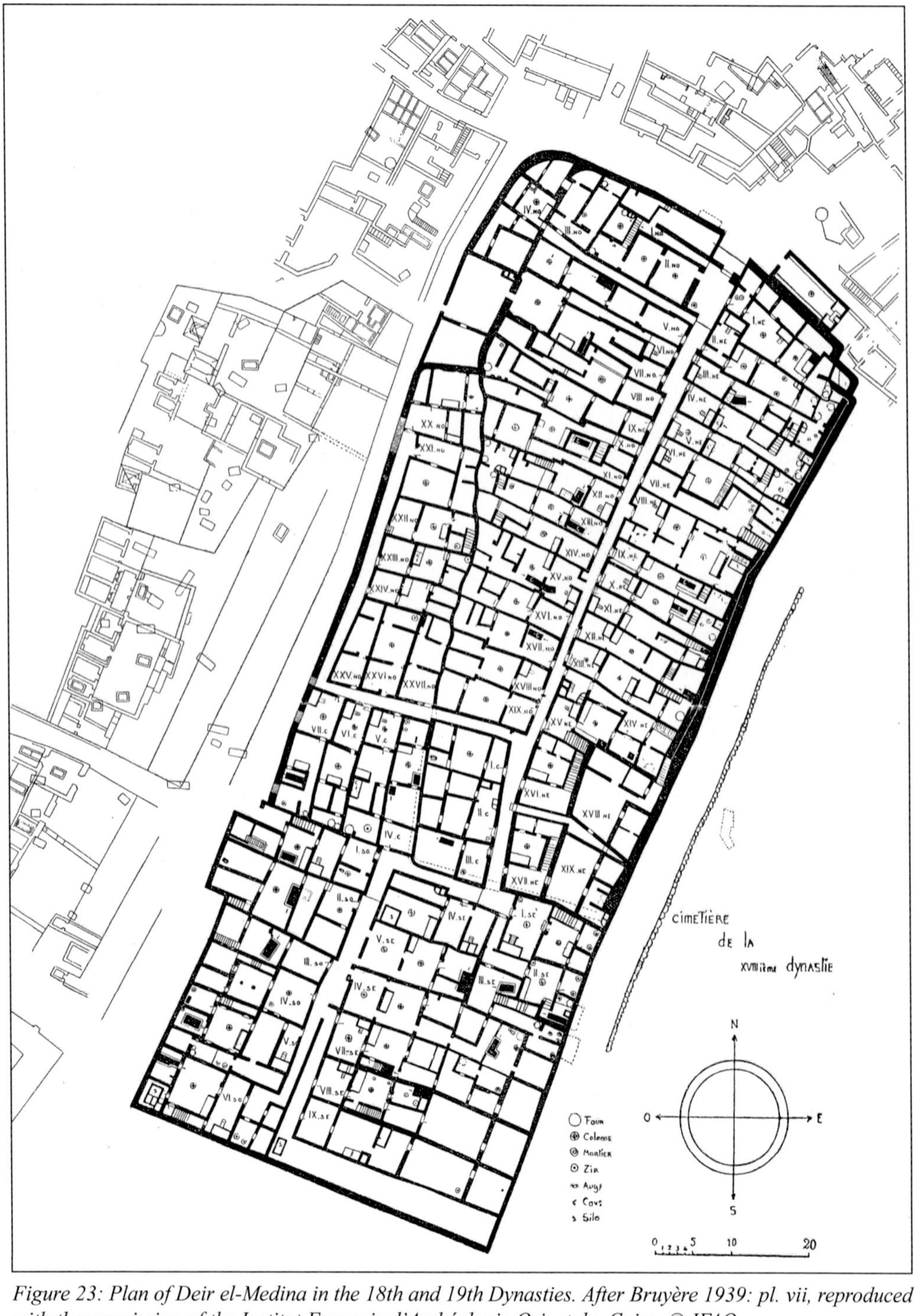

Figure 23: Plan of Deir el-Medina in the 18th and 19th Dynasties. After Bruyère 1939: pl. vii, reproduced with the permission of the Institut Français d'Archéologie Orientale, Cairo. © IFAO.

the *lit clos* to be redundant as a place of rest or childbirth, and given the size and shape of the structures, midwifery would be virtually impossible.

Niches

In Peet and Woolley's description of houses at Amarna,[74] there is often no clear distinction made between niches (understood here as small square or rectangular recesses in the face of walls, several brick courses above floor level), and false doors, which, in most cases, reached from floor to ceiling. Peet and Woolley were inclined, as was Borchardt before them and Frankfort and Pendlebury after them,[75] to consider niches or false doors opposite doorways as balancing architectural elements rather than ritually significant components, despite the discovery in house O.49.1 in 1911 of a falcon's head fashioned from mud that had probably fallen from the double niche above it.[76] Although Peet and Woolley conceded that some niches 'must have had a religious character',[77] they were not convinced that most niches were significant: 'The question of whether the niches in general were religious in origin or whether they were features purely architectural in origin and only afterwards adapted to a ritual use obviously cannot be answered.' To construct a house with essentially superfluous niches seems uncharacteristic of Egyptian design, however, and many of them appear to have some cultic associations or multiple functions.[78]

At Amarna fragments of inscribed plaster with a hymn to the Aten in vertical columns probably fell from the niche in house M.50.16, which was 0.9m above floor level and had a small empty vase buried up to its rim in the ground before it. The vessel was described by Peet and Woolley as a receptacle for offerings,[79] suggesting the original presence of a cult image in the niche. At Deir el-Medina Bruyère stated that on the ground below niches offering tables (either portable or inserted into the floor), stone basins, jars with stands, and lamps were discovered.[80] In house C. VI (room 1), a painted limestone bust was found at the foot of the wall below three niches; Bruyère believed that it probably came from the largest of them.[81] A fragment of a limestone stela dedicated to the [*akh iqer*] *en re* Mose, and a broken bust also derived from niches.[82]

---

one with webbing (Grandet 2002: 75, no. 3). Janssen (1975: 524) includes beds among items commonly purchased at Deir el-Medina. Peet and Woolley (1923: pl. xviii, fig. 2) found a bed at Amarna, complete with frame and webbing, upturned in the street, perhaps abandoned during the evacuation of the site. Some female 'fertility' figurines and several ostraca illustrating the 'birth-bower' scene show beds decorated with snakes (Pinch 1983: 406). At least one similar bed has survived (Cairo JE 27254; Mahmoud 2002: 149, no. 66; tomb of Sennedjem, TT 1); its whitewashed surface and painted decoration is worn, suggesting that, like the other furniture found in the tomb, it had been constructed for and used within the home.

74 1923.

75 Peet and Woolley 1923: 42; Frankfort and Pendlebury 1933: 9.

76 Frankfort and Pendlebury 1933: 9; also Ricke 1932: 29.

77 1923: 43.

78 Stevens 2006: 236–47.

79 1923: 43.

80 1939: 55.

81 1939: 309; cf. *ibid.*: 55, 261.

82 Keith 2011: 12.

Figure 24: Mud-brick and limestone pillar with niche for a bust, statuette or stela (Meskell's 'cultic cupboard'). House N.E. XII, Deir el-Medina. 19th Dynasty.

Mud-brick niches were ornamented with limestone jambs and cornices[83] and were dedicated to local deities and the dead.[84] Niches were located throughout houses (Figure 24), on the staircase, in the kitchen (where they probably held images of deities associated with food and abundance such as Renenutet, as well as more mundane objects including utensils), the second room, the first room, and the 'bedroom'.[85] At least some niches possessed doors, as shown by the fragmentary ebony example from the house of Sennedjem.[86] The small shrine in the house of Panehsy at Amarna also possessed wooden doors, and was thought by the excavator to have contained a cult statue.[87] Sennedjem's house contained several limestone lintel and cornice

[83] Sadek 1987: 77; Bruyère 1939: 194, fig. 86.

[84] E.g. Andreu 2002a: 74; Bruyère 1939: 203, fig. 93 (gods); Bruyère 1939: 320, fig. 190 (dead).

[85] Peet and Woolley 1923: 87, 89, 90; Sadek 1987: 77.

[86] Room 2, S.O. VI: Bruyère 1939: 332, fig. 204. Cf. the inscribed fragment of a naos door: Bruyère 1939: 196, fig. 87. For a virtually complete example from the Workmen's Village at Amarna see Peet and Woolley 1923: pl. xix, fig. 4.

[87] Pendlebury 1951: 27, pl. xxxi.

fragments from niches, along with an offering table and the roof stone of a niche, painted red and blackened by smoke from ritual performances.[88]

Lustration slabs

Libation was a central element in offerings made to the dead.[89] The Instructions of Ani state: 'Libate for your father and mother who are resting in the valley',[90] but do not mention where such an offering ritual should be carried out, whether in the necropolis, in the home, or both, as specified, for example, in P. Sallier IV.[91] There is evidence for at least 80 'lustration slabs' in Amarna houses;[92] traces of several more were probably discovered but not recorded during excavations, and many had been removed for reuse.[93] These limestone or sandstone platforms were usually found in the main room, and were provided with means of drainage along with additional stone slabs acting as splash-guards to protect adjacent walls; a similar arrangement of stone blocks was found in the washing area of 'bathrooms' at Amarna.[94]

The rectangular shape of the slabs, which often had a small rectangular runnel in front, is reminiscent of other objects associated with activities involving water such as offering tables, libation basins, and 'bathroom' trays, as well as *lits clos*. The fact that the slabs are found in houses both large and small[95] indicates that they had a significance across the social spectrum, and their prominence in the central room of the house suggests a cultic function.[96] Although they have been variously identified as troughs, jar stands, and places for washing[97] the location of one in front of a double false door[98] supports the view that they were intended for religious rather than mundane purposes. If niches containing stelae, busts, or other images or figurines of the deceased were set into the walls above the lustration slabs this could have been the location of some of the offering rituals depicted on stelae, such as that of Henut, on which a woman is depicted pouring water and burning incense before an anthropoid bust on a plinth.[99]

Offering tables

Stone offering tables were a common feature of New Kingdom artisans' houses. They may have had dual functions as part of cults for both gods and the dead. An example is the limestone offering table found in the second room of Sennedjem's house.[100] Several tables inscribed for

---

88 Bruyère 1939: 333.
89 Sadek 1987: 184, 186–7, 195.
90 Lichtheim 1976: 137.
91 'Make invocation offerings to the *akhu* in your house': Demarée 1983: 272; Friedman 1985: 96; cf. Sadek 1987: 82.
92 Peet and Woolley 1923: 40, 44–5.
93 Spence 2007: 285; Peet and Woolley 1923: 11.
94 Peet and Woolley 1923: 44–5; Spence 2007: 285–7.
95 Forty were found in Amarna houses in the North Suburb and the Main City (Stevens 2006: 234–5).
96 Spence 2007: 289, 291.
97 Petrie 1894: pls 38–9; Peet and Woolley 1923: 40; Borchardt and Ricke 1980: 17; Kemp 1989: 295–6; Stevens 2003: 155, 160.
98 House of Ramose P.47.19: Borchardt and Ricke 1980: fig. 13.
99 Vandier d'Abbadie 1946: fig. 1; Abdalaal 2005: 19.
100 S.E. VI; Meskell 2002: 120. Offering tables were found in Amarna houses including L.51.1, M.50.13,

ancestors were found at Deir el-Medina, including a fragmentary example dedicated for the *ka* of the *akh iqer en re* Paheripedjet in house N.E. XIX,[101] and that found in room 1 of house S.E. VIII for the *akh iqer en re* Nebamun.[102] A table for offerings made for the *ka* of the *akhet iqer en re* Iuy was discovered in the debris of house S.E. IX,[103] and an offering table with an attached libation basin dedicated to a woman, the *akhet iqer en re* Irynefer, was found in the second room of house C. VI.[104]

Baskets and reed mats may have been used as substitutes for stone tables in non-elite households. Anna Stevens suggests that mats and baskets may have been commonly used as an 'affordable and accessible means of delineating a sacred clean space'.[105] Such mats, made from dried grass and cord or leaves, were perishable and expendable, but examples have survived from tombs.[106] A 19th Dynasty letter links the use of mats with ritual activity: '… send us leaf-mats and garlands [on] day 18, because they are going to pour libations on day 19'.[107]

Statues and statuettes

It is possible that the seated figures depicted in the house of Djehutynakht are statues of the owner. Such figures could have been carved from wood[108] or even fashioned from clay: fragmentary clay/mud statues have survived in shrines and tombs at Deir el-Medina.[109] Four fragments of statuary were unearthed in domestic contexts at Kom Rabi'a; they had perhaps been smashed to recover reusable stone.[110] Stone fragments in house N.50.30 at Amarna may have derived from a statue that suffered the same fate.[111]

At least one statuette explicitly dedicated to an ancestor is known. The unprovenanced wooden standing male figure wears a short kilt and is identified as the *akh iqer* Ba'aref.[112] It is similar in type to other uninscribed, unprovenanced New Kingdom figures which might also represent the potent dead and have been set up in tomb chapels and houses as objects of

---

and nos. 16, 17, and 20 Long Wall Street: Peet and Woolley 1923: 87–9, pls i, iii.

101 Bruyère 1939: 262, fig. 137; Demarée 1983: 151–2.

102 Bruyère 1939: 275, fig. 147.

103 Bruyère 1939: 278, fig. 153; Demarée 1983: 147.

104 Bruyère 1939: 310, fig. 181; Demarée 1983: 148–9.

105 2006: 297.

106 Wente 1990: 164, no. 263, 139, no. 173. E.g. the reed mat from tomb 1389 at Deir el-Medina, *temp.* Thutmose III (McDonald 1982: 134), and the circular grass mat from Tomb 5 at Gurob, dating to the 19th Dynasty (Thomas 1981: 22).

107 O. DM 51: Wente 1990: 139, no. 173.

108 Problems of preservation: wood was difficult to obtain and therefore likely to be reused wherever possible. Secondly, there is the issue of survival: at Amarna, for example, most wooden objects were destroyed by white ants/termites (Peet and Woolley 1923: 38; Stevens 2008: 36–7). At Saqqara as elsewhere in Egypt, climatic and hydrological changes since the 19th century have led to raised subsoil humidity resulting in the obliteration of many ancient wooden objects (Raven 2001: 4, 6; Castel and Meeks 1970: 31, 40). Thirdly, it is possible that when sites such as Deir el-Medina were finally abandoned, people took the most valuable or practical portable possessions with them.

109 Sadek 1987: 71; Muhammed 1966: 31.

110 Giddy 1999: 305.

111 Peet and Woolley 1923: 27, pl. xi, no. 21/512.

112 Demarée 1983: 161–2.

veneration. A limestone statuette of a man in a typical *akh iqer* pose, seated in a high-backed chair and holding the stem of a lotus bud at the centre of his chest with the bud itself resting on his left shoulder, was found in the most south-easterly room in house T.35.4 at Amarna may be an example of an uninscribed ancestral figure.[113] Other examples include a pre-Amarna-style uninscribed limestone statuette of a seated man holding the stem of a water lily, from the northern buildings at Amarna,[114] and a wooden statuette of a striding man also holding a water lily stem surmounted by a bud, now in Turin.[115] It seems unlikely that such sculptures were isolated examples, and Schulman pointed to several other examples of figures holding lilies that may also have derived from domestic contexts[116] (Figure 25).

Votives, including female figurines

An aspect of fertility figures shared by Egyptians and the South Sotho of southern Africa[117] is that although the figurines signify the desire to have children, they are not in the form of children but of adults, mostly female. The majority of surviving examples were modelled from clay, fired and deposited, possibly as votive offerings, in a wide range of contexts, from temples to tombs and houses.[118] Pinch states that:[119] 'It is uncertain whether these objects were votive in the sense of being gifts offered in fulfilment of a vow, after an answered prayer … The numerous forms of magical 'coercion' employed in Egyptian funerary religion suggest that the offerings were made in anticipation of the desired effect.' However, Wood[120] notes that it is equally possible that the figurines were deposited in gratitude at a successful outcome, in this case conception or birth.

Ceramic snakes found in domestic contexts may have acted as guardians to protect against nightmares induced by the dead.[121] Examples have been found in houses at Memphis and Amarna.[122] Such protection may also have been the function of a Nineteenth Dynasty stela of Khonsu and Tentopet (probably from Deir el-Medina) with its appeal to Meretseger in snake form: 'May she grant pleasure without seeing horror'.[123]

---

113 Frankfort and Pendlebury 1933: pl. xxxvii, figs 1–4, cat. 29/331, Cairo JE 53249.

114 Freed 1999: 225, no. 173.

115 Curto 1984: no 174, N 3100.

116 1986: 307–8, n. 22. In addition there are tomb statues where the owner is depicted holding a blue water lily by the stem, e.g. Hawass and Garrett 2002: 50.

117 Pinch 1993: 198–234; Wood 1998: 45.

118 Temples: Kemp 1995a: 29; Waraska 2009; tombs: Pinch 1993: 226–32; cf. Iron Age Palestine: Bloch-Smith 1992b: 218–19; houses: Peet and Woolley 1923: 22, 24, pl. xii; Frankfort and Pendlebury 1933: 36, 40, 42; Bruyère 1953: 36; Bonnet and Valbelle 1976: 341.

119 1982: 139.

120 1998: 35.

121 For which see Ritner 1990; Stevens 2006: 323; Blackman 1927: 237.

122 Giddy 1999: 13–27; Kemp 1995a: 31–2; Peet and Woolley 1923: 66; Frankfort and Pendlebury 1933: 42, cat. 29/375.

123 Louvre E 13935: Kitchen 2000: 456.

Figure 25: Statuette of Mersu, dedicated by his brother, Mayamun. Painted limestine, from Deir el-Medina, 18th Dynasty. Turin 3092. © Fondazione museo Antichità Egizie di Torino – used with permission.

Stelae

According to Meskell:[124] 'ancestor stelae embodied a knowable, biographic thread that served to link generations and individuals through time.' Stelae specifically related to ancestors were found in several Deir el-Medina houses. In house C. VI, a broken bust, a further bust, and a fragment of an *akh iqer* stela of Mose were discovered in the first room, and a stela dedicated to the *akh [iqer] en re* Baki was found in the second.[125] The cellar of house S.O. II contained a stela dedicated to the *akh iq[er] en re* Khonsu and another dedicated to/for the Osiris, *akhet iqeret en re* Sheriure.[126] House S.O. V, room 4, contained a stela dedicated to the *akh iqer en re* Khaemwy and another for the *akh iqer en re* Pennub; the base of a limestone naos was found nearby.[127]

The atypical nature of settlements such as Deir el-Medina and Amarna, with their abnormally high number of inscribed artefacts (as well as documents at Deir el-Medina), can give the misleading impression that cultic activity did not extend beyond the deposition of such material. Juan Carlos Moreno García,[128] for instance, states: '... the high levels of literacy of its artisans and scribes led to the expression of the cult of the ancestors not by means of the letters to the dead or of oral performances and rituals, but, instead, through prestigious items like the inscribed stelae'. However, physical and oral acts need not be mutually exclusive, and oral petitions are by nature almost impossible to detect archaeologically. Kemp notes in regard to domestic cults that:[129] 'some texts demanded, when significant words were to be uttered, the use of ephemeral materials such as vulture feathers, pieces of wood, flowers and figures made of white bread.' The fact that these objects cannot be recovered does not mean that such practices did not take place. Pinch has suggested that hair or body fluids, including blood, may have been incorporated into fertility figures in order to enhance their potency;[130] if the figurines were mass produced, the secretions could have been added prior to deposition in a tomb, temple, or domestic shrine, activities that over time would have left little, if any, trace. On oral communication, Ben Haring comments that:[131] 'contrary to what the word 'oral' suggests, information is by no means restricted to words, but includes gestures, such as facial expressions and movements of the hands, as well as circumstances such as the presence of witnesses.'

Female involvement in the cult of ancestors is illustrated on the stela of Henut and BM EA 270,[132] where women are depicted alone worshipping and libating before busts on plinths. Women were involved in commissioning stelae, as indicated by a 19th Dynasty ostracon, on which the lady Senetneferet is recorded paying a draughtsman for two stelae for the temple of Hathor and one for the temple of Amun at Karnak.[133] At least three stelae from Mirgissa were decorated by

---

124 2004: 73.

125 Bruyère 1939: 309–10, fig. 179.

126 Bruyère 1939: 317–18, figs 186, 187.

127 Bruyère 1939: 327, fig. 198.

128 2007: 11.

129 1995: 26.

130 1993: 340.

131 2003: 256.

132 Vandier d'Abbadie 1946; Harrington in Keith 2011: 324–6.

133 O. Berlin 14256: Demarée 1982: 104. Examples of votive stelae dedicated by women include Roemer- und Pelizaeus-Museum, Hildesheim 380 and Kestner-Museum, Hannover 2938 (Holden 1982: 298, no. 408; 300–1, no. 410), which date to the 19th Dynasty and show women before statues of Ramesses II

or for women, and Kemp comments in relation to the latter:[134] 'the thought naturally follows that some, perhaps all of the votive material also derived from them.' It may be that, as in Iron Age Palestine,[135] women provided for and consulted ancestors and acted as mediators between generations. Equally in twentieth century Nubia, it was the female members of the family who made libations at the graves of their relatives, as it is in Egypt today.[136]

An example of a stela as the focus of ancestral cult in a domestic context was found at Askut: the stela of a man named Kuttamuwa found at Zincirli in Turkey dating to the Syro-Hittite Iron Age (*temp.* Panamuwa II, *c.* 732 BC) is comparable insofar as it was discovered in a domestic context and would have been accessible only to kin and invited guests. It was probably intended to provoke respect in those responsible for the mortuary cult associated with it, and the inscription states that the spirit of the deceased will be present in the stone. There is evidence for burning in front of the stela, and an offering dish was found in the same room.[137] An analogous Egyptian example is the shrine incorporating a stela dedicated to the house owner Meryka, which was erected in the 18th Dynasty in the same area where a late 12th Dynasty household shrine had stood. The stela itself dates to the Second Intermediate Period, indicating the continuous veneration of the same ancestor for more than 200 years.[138]

Incense burners/evidence of burning

Limestone offering grills with traces of burnt residue,[139] portable incense burners,[140] and dishes containing resinous matter[141] are indicative of cultic activities, presumably relating to both the gods and the dead (for a discussion of the significance of incense in rituals see Chapter 4). Several ancestor busts have carbonized residue on the front indicating that they were in close proximity to smoky fires, and thus that incense had been burned before them.[142]

Buried objects

At Gurob, groups of valuable, burnt objects were discovered buried in holes beneath the floors of houses. Petrie interpreted these remains as evidence of foreign influence in the form of sacrificial pyres, burnt at the house-owner's death.[143] It is equally possible that the items, which included

---

and Amun-Re, and BM EA 8501 depicting a woman worshipping Meretseger (Bierbrier 1982: 38, pl. 88, fig. 1).

134 1995a: 29.

135 Bloch-Smith 1992: 219.

136 Blackman 1916: 31; El-Shohoumi 2004: 320, pl. 24 C.

137 Struble 2010.

138 The shrine was located in an Egyptian complex in Askut, Nubia. Smith 1997: 73–5, fig. 5.5.

139 E.g. houses N.O. XIX, S.O. III at Deir el-Medina: Bruyère 1939: 296, fig. 166; 320, 206; McDonald 1982: 111, no. 92. A comparable inscribed grill was found in the West Hall of the Ptah temple at Memphis: Hayes 1959: 274.

140 Bavay 2002: 248, no. 196.

141 E.g. at Amarna: House 2, Main Street, main room, found in association with a limestone offering tray; House 11, Long Wall Street, main room: Peet and Woolley 1923: 75, 85.

142 Keith 2011: 32–3.

143 Thomas 1981: 13, referring to notes in Petrie's journals.

pottery, faience and glass vessels, cosmetic items, and jewellery, may have been offerings. The fact that in one case they had been 'covered over with a layer of potsherds carefully placed' before the pit was backfilled may suggest that some element of ritual was involved.

Early excavators at Amarna rarely investigated sub-floor or sub-wall contexts where buried deposits might be expected.[144] The burial of items and dead infants[145] beneath the floor of houses[146] may be related to rituals involving the dead or the gods, but without further evidence it is not possible to be certain. Concealment of objects, and in some cases names, must have been a significant act at Deir el-Medina (and elsewhere). For instance, the ink inscription on the ancestor bust of Khanser was written on the underside of the base even though there was plenty of space on the front and back for text.[147] The concealment of names is also apparent in a chapel of Amenhotep I at the artisans' settlement, where a limestone pillar base inscribed with the names of ten men would have been covered by the pillar itself.[148] This is atypical of architectural features: high temple inscriptions, for example, may not have been discernible from the ground, but they were not hidden by another object.

The proximity of the living and the dead is illustrated in houses where cellars had been formed from existing tombs.[149] On excavation some of these cellars were discovered still to contain mummies along with their coffins.[150] The fact that these bodies were not removed and reburied elsewhere, but remained in actively used storerooms, provides some insight into how the Egyptians viewed the dead. Burial beneath or in the vicinity of the house was uncommon. Tombs built inside houses or their courtyards forming small family cemeteries exist at Tell el-Daba, and in Mesopotamia.[151] Isolated cases include the man and woman interred in the courtyard of house T.35.6 at Amarna.[152] The woman's body was buried with a red pot and dish, while the man was placed in a subterranean brick-lined storage chamber, which had been broken through at one end to accommodate the corpse.

Items not obviously associated with cultic activity

With regard to religious practices at Amarna, Anna Stevens comments: 'Stone offering tables, pottery offering-stands, pottery and stone vessels and perhaps free-standing wooden shrines could all have served to focus religious conduct, and similar emplacements could have been destroyed or removed, or have a multi-purpose nature that obscures religious function'.[153] Modern examples of items whose function would not be obvious include human hair and blood-soaked date stones hidden between bricks in house walls for protection from malign influences and to

144 Stevens 2006: 232.

145 E.g. Amarna: Peet and Woolley 1923: 17, 85, pl. xx, fig.1, no. 22/83.

146 For example the 'treasure chest' sealed beneath the floor in house N.49.11 at Amarna (Peet and Woolley 1923: 21, pl. vi, fig. 3); and deposits of miniature vessels/remains of cultic meals in unmarked places under the floors of houses during the late Hyksos Period at Tell el-Daba (Müller 1997: 799; Bietak 1996: 54).

147 Keith 2011: 204–5.

148 Cairo JE 51512: Sadek 1987: 80; Černý 1927: pl. ix.

149 E.g. houses S.E. VIII, room 3, C. VII, room 3; Bruyère 1939: 275, 311.

150 Bruyère 1939: 319–20.

151 Müller 1997: 796, which may not be culturally Egyptian; Scurlock 2002: 5.

152 Frankfort and Pendlebury 1933: 43.

153 Stevens 2006: 297.

prevent conception respectively.[154] Examples from the New Kingdom may include mud or clay balls, sometimes containing human hair, found in domestic contexts at Amarna.[155]

Statues of local and household deities may have been used in tandem with ancestral objects to harness both the power of the gods and of the blessed dead simultaneously at times of greatest need, for example during illness or childbirth. The presence of figurines of Bes, Taweret, and deified royalty within the home is indicative of the importance of divine presence in a domestic context, and is in keeping with Jennifer Dornan's view that 'there is arguably a shared human drive for some form of direct experiential access to the sacred'.[156] The discovery of images of deities in domestic contexts suggests a situation similar to that found in ancient Syria, where ancestor cults and worship of the gods were performed side-by-side.[157]

Tombs/tomb chapels

Geraldine Pinch cautions against assuming that all material found in burial grounds constituted offerings for or artefacts associated directly with the dead:[158]

> *Objects may be found in cemeteries because they were votive offerings for the dead, objects buried to utilize the heka (magic) of the dead, or objects used to work magic against the dead ... Other types of objects could be offered to the dead to reinforce a prayer, particularly in liminal areas of tombs or cemeteries that could be regarded as the threshold between the realms of the living and the dead ... It is not always easy to distinguish between offerings to the dead and objects used in everyday magic that were deposited in or near tombs to activate or perpetuate a spell ...*

A grave is, by its nature, a liminal space, occupying an ambiguous and unstable position between two spheres of existence,[159] because it is located simultaneously in the realm of the living and the underworld. This liminality combined with the latent power of the dead meant that the tomb acted as a space in which the ancestors and their descendants could come together. Here, through the creation of the appropriate environment through ritual, dance, and/or intoxication, the borders between worlds became permeable and allowed the living to interact directly with the dead (see Chapter 4).

The Egyptian tomb was divided into three parts corresponding to the three zones inhabited by the deceased: the solar/heavenly realm (superstructure, pyramidion, stelephorous statue in recess), the earthly realm (courtyard, tomb chapel, stelae, false door, statues, shaft entrance), and the underworld (substructures, shaft, burial chamber).[160] The diagrams in Figures 26 and 27 are based on New Kingdom Theban tombs, but the division between the solar and chthonic domains was apparent in the Pyramid Texts, and the tomb chapel or graveside would presumably have always been the location for interaction between the living and the dead, and the place

[154] Blackman 1927: 108, 224.
[155] Peet and Woolley 1923: 26, 80; Blackman 1927: 290, fig. 161.
[156] 2004: 31.
[157] Van der Toorn 1995: 47.
[158] 2003: 445.
[159] Anderson 2002: 232.
[160] Termed by Kampp-Seyfried 'Upper, Middle and Lower levels' (1998: 250; 2003: 8).

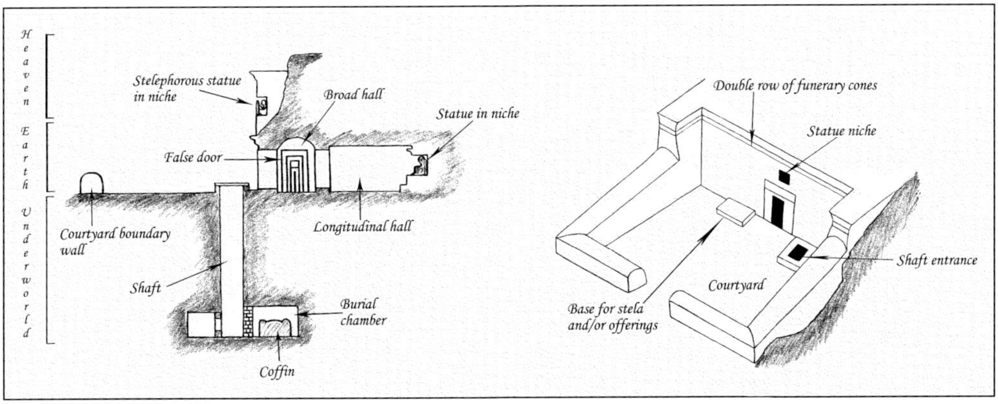

Figure 26: A sketch of a typical 18th Dynasty elite Theban tomb, showing the main constituent parts and the division of the tomb into sectors. Based on Kampp-Seyfried 2003, 8–9.

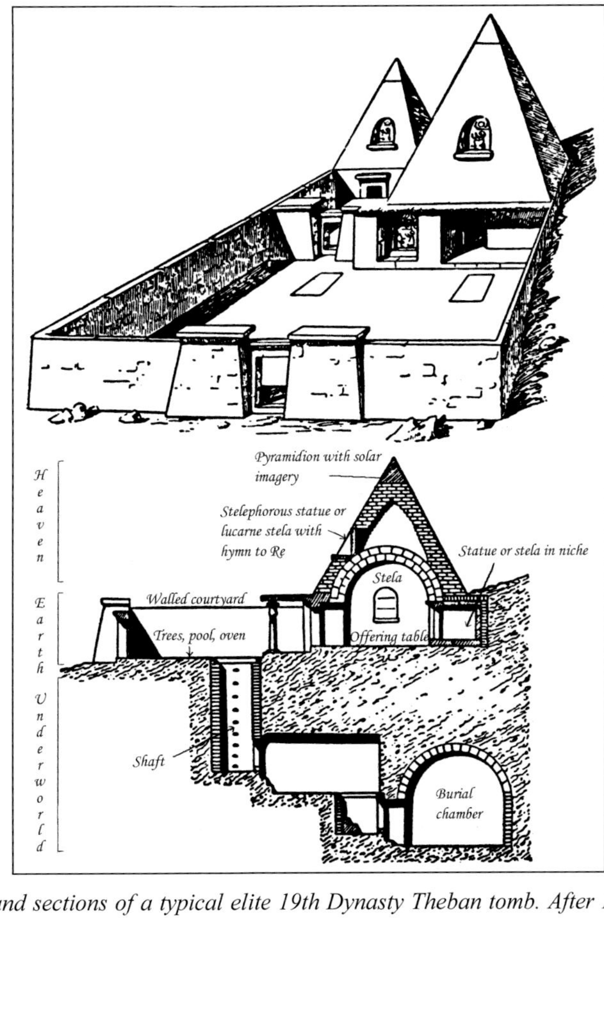

Figure 27: Profile and sections of a typical elite 19th Dynasty Theban tomb. After Muhammed 1966: pl. 79a.

to which offerings could be brought and petitions heard.[161] The parts of the tomb accessible to the living once the burial had taken place were the courtyard and the chapel.

Chapels

Tomb chapels were a point of contact between the living and the dead as well as between the dead and the gods. Letters to the dead such as the Kaw bowl and the Cairo linen contain requests for the dead to defend the interests of the living at the divine tribunal, which Sylvie Donnat suggests took place within the chapel (ꜥꜣ).[162] The need to maintain the purity of the tomb while at the same time encouraging visitors to libate and offer to the dead created a tension between restriction and accessibility.[163] This may have been partially resolved by offerings presented in the courtyards to the stelae and statues or other images of the deceased located there.

Tomb chapel stelae present an idealized view of activities that were meant to take place in the vicinity of the dead. For example, the 19th Dynasty stelae of Irinefer and Mesu[164] show the deceased in the presence of the gods, seated before offering tables[165] receiving libations, incense and floral garlands from all members of their families, including young children in the case of Irinefer. The early 18th Dynasty stela of Nebnakht from Sedment el-Gebel[166] was 'found in the niche of the family funerary chapel, with an inscribed offering table of a man named Amenmose and a stelephorous statue of the scribe Minmose in front of it',[167] enabling several deceased members of a family to participate simultaneously in activities within the chapel and its environs. The discovery of offering tables dedicated to several different individuals in a single tomb[168] may indicate that many ancestors were worshipped there simultaneously (Figure 28).

Anthropoid busts have been found in tomb chapels, though not at Deir el-Medina with one possible exception.[169] A further bust was discovered by Bruyère between tombs 290 and 214, but it is not clear whether it originated from a tomb or nearby house. The faience bust found in Tomb 603 at Gurob was associated with a jug and vase,[170] possibly indicating that it was the recipient of cult practices. The atypical busts of Mutemonet and Paendjerty were plastered

---

161 It may be significant that the earliest known 'votive ears' derive from an undisturbed shaft tomb (Northern Cemetery at Abydos, Middle Kingdom: Richards 2006: 234) that did not have a superstructure, sharing a mud-brick chapel with the graves of family members buried nearby.

162 2003: 168–9. Evidence for cultic activity in tomb chapels, particularly in the form of ceramic vessels, is often compromised or inadequately recorded – see e.g. Rose 2003. 'Offering pottery' in the chapel of Senneferi (TT 99) was scattered by later activity (*ibid.*: 203), presumably including tomb robbery.

163 Chauvet 2008: 45.

164 Louvre C 311 and C 280: Andreu 2002b: 116–17, nos 57, 58.

165 Offering tables from tomb chapels include: that in front of a stela in TT 125 dating to the reign of Hatshepsut (Kampp 1996: 416, fig. 307); an offering table and libation basin combined probably from the tomb of Amennakht (TT 266; Pierrat-Bonnefois 2002: 251, no. 200); and an offering table from tomb 1164 (Pierrat-Bonnefois 2002: 250, no. 199).

166 Cairo JE 4699; Petrie and Brunton 1924: 169.

167 Sullivan 2002: 93.

168 TT 216; Bruyère 1925: pl. xii.

169 DMB 2, from 'cult chamber E I' in the Western cemetery, associated with TT 250, Ramose: Keith-Bennett 1981: 47.

170 UC 16031; Thomas 1981: 83, pl. 55.

Figure 28: The stela/offering table/commemorative monument of Senpu and his family. From Abydos. 11th Dynasty. 20.5 cm high. Louvre, E 11573.

into niches on the west wall of the transverse hall of the tomb of their son Amenmose.[171] Their inscriptions are concerned with the provision of the deceased in the afterlife, and the busts' placement in the tomb suggests that their function was to ensure that Amenmose's parents would benefit from offerings brought to the chapel. Ancestor busts are known from tombs at Sedment and Saqqara, but their exact findspot is not recorded.[172] Busts were also found in tombs at Abydos.[173]

Female figurines found in tombs[174] were probably deposited as part of a ritual act focussed on the desire for children or in gratitude at a successful birth. A custom of petitioning the dead

171 TT 373; Porter and Moss 1960: 428, 433; Seyfried 1990: 299.

172 Sed II, from Grave 263; Keith 2011: 292–8.

173 Keith-Bennett 1981: 51, 56; Randall-MacIver and Mace 1902: 90, pl. xlviii.

174 Pinch 1993: 226–32.

at tombs is indicated by a First Intermediate Period letter to the dead, which asks: 'let a healthy son be born to me, for you are an *akh iqer*' as well as Middle Kingdom inscribed figurines.[175] The placing of pottery models and figurines in areas frequented by ancestors, particularly graves and houses, in order to ensure fertility (both human and agricultural) is found in neighbouring Mediterranean cultures, including those of Bronze Age Cyprus and Iron Age Palestine.[176]

Courtyards

Pottery from the tomb of Ramose at Saqqara provides an example of the difficulties encountered in the excavation of possible funerary/mortuary deposits.[177] Earlier excavators' priorities in the clearance of tomb courtyards left major gaps in the archaeological record, as exemplified by the approach of Norman de Garis Davies in his report of work at TT 110:[178] 'Its real doorway ... is deeply buried at present and, as the thicknesses of the entrance do not appear to be decorated, little or nothing is likely to be gained by its complete clearance.' Davies noted that archaeologists at Amarna were selective in their treatment of finds:[179] 'heaps of sherds outside the chief tombs ... were thrown out by the excavators, and were already broken for the most part. Professor Petrie describes Tomb 16 as containing 'burials in palm-sticks, coffins, etc.' and this was also the case doubtless in the other tombs. Most of these remains were destroyed, I believe, by the excavators.' It is likely that much of the evidence for rituals carried out in the vicinity of tombs has been irretrievably lost.

Directly in front of the tomb of Sennedjem at Akhmim, excavators found layers of sand, rubble and broken pottery bowls, along with fragments of a ceramic altar.[180] The presence of the altar suggests that the vessels may provide evidence of mortuary cult practices taking place in the courtyard. Such practices evidently occurred in the forecourt of Tjanuni's tomb, where fragments of pottery, reed mats, and other debris associated with feasting were recovered.[181] Maarten Raven found evidence of an offering cult in the forecourt of the 18th Dynasty tomb of Maya and Meryt at Saqqara,[182] including a pottery assemblage, offering stands, an offering table, a basin, and a votive tablet, along with an unfinished anthropoid bust on the ledge surrounding the stairway of the substructure of the tomb.[183] The excavator comments: 'it is hard to conceive the function of such an object in the underground parts of the tomb.'[184] However he also states that several broken offering tables and a rock-cut stela were found in the vicinity, and that the area may have been accessible before the burial of Maya: 'Perhaps the stela and offering tables are evidence from the period between the earliest burials (in Chamber R, and later in Chamber O) and the death of Maya himself, when this part of the tomb was still accessible whereas the offering chapels of the superstructure may still have been unfinished.' Thus an offering cult may

---

175 Wente 1990: 213; Donnat 2003: pls 571–6, l, li.

176 Keswani 2004: 151; Bloch-Smith 1992: 219.

177 Martin *et al.* 2001: 54; see also the tomb of Pabes, *id.*: 58.

178 1932: 279.

179 1908a: 14, n. 5.

180 Ockinga 1997: 5.

181 TT 74: Brack and Brack 1977: 60; Hartwig 2004: 12–13, 43–5.

182 2001: 8.

183 Chamber G; Raven 2001: 8; cat. 6, pl. 14.

184 2001: 8.

have been set up for Maya's ancestors, including his parents, and his wife prior to his death. Upon his demise and burial the temporary ceremonial area would have been sealed and rituals transferred to the chapels built for the continuing mortuary cult.

Pits and depressions[185] may be significant for activities performed in mortuary cults, particularly if, as in TT 189,[186] the depression lies before a stela or statue. Such indentations may have been created to receive vessels. The area before the first courtyard in the tomb of Neferhotep contained an offering basin in the form of a reused amphora.[187] Excavations at Amarna revealed a similar use of vessels: jars were partly or completely buried up to the rim in the floor of houses in the same room as offering tables and stelae.[188] In the courtyard of the tomb of Sennedjem at Akhmim a large jar with a pointed base was found standing upright in a hole in front of the portico; a piece of limestone had been used as a lid.[189]

Larger depressions labelled 'Osiris beds' or 'flowerbeds'[190] could well be the remains of small pools surrounded by vegetation that provided the tomb owner and his *ba* with the drinking pool often illustrated in tomb scenes, and visitors with a water source for libations. The importance of this feature is emphasised by its appearance in tomb decoration (Figure 29) and texts:[191]

> *Going into and out of the garden with its pond*
> *To cool the heart under its trees.*
> *... drinking water from his bird pond,*
> *Smelling lotus blossoms and picking buds by N.*

> *I have presented [you] with this cool water that [your] heart may be refreshed thereby – this water that comes from [your] pool in the necropolis in the west of Thebes ... [your* ba *sits] in my shade and drinks water to its heart's content*

The presence of alluvial mud around a T-shaped basin in the forecourt of Chapel 529 at Deir el-Medina indicated that a small garden surrounded the basin,[192] and the associated brick projection designed to hold a jar led Bomann[193] to suggest that this might be the location of libations for the *ba*s of the deceased, as illustrated in tree-goddess scenes.[194] She notes that at Deir el-Bahri and Deir el-Medina, T-shaped basins were found in connection with funerary gardens, and that the presence of a token garden would have provided sustenance and pleasure to the deceased.[195] Mortuary texts indicate that the garden was one of four places that an individual wished to visit after death, the others being his house (to see his wife and children), the tomb (to receive offerings), and festivals at Abydos, Memphis, Thebes, and Busiris.[196]

---

185 E.g. TT 160, TT 49: Kampp 1996: 226, 253, figs 127, 149.

186 Kampp 1996: 478, fig. 375.

187 TT 216, *temp.* Ramesses II: Kampp 1996: 495.

188 Peet and Woolley 1923: 70–2, 77.

189 Ockinga 1997: 4–5.

190 Kampp 1996: 409.

191 TT 85, Amenemheb: Assmann 2005: 221; Davies 1927: 19. Cf. the tombs of Huya and Pentju at Amarna: Davies 1905: 16, pl. xxii; 1906: 30, pl. iv.

192 Compare the description of Maruaten at Amarna by Peet and Woolley 1923: 116.

193 1991: 104.

194 E.g. TTs 51, 178 and 296: Hofmann 1999: 19, fig. 18; pl. viii, figs 22, 23.

195 Bomann 1991: 62, 108; cf. Kemp 1995b: 452–3.

196 Assmann 2005: 51.

Figure 29: The ba *hovers over the T-shaped basin, while the tomb owner in human/*akh *form drinks from the water below. To the right, the goddess of the sycamore tree provides sustenance for the* ba, *and the* ka*-table is visible. To the left, the beginning of the harper's song may be seen. Tomb of Tjanefer (TT 158), Dra Abu el-Naga, 20th Dynasty. © Schott-Archiv (Ägyptologie der Universität Trier), reproduced with permission.*

Some courtyards contained permanent cultic emplacements in mud-brick, including platforms for stelae and/or offerings and enclosed areas, possibly Osiris beds.[197] The tomb courtyard of Sobekhotep contained various mud-brick features that were probably intended to facilitate mortuary offerings, including a pot-stand, offering table, altar, and a bench probably for a stela.[198] The significance of offerings made in the courtyard[199] may lie partially in the fact that this was the last place that the mummy rested before it was taken to the burial chamber. The Opening of the Mouth ritual that took place at the tomb entrance[200] enabled the corpse to consume food

[197] E.g. TT 120, *temp.* Amenhotep III: Kampp 1996: 409, fig. 299. For a brief discussion of corn mummies and Osiris beds, see Ikram and Dodson 1998: 120. For corn mummies, see Centrone 2005, 2006.

[198] TT 63, *temp.* Thutmose IV/Amenhotep III. Kampp 1996: 280, 283, fig. 172.

[199] E.g. Kitchen 2000: 441: the offering table of Pay includes a request for water poured onto his offering slab at the doorway of his tomb every day. An inscription on the outer thickness of the doorway of the tomb of Ahmose-Pennekhbet at Elkab mentions '[all things] good and pure at the entrance of your tomb' (Davies and O'Connell 2011: 3), again suggesting that doorways were focal points for cultic activity.

[200] Muhammed 1966: 171; see Chapter 4.

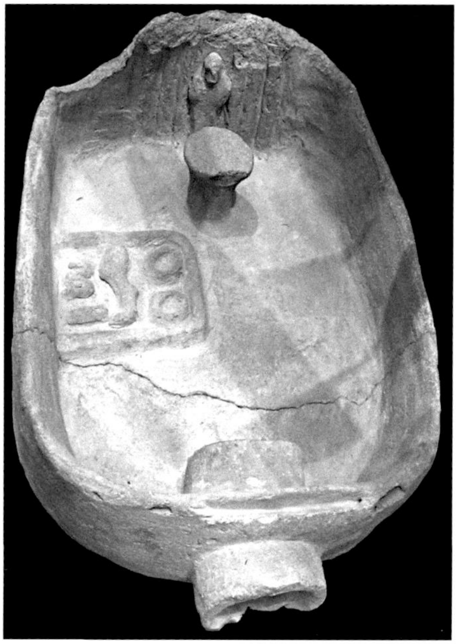

Figure 30: Model of a tomb courtyard with the deceased emerging from a (false?) doorway to receive the offerings laid out on the offering table and a low plinth. Middle Kingdom. Ceramic. Louvre E 26927.

Figure 31: Burial, resurrection, and the activity of the ba, *which flies down the tomb shaft holding sustenance for the corpse in the burial chamber, while the deceased emerges as an* akh *to 'go forth by day'. Book of the Dead of Nebqed, 18th Dynasty. Louvre, N 3068.*

and drink so it was an appropriate place for sustenance to continue to be offered and rituals to be performed (Figure 30).

A vignette from the Book of the Dead of Nebqed associated with the Opening of the Mouth scene (Figure 31) shows the passage of the *ba* taking provisions to the mummy in the burial chamber, and the proximity of the shaft to offerings made in the courtyard may have been relevant to this conception. Statues and stelae in the forecourts would equally have had the potential to enhance offering rituals, as well as perpetuating the memory of the tomb owner and his wife. Food preparation was carried out in at least some tomb forecourts, as is indicated by the presence of ovens.[201] Due to the rituals carried out in courtyards in the Ramesside period at Thebes, Assmann refers to forecourts as places of transition, initiation, purification and consecration.[202]

The modern Egyptian equivalent of mortuary offerings made at the tomb might be *et-Tala*, literally 'coming forth' or 'going up', when the souls of the dead are believed to return to the graves on the expectation of meeting visitors and receiving offerings.[203] Dates for visiting tombs in the ancient world included festivals and anniversaries: 'Month 1 of Akhet, Day 1, the day

201 E.g. TT 63; Kampp 1996: 667, figs 572, 573.

202 2003a: 51.

203 El-Shohoumi 2004: 75, 77, pl. 4; Blackman 1927: 117.

of the death of my sister: 4 *mḥt* jars and 8 *p3wt* loaves'.[204] It is probable that annual feast days, such as the Beautiful Festival of the Wadi were celebrated in tomb forecourts.[205]

Activities related to mortuary cults need not necessarily have taken place at the tombs themselves; it has been suggested, for instance, that the desert altars at Amarna were linked with the mortuary cult of nearby tombs.[206] Juan Carlos Moreno García[207] states that the presentation 'of bowls at specific locations, as well as of offerings, funerary equipment or the celebration of ritual meals needed some kind of appropriate commemorative building which could be visited by relatives; these elite rituals were probably seldom accomplished in the cases where the corpse was simply inhumed in a pit dug at the border of the desert.' The discovery of burials containing non-mummified bodies with funerary, and probably mortuary, offerings adjacent to them, yet no individual 'commemorative buildings,' at the South Tombs Cemetery at Amarna[208] challenges this view. Kemp[209] has suggested that the graves may have been served by a communal shrine as a focus of their mortuary cult. Equally, commemoration could take place in the house or at the graveside while the deceased remained within living memory and the location of the interment, if not marked, was still known.

The doorway as a liminal place has been highlighted by Violaine Chauvet in relation to Old Kingdom private tombs,[210] where the portico (*tp i3?*) was seen as a point of transition between the outside world and the sacred, ritually pure tomb environment: a boundary or transitional point between the realm of the living and that of the dead. For example, the tomb of Tiy at Saqqara had a serdab in a corner of the portico, which meant that it was not necessary to enter the tomb itself in order to perform rituals for the tomb owner, as the portico was considered part of the internal space (shown by the use of raised relief) even though it was physically outside the tomb proper.[211] Equally the tomb of Hesy had a false door placed in the portico providing a ritual space outside the tomb but with raised relief indicating that it was an extension of the tomb's interior. Texts not addressed to the public, and only intended to be read by those with access to the sacred tomb interior, were produced in raised relief (e.g. depictions of rituals being performed) – those accessible to the public and therefore approachable by all (e.g. the address to the living, curses, names and titles, offering lists) were carved in sunk relief which was a faster and cheaper method of decorating stone.[212] The duplication of some scenes inside and outside tombs may have been a means of allowing those who could not enter the buildings (because they were ritually unclean, for example), to gain access to the deceased and be able to leave offerings for them.

The principles outlined above can be applied to New Kingdom tombs, both carved and painted (Table 4), and may provide an indication of the areas of the tomb accessible following the owner's burial. It seems that sunk relief was used as a means of symbolically bringing part of the outside world into that of the dead, with images of the deceased (and often his wife)

---

204 Černý and Gardiner 1957: pl. 60, no. 2.
205 Shedid and Seidel 1996: 17.
206 Pendlebury 1933: 102; Kemp 1995b: 448–52; Stevens 2006: 326.
207 2007: 5.
208 Stevens 2006: 294; Kemp 2007: 31.
209 2008: 25, 41–2.
210 2010, 2008.
211 Chauvet 2008: 44.
212 Chauvet 2010.

Name/ TT no	Location	Dyn.	Internal raised relief	Sunk relief	Painted text sections
Roy, TT 255	Dra Abu el-Naga	18	None	Outside only	Praise to Ennead; name and titles on wall panels; ceiling strip
Userhet, TT 56	Sheikh Abd el-Qurna	18	None	Outside only	Stela text; king in shrine; text around statue niche; doorways; ceiling strip
Khonsu, TT 31	Sheikh Abd el-Qurna	19	None	Outside	Above doorway; in kiosk; offering to barque of Montu in festival
Khaemhet, TT 57	Sheikh Abd el-Qurna	18	Figures; most text; Opening of the Mouth implements	Outside; text above offering bringers and Renenutet; texts over doorway; texts and figures inside entrance; offering lists beside statues; statue texts; ceiling strip	None
Ramose, TT 55	Sheikh Abd el-Qurna	18	Figures; most texts	Name and titles around figure of tomb owner	None
Inherkhau, TT 359	Deir el-Medina	20	None	Text around doorway to burial chamber	Yellow paint used to highlight sections including harpist's song in burial chamber
Benia, TT 343	Sheikh Abd el-Qurna	18	Some figures and texts, rest painted	Statue texts (on central strip)	None
Nefersekheru, TT 296	Khokha	19	None	Outside; figures and text inside entrance; statue texts	White paint used to highlight text next to statues, names of gods, harpist's song, funeral scene. Yellow paint used as background for all other text
Neferrenpet, TT 178	Khokha	19	None	Outside; figures and text inside entrance	White paint used to highlight stela text (burial scene) and text on tomb itself; text around priests and mourners; text on ceiling near *ba*-birds; text above workers (mostly names and titles); Opening of the Mouth scene (mostly names and titles); ceiling text in white on yellow background. All other text is in black or coloured paint on a yellow background
Djehutynakht, TT 189	Assasif	19	None	Outside; text in doorways; false door	Black paint on a red background form most of the texts
Kheruef, 192	Assasif	18	Figures and text	Outside; text in doorways	Ceiling strip text painted blue; cartouches and text around royal kiosk painted yellow
Djehuty, TT 295	Khokha	18	None		Most text is painted in a variety of colours but text relating to the Opening of the Mouth ritual is painted in black, and table below is written in red. Text above offering scenes is also monochrome – above the banquet is multicoloured; ceiling strip not filled in – had yellow background

Table 4: Examples of New Kingdom tombs where sunk and raised relief and paint were used to highlight texts and images.

Figure 32: (left) Deceased greeting the sun. The scene is located within the tomb, but the sunk relief indicates an external space. Tomb of Khaemhet (TT 57), Sheikh Abd el-Qurna, 18th Dynasty.

Figure 33: (right) An inscription around a doorway in sunk relief in a tomb that has painted rather than relief decoration and texts. Tomb of Inherkhau (TT 359), outer chamber F, Deir el-Medina, 20th Dynasty.

greeting the sun in a carving style developed for the exterior of buildings (Figure 32).[213] The fact that the text is also in sunk relief suggests that those entering the building were meant to read the inscriptions as well as those on the doorways, effectively leading visitors through the tomb towards the statues of the deceased at the back (also bearing sunk relief inscriptions) where offerings could be made. The sunk versus raised relief model works for most New Kingdom tombs whether they are predominantly carved, such as Kheruef (TT 192), Ramose (TT 55) and Khaemhet (TT 57), or painted (with the apparent exception of monochrome examples) wherein sunk relief may be used around doorways (e.g. Inherkhau, TT 359; Figure 33) or certain texts

[213] But compare, for example, the tomb of Paser (TT 106: Hawass 2009: 51), where the figure of the tomb owner is in raised relief but the text surrounding him is in sunk relief.

highlighted in paint.[214] The model may also extend to stelae, which are most often carved in sunk relief suggesting that the text was intended to be read for the benefit of the gods and/or the dedicatee, and was symbolically outside (and accessible) despite placement inside a temple, tomb or shrine. Even in examples where figures have been highlighted in raised relief, inscriptions are incised,[215] suggesting that the choice of one form of carving over another was not simply a matter of cost or labour.

Shrines and chapels

In her discussion of the garden shrines at Amarna, Salima Ikram refers to the fact that they only appear in association with medium-sized or large houses and were 'probably built by important and rich officials' who wished to demonstrate their loyalty, wealth, and piety in a public, or at least semi-public, arena.[216] She does not mention the possibility that the shrines, whose size and complexity she notes hardly relate to that of the houses with which they belong, could also have been used by the occupants of nearby houses as a communal place of worship.[217] In designating the shrines as places of Aten worship through the medium of the royal family, Ikram[218] does not take into account the presence of inscribed material and artefacts indicative of other religious beliefs and practices, such as the disc with horns from the inner court of Chapel 529, and the stelae from Chapel 525 dedicated to the god Shed.[219] Each chapel at Amarna originally had a T-shaped water basin, considered by Peet and Woolley to be for purification purposes,[220] though Bomann[221] concludes that it was 'primarily associated with the funerary cult.' While it is not depicted as a washing vessel, it is commonly shown being used by the deceased, his wife, and their *ba*s as a source of drinking water.[222]

Lynn Meskell suggests that the area at Deir el-Medina between the Ptolemaic temple enclosure and the northernmost village wall 'represents a liminal zone, incorporating rituals for the living and the dead'.[223] This sector contained a group of independent private chapels (*ḫnw*)[224] dating

[214] E.g. Menna, TT 69: Porter and Moss 1960: 298–300; 105–11; 113–19; 421–4; 134–9. In relation to Old Kingdom tombs, Chauvet (2008: 47) observes that 'the carving technique physically breaks up the decoration of the portico, setting aside the elements pertaining to the life of the tomb owner from those contributing to the afterlife of the deceased.' A similar means of dividing such elements may be seen in New Kingdom scenes with the use of different coloured paint for blocks of text (e.g. TT 52, Nakht: Shedid and Seidel 1996: 56–7, 34–5).

[215] E.g. the stelae of Qenherkhepeshef (Vernus 2002: 243, no. 192); Huy (Cabrol 2002: 266, no. 215); and Nakhtamun (Rigault: 2002b: 151, no. 94).

[216] 1989: 100.

[217] For which see Stevens 2003: 88.

[218] 1989: 100–101.

[219] Peet and Woolley 1923: 100; Bomann 1991: 62, 66.

[220] 1923: 100.

[221] 1991: 114.

[222] And less frequently is depicted as a fishing pool (Vandier 1969: 605–9). For T-shaped basins, see Bomann 1991: 101–17, figs 57–74.

[223] 2000b: 271.

[224] For this term see Bomann (1991: 119–21); Meskell (2000b: 270, n. 1); Sadek (1987: 60–1); Janssen and Pestman (1968: 161–2). The *khenu* was clearly a building that belonged to individuals and could

mostly to the 19th and 20th Dynasties with one or two courtyards, benches, and columns or pillars.[225] Artefacts found in the vicinity of the chapels and their courtyards include statues, stelae, offering tables, basins, cultic pottery, portable altars, offering bowls, incense vessels, unguent vases, and amphorae for water, wine, oil, honey, and beer.[226] Some chapels possessed ovens[227] indicating that preparation of food took place in forecourts, perhaps on feast days. In the lower strata of Chapel 561 naturally occurring flint nodules were found that resembled worked objects; one of them incised with the hieroglyph *wἰ3*.[228] Bomann believes that these may have been offerings to a deity or ancestors.[229] At the Mirgissa shrine dedicated to Hathor, depositions of natural stones with 'arresting nodular shapes' suggesting fat or pregnant women and phalli were discovered; Kemp and Pinch,[230] propose that such objects were considered as suitable votive offerings to the gods.[231] A painted flint 'pregnant' female figure[232] may have derived from a house, tomb, or chapel, deposited as a votive object with the intention of increasing the prospects of conception through the intercession of the gods or the dead, or in gratitude at an incident-free pregnancy and birth, as may also have been the case with female figurines. Flint objects of this type can still be found in the Theban desert, and are sometimes collected by locals as good luck charms.[233]

In Bomann's study of the private chapels at the workmen's village at Amarna,[234] there is an implicit assumption that unless these were obviously given over entirely to the worship of deities, they were all at least partly dedicated to cults of the dead. However, only the occasional unfinished shaft in proximity to a tomb might directly link any of the chapels to an ancestor cult. Stevens[235] believes that the chapels probably served ancestor cults because they were situated close to a small cemetery, as well as having the tomb shafts and decoration that 'communicated themes appropriate to ancestor worship'. At Deir el-Medina at least eight anthropoid busts were excavated from the northern area of the votive chapels and temples, with three found in the

---

be inherited along with houses and tombs (Janssen and Pestman 1968: 161), but could also be used for storage when necessary (*ibid.*: 148; as could tombs: Wente 1967: 38), and may in some cases refer to a tomb chapel (Janssen and Pestman 1968: 162).

[225] Bruyère 1929: 16; Sadek 1987: 80.

[226] Meskell 2000b: 271.

[227] Chapel 561, annexe 450 had an oven and a semi-circular enclosure that was possibly niche for a statue of Renenutet (Bomann 1991: 59). Chapel 535 also had an oven (*ibid.*: 67). Building 528 was associated with chapels 528, 529, 530, 531, and contained an oven, a series of receptacles and a T-shaped basin, a combination that led Bomann (1991: 61–2) to conclude that it had been designed as a mortuary garden (see also Kemp 1986: 21).

[228] Petrie 1903: 27, pl. ix.

[229] 1991: 58, 77, n. 17.

[230] 1995a: 28; 1993: 210.

[231] Other possible votive offerings formed from unworked flint include the Hathor cow (UC 33193) of unknown provenance (Page 1983: 8–9, no. 10), a crocodile, and the nodule associated with the solar cult found in the second room of house C. VI at Deir el-Medina (Bruyère 1939: 276, fig. 149; 199–200, pl. xxiii).

[232] Keimer 1940: 8–9, pl. 7.

[233] See Graves-Brown 2006: 47–9.

[234] 1991.

[235] 2006: 294.

vicinity of Chapel 1213, and two to the south of the Ptolemaic temple.[236] *Akh iqer en re* stelae have also been found in votive chapels at Deir el-Medina.[237]

Chapel G in the south-western group on the path between Deir el-Medina and the Valley of the Queens may have been intended to perpetuate the cult of a man called Amenmose, whose name was erased and whose smashed offering table was unearthed in the pit and chamber below the vaulted shrine.[238] Niches in the decorated hall once held stelae, possibly including an *akh iqer* stela. The damage could be indicative of some form of execration ritual or *damnatio memoriae* for the owner (see Chapter 5). Chapel F contained a burial chamber and niches for more than a dozen private stelae. Sadek[239] states that it may have been a re-used tomb chapel but equally, given the precedent of honouring certain individuals within the community, such as those to whom several *akh iqer* stelae were dedicated, it might have been the tomb chapel of a particularly venerated local official that later became a shrine.[240]

Temples

Since non-elite individuals had restricted access to the gods, and 'could rarely hope to penetrate further than the enclosure wall or the first courtyard of a temple',[241] intermediaries were necessary for them to participate in state religion other than during festivals.[242] Indirect access could be afforded by colossal statues of kings at temple gateways, some of which bore the epithet 'He who listens to prayers',[243] or by intermediary statues of officials.[244] By the New Kingdom it seems that people desired a closer relationship with gods,[245] as evidenced by the increased salience of 'personal piety',[246] which in turn was presumably the catalyst for the production of objects associated with ancestral cults for use within the home.

The discovery of anthropoid busts and an *akh iqer* stela in the Sety I temples of Hathor and Amun at Deir el-Medina suggests that ancestors and deities were worshipped simultaneously in these buildings.[247] Busts were also found in a temple at Gurob and in a temple drain at

---

236 Keith 2011: DM 4004, DM 4011, DM 4017. For Chapel 1213, see Bomann 1991: 69–70.

237 Panakht stela from Chapel II (Louvre E 16367; Demarée 1983: 43–4, 287, pl. v, A 13; Sadek 1987: 63); Hapy-a stela from Chapel 1215 (Bomann 1991: fig. 26; Demarée 1983: pl. viii, A 29).

238 Sadek 1987: 73.

239 1987: 73.

240 Demarée 1983: 282. Cults of local rulers or officials may be relevant in this context (Kemp 1995a: 38–9, 41; Morena García 2007: 4, 8; cf. van der Toorn 1995: 47; Whelan 2007: 46). At Asyut, a Middle Kingdom official's tomb became the focus of a New Kingdom cult that saw the deposition of six hundred votive stelae mostly dedicated to Wepwawet (the 'Salakhana trove') and a cache of demotic papyri (DuQuesne 2007).

241 Pinch 1982: 138.

242 This exclusivity may be found elsewhere, in the Hittite world, for example (Bryce 2002: 154).

243 Pinch 1982: 139.

244 A similar situation existed in the Classic Maya religious system (Dornan 2004: 32).

245 Pinch 1982: 138.

246 E.g. Vernus 2003; Assmann 1995: 190.

247 Sadek 1987: 65; Keith 2011: 13.

Karnak.[248] The Gurob bust was discovered with a dish, possibly for offerings, buried about fifteen centimetres below the surface near the central column of the temple: the head and its support, broken apart in antiquity, were placed together on a sherd and covered with an inverted saucer.[249] The breakage may have led to the deposition of the bust in a sacred place; the fact that the sculpture was buried rather than discarded suggests that the person represented by the bust may still have been within living memory.

In the private statue cult in temples, a reciprocal agreement between officials, the king and the gods was clearly assumed. The steward of Memphis, Amenhotep-Huy, for example, contributed towards the cult statue of Amenhotep III in the temple of Ptah; in return he was rewarded with a statue of himself set up within the same temple and entitled to share in offerings made to the statue of his king, thus perpetuating his own statue cult.[250] Although the donation was made to the intermediary statue (*twt*) of the king, reversion offerings were to be provided by the cult/processional statue (*ẖnty*) already set up within the temple. By establishing a statue cult with his son as its mortuary priest, Amenhotep-Huy was also ensuring that revenue from the associated estate would remain within his family.[251]

Naophorous statues erected in temples represent elite men embracing and thus protecting cult images of the gods, and by so doing ensuring their own protection and renewal.[252] The same reciprocity extends to 'intermediary statues',[253] through which petitioners could address the gods in return for offerings made on behalf of the statue owner (see Chapter 2). Except for these statues of officials, New Kingdom temples were the least common location for interaction between the living and the dead, indeed, they were barely places of interaction between people and deities.[254] The deceased worshipping Hathor, and less frequently, Taweret, is often depicted in tomb scenes and Book of the Dead Papyri vignettes.[255] It may be that the scenes showing Hathor emerging both from the western mountain and a papyrus clump, sometimes with a diminutive statue of a king in front of her, represent variations of the sculpture in the chapel in the temple of Thutmose III at Deir el-Bahri.[256] The sculpture was apparently adapted for the tomb of Netjerumose at Saqqara,[257] which indicates the importance this aspect of the goddess in the cult of the dead. It may be significant that in the Book of the Dead of Ani, the tomb[258] is illustrated on the opposite side of the mountain from both Hathor and Ipet/Taweret (who stands on a low plinth, perhaps representing her chapel at Deir el-Medina; Figure 34).

---

248 Keith-Bennett 1981: 55, 57. This bust, unusual in that it has bronze inlaid eyelids, is also published by Hawass (2002: 38), who incorrectly dates it to the Middle Kingdom.

249 Thomas 1981: 83, pl. 55, no. 711.

250 Ashmolean 1913.163: Kemp 1995a: 36; Gardiner 1913: 33, pl. 78; Morkot 1990: 331. The statue has been much rubbed by worshippers, showing that it was used regardless of whether or not its original meaning survived.

251 Morkot 1990: 331–33.

252 Van Dijk 1993: 132.

253 See Keswani (2004: 157) for the social implications of the elite as intermediaries and their appropriation of the powers of the ancestors in Bronze Age Cyprus.

254 Spalinger 1998: 260.

255 Spell 186, a spell for Hathor, Mistress of the West, e.g. P. Ani: Faulkner 1985: 186–7; Dondelinger 1987: 130–2, figs 29–32.

256 Saleh and Sourouzian 1987, no. 138.

257 Zivie 2003: 80, fig. 4.

258 *Contra* Richards 1999: 88.

Figure 34: Deities representing chapels on the West Bank of Thebes at Deir el-Medina and Deir el-Bahri? Book of the Dead of Ani, Spells 185 and 186, 19th Dynasty. British Museum, EA 10470, 37. © Trustees of the British Museum.

These scenes may depict the desire of the deceased to visit local temples and chapels as they had done during their lifetimes. This would fit with Assmann's[259] assessment of the desire of the dead to return to earth for the purpose of following the gods in festival and worshipping them.

Conclusions

Toivari-Viitala notes:[260]

> *The dead clearly played a notable part in several aspects of the daily life of the people living at Deir el-Medina. One rather gets the impression that dead ancestors count among the 'actual' inhabitants of the village at any particular time, as their presence was made visible through stelae, busts, inscriptions etc. in people's homes, nearby shrines and tombs.*

The need for access to ancestors in the home in addition to tombs, chapels and, to a much lesser extent, temples, is probably a result of activities within the home that required divine assistance: as Kemp states:[261] 'personal crisis would have been a common preoccupation'. The

[259] 2003: 51.

[260] 2001: 225.

[261] 1995a: 29.

dead who were still within living memory might be perceived of as providing greater support at times of personal distress or danger than more remote deities. Such difficulties would have included sickness, childbirth, infertility, protection against nightmares, snakes, scorpions and the spirits of the malevolent dead, death, and subsequent periods of mourning.

As well as acting as intercessors between individuals and the gods, the ancestors could be turned to for advice and comfort, in addition to being the focus of veneration and respect, and providing a link to past generations through their association with the house. Archaeological materials and textual references suggest that, as within the early farming groups of later European prehistory and early 20th century Japan,[262] the Egyptian house was the seat of ancestor worship, and the place where most of the regular cultic activity in relation to the dead took place. Indeed, as Chapman points out in relation to prehistoric eastern Hungary:[263] 'The frequent comparison between houses and tombs, the latter being seen as houses for the dead, reinforces the biographical symbolism of the living house; the architecture here mediates between the living and the dead as a liminal zone.'[264] The diagram below shows the contact that the majority of Egyptian citizens (or at least the elite) may have experienced with the divine in the New Kingdom, based on evidence from Deir el-Medina. To this could be added the festivals and oracles when gods and deified kings were more accessible through their cult images.[265] The overall pattern of worship suggests a trend towards localism,[266] as well as a certain level of exclusivity regarding state gods and their relationship with the king.

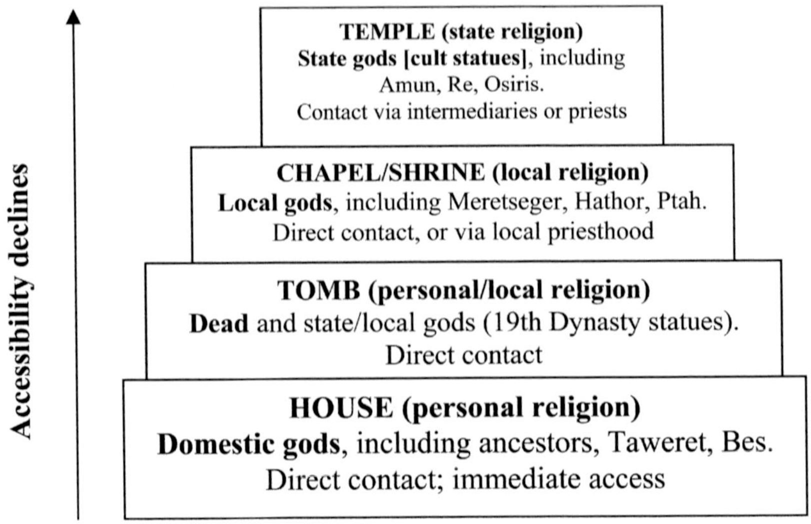

262 Chapman 1994: 74; Nozumi 1901: 45.

263 1994: 52.

264 *pr (n) ḏt*. See el-Shohoumi 2006: 353, n. 8 for further parallels.

265 E.g. Černý 1927: 182–5.

266 Meskell 2002: 49.

Chapter 4

Times of interaction between the living and the dead: funerals, festivals, and banquets

Funerals

> *That the dead do not bury themselves may seem obvious and banal. It is, however, the starting point for considerations of the social context in which an individual's death was celebrated and commemorated. Funerary practices are products of 'political' decisions (or sequences of decisions) in which the corpse is manipulated for the purposes of the survivors. Their treatment of the deceased is conditioned by their perception of death and their relationships with each other as much as by their relationship to the deceased whilst alive.*[1]

The main purpose of a funeral is to separate the living from the dead; it is an act of severance from the community.[2] The disruption to society caused by biological death[3] was countered by adherence to established patterns of behaviour, and by continued communication with the deceased via regular visits to the tomb and through media such as anthropoid busts and stelae. Although there are many representations of funerals or rituals related to them, very little is known about the actual ceremony, particularly prior to the New Kingdom.[4] Tomb scenes indicate that emotions were freely expressed: weeping, fasting,[5] and lamenting were part of the socially acceptable (and expected) response to the loss of close kin. The Prophecy of Neferti, dating to the 12th Dynasty but commonly copied in the New Kingdom, creates an image of an inverted world where 'one shall not weep at death/ one shall not spend the night fasting for death/ a man's heart concerned with himself alone./ One shall not make mourning today, the heart turning from it entirely'.[6]

Harold Hays[7] identifies seven 'major complexes' of Egyptian funerary rituals on the basis of scenes in the tomb of Rekhmire:[8]

1. Procession to the necropolis – *dw/rdit r tꜣ, smr tꜣ* ('landing'), involved crossing over to the West Bank by boat

---

[1] Parker Pearson 1993: 203.

[2] Watson 1988: 15, n. 40; or, as Davies (1994: 30) states: 'Funerals kill the dead'.

[3] Thompson 1988: 73.

[4] Assmann 2005: 299.

[5] Frandsen 1999: 135–6.

[6] Parkinson 1991: 34–5.

[7] 2010: 2, 5–6.

[8] TT 100: Davies 1943. For funerary cult in the Middle Kingdom and the roles of priests within it, see Russo 2007.

2. Procession to the embalming place – *prt ḥr tꜣ* ('disembarking')
   spr r sḥ-nṯr ('approaching the god's booth')
3. Embalming and mummification – *wt* ('wrapping'), including three-day purification in an *ỉbw* or *sḥ-nṯr* tent, followed by mummification in the pure place – *wꜥbt* or *pr-nfr*[9]
4. Post-embalming rituals – including a night vigil[10]
5. Procession to the tomb/funeral – *ỉrt ḳrst nfrt* ('making a perfect burial')
6. Opening of the Mouth ritual – *wpt rꜣ*
7. Mortuary service – *prt-ḫrw* ('coming at the voice')

To this could be added any rites or activities taking place in the house immediately after an individual's death, including public notification by wailing and other expressions of grief for which no New Kingdom evidence survives, though it is known from the Old Kingdom as well as from other cultures.[11]

Of these stages, two were rarely if ever depicted in tombs: embalming and mummification are known only in TT 41, scenes that were later copied into TT 23,[12] while the vigil on the night before the funeral is never illustrated unless the scene of Anubis attending a mummy beneath a canopy is an abbreviated version of pre-burial rites (Figure 35). The latter is referred to by Assmann as a 'wake',[13] during which mourning, punishment of the enemy, beating of drums, and embalming by a priest wearing an Anubis mask took place.

It seems that prior to interment the deceased was considered to be particularly vulnerable to attack: Coffin Texts Spell 62, to be recited in the context of the wake, states that the enemy who comes in the night will be repulsed, as will the robber at dawn.[14] Whereas in many societies, 'much of the ritual at funerals is aimed specifically at settling the volatile and disorientated spirit of the recently dead',[15] the night rituals were apparently aimed at preparing the corpse for (a theoretical) eternity and protecting it, as well as mourning the individual's death.

Following the procession to the tomb, the next stage at which people are depicted as gathered together was the Opening of the Mouth. The main purpose of conducting this ritual on statues was to enable them to receive offerings,[16] but in principle it was performed on any object required to operate on behalf of the deceased: shabtis, coffins, heart scarabs, and the mummy itself,[17] a feature shared by the Mesopotamian *mīs pî* (mouth-washing) ritual.[18] The mummy and its anthropoid coffin were subject to the ritual, perhaps in an abbreviated form compared

[9] If, as mortuary texts indicate, the embalming process took 70 days (Assmann 2005: 31), it is likely that the funerary process took place in two stages – pre- and post-embalming.

[10] See Assmann 2005: 260–70.

[11] Simpson 1976: 21–3, pls xviii–xx, fig. 35. Cf. modern China: Watson 1988: 12. See Lane (1835: 517) and Blackman (1927: 109) for such behaviour in 19th and 20th century rural Egypt.

[12] Assmann 2005: 305.

[13] 2005: 295.

[14] Assmann 2005: 271; cf. Faulkner 1973: 58; de Buck 1938: 268 g–j. The newly dead were thought to be as susceptible to malign beings as newborn infants (Bourriau 1991: 13, 14).

[15] Watson 1988: 9.

[16] Finnestad 1978: 126. For the Opening of the Mouth see Otto 1960 and Fischer-Elfert 1998.

[17] Blackman 1924: 57; Bjerke 1965: 207; Lorton 1999: 148.

[18] Walker and Dick 1999: 71. For comparisons between the Opening of the Mouth and *mīs pî* or *pit pî* ceremonies, see Blackman 1924; Roth 1993: 77–8. Similarities between the rituals are regarded as coincidental by Lorton (1999).

to that performed on the statue,[19] as the mummy would not be accessible following burial, whereas the statue was required to sustain the tomb owner both in the world of the living and in the afterlife, and it may have acted as a substitute should the corpse be destroyed.[20] The aim of the Opening of the Mouth on private statuary was the restoration of the deceased's faculties, including their memory and consciousness. The importance of regaining awareness following death is expressed during the New Kingdom in the daily cult ritual and in earlier texts as the act of restoring the heart to the body.[21] In the Opening of the Mouth, the presentation of the bull's heart provides the consciousness essential for the continued existence of the individual.[22] Pinch suggests that the dedication of votive objects in a temple's open court 'could have been marked not just by spoken prayers, but by chanted invocations to the deity, singing, dancing, and the playing of musical instruments.'[23] Perhaps we should envisage similar activities taking place in tomb forecourts during offering ceremonies and banquets for and with the dead.

The Opening of the Mouth ritual took place outside the tomb's entrance[24] prior to the deposition of the deceased in the burial chamber:[25]

sʿḥʿ.tw sʿḥ.k n rʿ	Your mummy is erected for Re
m wsḫt nt i͗s.k	in the court of your tomb[26]

Assmann (2005: 318) has proposed that the ceremonies took place at midday when the sun would be shining directly on the mummy – symbolically endowing it with new life prior to its being placed back into the coffin for burial. Either mummies with masks (Figure 35) or anthropoid coffins may be depicted in Theban tombs.[27]

The addition of a partially closed court to tomb architecture during the New Kingdom may relate to the performance of rites there.[28] Based on depictions on stelae,[29] papyri, and tomb scenes, it is possible to suggest the positions of those attending the funeral within the courtyard (Figures 37 and 38). Although Assmann[30] states that the Opening of the Mouth ritual was carried out on the mummies of the tomb owner and his wife, this is debateable since the couple were unlikely to die at the same time, or for one mummy to be set aside

19 Assmann 2003a: 60.

20 Ranke 1935: 45–6; Finnestad 1978: 129–30, n. 43.

21 Assmann 2005: 272–3; Lorton 1999: 140.

22 Lorton 1999: 165; Otto 1960: II, fig. 1, scene 44.

23 1993: 340.

24 The sacredness of this area was maintained by ongoing cultic practices; for example the harpist's song in the 19th Dynasty tomb of Piay (TT 263: Lichtheim 1945: 204–205; Porter and Moss 1960: 345 (3) II) states: 'There is made for you a great sacrifice out[side] of your tomb. Your *ba* comes forth at the voice of the *ka*-priest to receive the offerings laid down for it (*r šsp ḫt wꜣḥ n.f*).'

25 E.g. TT 178, Neferrenpet/Kenro, *temp.* Ramesses II: Assmann 2003a: 60; Hofmann 1995a: 62, text 116.

26 Kitchen (2000: 237, no. 153/3) renders 'broad hall', but the deceased being in the presence of Re makes the courtyard a more likely place for the mummy to be set up.

27 E.g. black and gold anthropoid coffins are illustrated in the tomb of Nebamun and Ipuky (TT 181: Taylor 2001: 137, fig. 97). Coffins or mummies are often shown supported by mourners or priests, but on a 17th Dynasty rishi coffin, an anthropoid coffin is depicted tied to an upright board outside the tomb entrance (Hayes 1959: 30, fig. 14).

28 Assmann 2003a: 60.

29 Schulman 1984.

30 2005: 317.

Figure 35: Tomb owner's mummy tended by Anubis. Tomb of Sennedjem (TT 1), Deir el-Medina, 19th Dynasty. © Heidelberger Ramessiden-archiv, 40117. Reproduced with the kind permission of Eva Hofmann.

Figure 36: Opening of the Mouth scene, showing the mummy with a mask. Book of the Dead of Hunefer, Chapter 23, 19th Dynasty. British Museum EA 9901, 5. © Trustees of the British Museum.

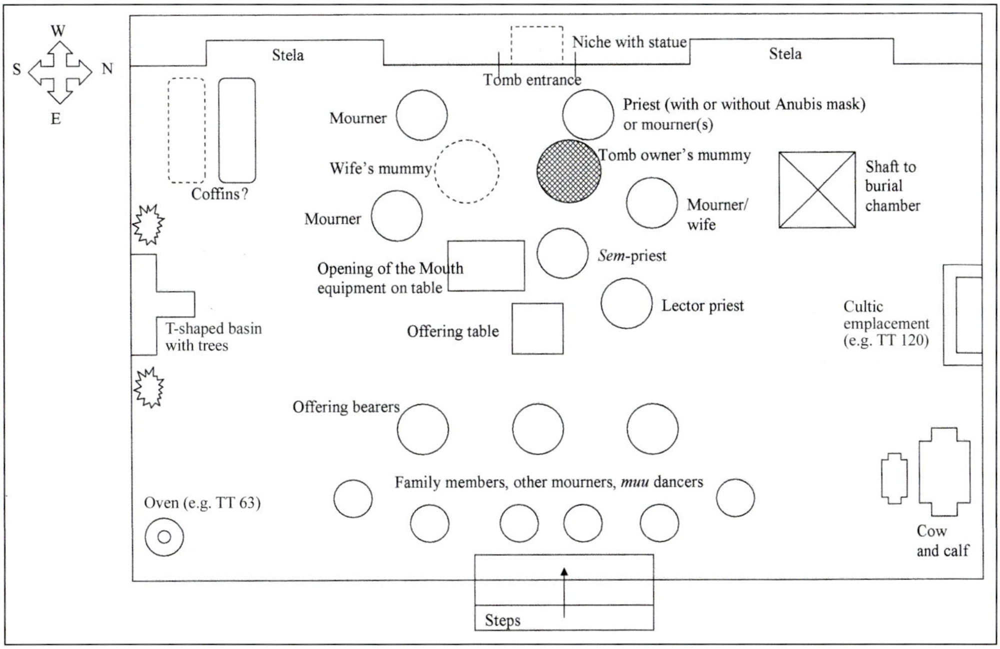

Figure 37: Opening of the Mouth outside the tomb entrance. Diagram based on tomb scenes and stelae.

Figure 38: Tomb courtyard with shallow stela niches on either side of the entrance. Tomb of Khonsu (TT 31), Sheikh Abd el-Qurna, 19th Dynasty.

until the survivor died and a joint funeral could be held. Instead it seems more likely that this is a pictorial convention, in the same manner that a wife may be shown as both mourner – when she might have predeceased her husband – and mummy in the same tomb.[31] Kathlyn Cooney, in contrast, interprets the two anthropoid forms not as the coffins of husband and wife or as mummy and coffin, but as a set of *wt* coffins that lack scale and belong to the male owner of the tomb.[32]

The *muu*-ritualists that accompanied the coffin funeral procession represented the ancestors, and welcomed the deceased at the entrance to the tomb and thence to the underworld.[33] Once the mummified, coffined corpse had been placed in the burial chamber and the chamber had been sealed, the mourners and other attendants presumably partook of the funerary banquet depicted on tomb walls, in the symbolic company of the recently deceased. The tomb would then be closed, with the door opened for the performance of the mortuary cult and for future festivals, banquets, and funerals. The events described above relate to high elite funerals, but may have occurred in modified form lower down the social scale.

The transformative nature of funerals

During the funeral, the deceased was transformed into an *akh* by the recitation of *sakhu* (*s3ḫw*) liturgies and the accompanying rituals. These texts first appeared in Old Kingdom pyramids and were used throughout Egyptian history to transfigure the dead.[34] Formality, performance and structure are fundamental to the enactment of rituals[35] and particularly important to the re-establishment of order following the damage to the social fabric caused by a death.

> *... regardless of the particulars of a society's belief system, religious observances, burial practices, and acts of commemoration, people throughout the world must work to transform the social body and person who has died into something else, and this process involves the distillation of the living people's memories through a complex process of remembering and forgetting. The transformative work of distilling a social person into a non-living entity often involves commemorative rites, expressions of mourning, religious observations, sanctioned processing of the physical bodies of the dead and the living, as well as remembering certain aspects of that person and his or her life while forgetting others.*[36]

Shafer[37] remarks that: 'ritual is not *primarily* a catharsis for unresolved personal or societal neuroses nor *primarily* a source of psychological security in the midst of a dangerous world – although ritual may provide catharsis and security.' The involvement of the tomb owner's children in his funeral served to bolster this security by emphasizing the continuation of life after death; children were also a means of survival for an aspect of the deceased, whose

---

31 Sweeney 2001: 30; Assmann 2005: 312.

32 The coffin with a divine beard would represent the outer piece and the coffin with the short beard or without facial hair the inner one (Cooney 2008: 21, n. 4).

33 Seyfried 2003: 62; Altenmüller 1975: 30.

34 Assmann 2005: 240. Assmann suggests that *sakhu* means 'to have spirit power' (2005: 244).

35 Laneri 2007: 2.

36 Chesson 2007: 109.

37 1997: 19.

ka was passed on through successive generations.[38] As Bell notes:[39] 'Individuals could not survive death intact, but families could endure forever, defeating death through lineage.' The importance of the existence of heirs to care for the deceased is emphasised in modern Egyptian laments: without children a man will be abandoned in the graveyard, his name and memory forgotten.[40]

Funeral laments

Lamenting is associated with the goddess Isis, whose cries awoke her husband Osiris and enabled him to transform into an immortal spirit and descend to the netherworld,[41] but it is also a means of expressing shared sorrow in a communal setting. Women are frequently shown mourning more expressively than men in tomb scenes[42] but this may be an iconographic convention rather than a reflection of reality, perhaps linked to the iconography of Isis and Nephthys (Figure 38): as Deborah Sweeney points out, 'the scenes in tombs are often an interpretative rendering rather than a record.'[43]

However, in modern Upper Egypt it is the women who are responsible for lamenting (*'idid*) at funerals,[44] particularly those who are post-menopausal since they are immune to the dangers of crossing the boundary between the living and the dead that may harm fertility.[45] Death pollution (*mushahara*) is thought to afflict lactating women or those of child-bearing age if they come into contact with recently bereaved widows or women who have just left a funeral.[46] This does not seem to have been the case in the New Kingdom, where infants are depicted carried by children,[47] presumably while their mothers participate in mourning rituals. Funerals can be a forum for the display of social solidarity,[48] and communal wailing/lamenting served to remind funeral attendees of the shared loss, and to inform the bereaved wife that she was not alone.[49]

Among the many euphemisms for death,[50] the image of travelling and being distant from family members is common: death as departure is a feature of several funerary laments, in which the immediate family, particularly wives and sons, plead with the deceased not to leave,[51] and

---

38 Assmann 2005: 44.

39 1997: 286, n. 39.

40 Wickett 2010: 28–9.

41 Assmann 2005: 245.

42 E.g. Sweeney 2001: 46.

43 2001: 29. See also letters to the dead P. Leiden I, 371 (Gardiner and Sethe 1928: 8–9, pls 7–8; Schott 1950: 150–1) and O. Louvre 698 (Frandsen 1992), where male grief is expressed.

44 El-Shohoumi 2004: 256–62.

45 Wickett 2010: 108.

46 Wickett 2010: 67, 107.

47 E.g. Khaemhet, TT 57: Malek and Miles 1989; Toivari-Viitala 2001: 166, n. 129. For New Kingdom laments, see Lüddeckens 1943: 31–160.

48 Tonkinson 2008: 49.

49 It was an expression of '*marlpa*' or 'company': Musharbash 2008: 32.

50 Zandee 1960: 52–4, 85–6.

51 E.g. TT 10, Penbuy and Kasa, and TT 219, Nebenmaat: Kitchen 2000: 494, 509. This fear of being left behind is also apparent in Aboriginal laments (Strathern and Stewart 2008: xv), among others.

Figure 39: Female mourner. Terracotta. Provenance unknown; late Middle Kingdom–early New Kingdom. 25 cm high. Louvre, E 27247.

is illustrated in Opening of the Mouth scenes, where the widow[52] clasps her husband's coffin or mummy (Figure 40).

The attribution of the laments to the deceased's family sets modern and ancient lamenting apart. Those who compose and lead laments in modern Luxor (*badaya*, 'the one who begins') are not necessarily related to the deceased's family but are highly regarded by other women, while professional mourners (*naddabat*), who rip their clothes and pour dust onto their hair, are extremely poor and often subsidise their income by prostitution.[53] Bereaved widows still rend their clothing, unplait their hair and daub their faces with mud, partly in emulation of the state of the dead, since a deceased woman's plaits are unravelled prior to burial.[54] Ancient burials, such as those at Diospolis Parva for example,[55] show that at least some women were interred with plaited hair,[56] suggesting that the loose and dishevelled hair of mourners depicted on, for

[52] Occasionally children are shown instead, as in the Ramesside tomb of Nebenmaat (TT 219: Goyon 2000: 24).

[53] Wickett 2010: 33.

[54] Wickett 2010: 156, 71, 137.

[55] Bourriau 2009: 74, 81. Also South Tombs Cemetery at Amarna (Stevens 2008: 21), and the burial of Senenmut and Hatnefer (Dorman 2003: 32).

[56] Plaited hair was symbolic of control and appropriate appearance (e.g. P. Harris 500, Colln II, 8:

Figure 40: Widow weeping and throwing dust onto her hair at the foot of her husband's anthropoid coffin. Tomb of Nebamun and Ipuky (TT 181), Khokha, 18th Dynasty. After Mekhitarian 1978: 128.

instance, Middle Kingdom coffins and New Kingdom tomb walls was not a display of empathy with the deceased but rather an aspect of the chaos created by death.

The laments inscribed above funeral procession scenes are superficially similar to harpers' songs in their apparently 'heretical' approach to death and the afterlife.[57] They are characterised by a subversive pessimism in which no comfort counters the overwhelming negativity they express.[58] For example: 'He who liked to get drunk is now in a land without (even) water.'[59] Book of the Dead Spell 175b, a spell for not dying again, which seems to question orthodox views regarding the afterlife is countered by explanations from Atum, and equilibrium is thus restored:[60]

> *O Atum, what means it that I proceed to the necropolis, the silent land, which has no water and no air and is very deep and very dark and (all) is lacking, wherein one lives in quietness of heart and without any sexual pleasures available? 'I have given blessedness instead of water, air, and sexual pleasures, quietness of heart instead of bread and beer,' says Atum.*

Funerary laments are a form of communication with the dead. They articulate feelings of bereavement and longing while also being a forum for the expression of unorthodox views about death that, aside from the harpers' songs which were also inscribed in tombs, are otherwise rare in written sources. They also create 'an environment for the enactment of emotions of sorrow, anger and loss, and [empower] women to display these sentiments.'[61] The inscribed laments may only represent a fraction of those performed, since the performers were probably illiterate and the laments would therefore have been part of oral tradition, passed from mother to daughter.[62] Werbrouck suggested that lamentations and images of lamenters were incorporated into tomb decoration so that their presence would provide the *ka* of the deceased with a continuous state of wellbeing in the afterlife.[63] This is questionable given the content of the laments:[64] would the deceased be comforted by re-experiencing his funeral? Rather, laments were intended then as now to benefit both the living and the dead,[65] during the funeral rather than afterwards.

Landgráfová and Navrátilová 2009: 111).

57 Assmann 1977: 76.

58 Sweeney 2001: 44–5; Zandee 1960: 91.

59 TT 137, Mose: Sweeney 2001: 44; Lüddeckens 1943: 134, no. 64; Kitchen 2000: 303.

60 Lloyd 1989: 131; Allen 1974: 184.

61 Wickett 2010: 100.

62 Toivari-Viitala 2001: 226. Cf. Wickett 2010: 166, 235.

63 1938: 144.

64 Sweeney 2001: 48; Enmarch 2008.

65 Wickett 2010: 168. Funeral scenes are not common in the Old Kingdom, possibly because the funeral was a one-time venture, so there was no need to repeat it, even in representation (Rzeuska 2006: 297).

Festivals and banquets

Tomb inscriptions often express the wish for the deceased to be present at a range of festivals including:[66]

> *the monthly feast, the sixth-day feast, the half-monthly feast, the great procession, the rise of Sothis, the wag-feast, the Thoth-feast, the first-birth feast, the birth of Isis, the procession of Min, the procession of the sem-priest, the evening meal, the rise of the river – the feasts of heaven on their fixed days, in accord with daily custom.*

The need for the dead to participate in regular feasting is indicated by expressions such as: 'Follow your heart at the season of your desiring, your tomb being festive every day'.[67]

An analysis of tomb scenes indicates that following the burial a meal was consumed, probably in the tomb courtyard. This repast marked the end of the fasting period that began prior to the funeral, and it established a pattern of eating in the presence of the dead that was intended to continue indefinitely. Depictions of the post-funerary meal differ from banquet scenes by the absence of musicians, servants, as well as the static nature of the participants, who are shown seated rigidly on chairs (as opposed to stools or mats) facing the deceased and his wife. The apparent sobriety of these scenes[68] may reflect the exhaustion and grief experienced by the family at the culmination of the official mourning process.

The origins of the banquet scene may be traced to the Middle Kingdom:[69] by the 18th Dynasty it had become a standard feature of elite tomb decoration, but during the 19th Dynasty, with its greater emphasis on the relationship between the deceased and the gods, the banquet scene disappeared leaving only the harpers' or lutists' songs remaining. Unlike the fishing and fowling scenes, which are generally acknowledged to be purely symbolic in nature having remained largely unchanged from the Old Kingdom onwards, the banquet was based on the principal that regular feasting would occur in the vicinity of the tomb. Meals with the dead, be they personal (anniversary of death), local (cults of deified kings or local gods), or regional (feasts of Osiris, Amun etc.), are unlikely to have been as extravagant as the scenes depicted, since they represent an idealised image intended to satisfy the tomb owner during his lifetime as well as after his death.[70]

While no two banquet scenes are identical, they all contain elements that make them instantly recognisable and distinctive as a genre. Guests are seated on chairs, stools, or reed mats, and attended to by servants, who pour drinks, tie floral collars,[71] apply oil to the arms, and anoint with unguent (in the form of a cone).[72] Festival participants turn to one another as if conversing,

---

66 Paheri, EK 3 at Elkab: Tylor 1895, pl. xvi; Lichtheim 1976: 16.

67 Tomb of Ay (no. 25 at Amarna); Murnane 1995: 119; Davies 1908: 35, text 11, E, 34. Cf. *ibid.* text 11 D, pl. xxxiii.

68 For an analysis of the difference between these 'funerary' meals and banquet or 'mortuary' feasts, see Harrington 2012.

69 E.g. Chapel of Senwosret from Abydos, Louvre C 16: Ziegler and Rutschowscaya 1990: 34.

70 Bolshakov (1991) suggested that tomb cults were established and functional during the life of the owner. This idea, though controversial, finds support in texts such as 'your tomb being festive every day just as when you were alive' (tomb of Ay, Amarna no. 25: Murnane 1995: 119; Davies 1908: 35, text 11 D, pl. xxxiii).

71 *wꜣḥ*-collars are worn by both the living and the dead and are a feature of many anthropoid busts, perhaps due to the regenerative properties that they were thought to possess (Hartwig 2004: 99; Keith 2011: 59).

72 Perfumed matter was a means of creating a festal and sacred atmosphere as well as being suggestive of

Figure 41: Women passing and smelling mandrake fruit. Tomb of Nakht (TT 52), Sheikh Abd el-Qurna, 18th Dynasty.

Figure 42: Banquet scene, tomb of Djeserkareseneb (TT 38). After Davies 1963: pl. vi.

Figure 43: Banquet guests and musicians. Fragment from the lost tomb chapel of Nebamun. British Museum, EA 37984. © Trustees of the British Museum.

pass mandrake fruit around (Figure 41), and support those who are physically sick as a result of excessive alcohol consumption (Figure 42).

The atmosphere is one of celebration, with musicians and dancers providing entertainment (Figure 43), drink (and food)[73] freely available, and guests wearing perfumed oils and fresh white linen. 'Banquet' is considered by some scholars to be a misnomer because participants

ritual purity: Thompson 1998: 242–3. Oils or unguent, indicated by the orange/red shading on garments, may have represented the association of the deceased with the divine. The portrayal of scent on those approaching a deity may be symbolic of ritual cleanliness and the pure, elevated state of the justified deceased and his family. Thus unguent was worn in the presence of the divine (which included the justified deceased) and by those wishing to be recognised by the gods as one of them (for example, the deceased before Osiris). For a discussion of unguent cones and the use of oils, see Harrington 2012.

[73] In several scenes piles of food are depicted near to the guests, in others only drinks (wine or beer) are offered. The tomb owner and his wife (or mother) are always seated before an offering table apparently heaped with food, and it is likely that the offerings would revert to the festival participants once the deceased were deemed to have taken what they required.

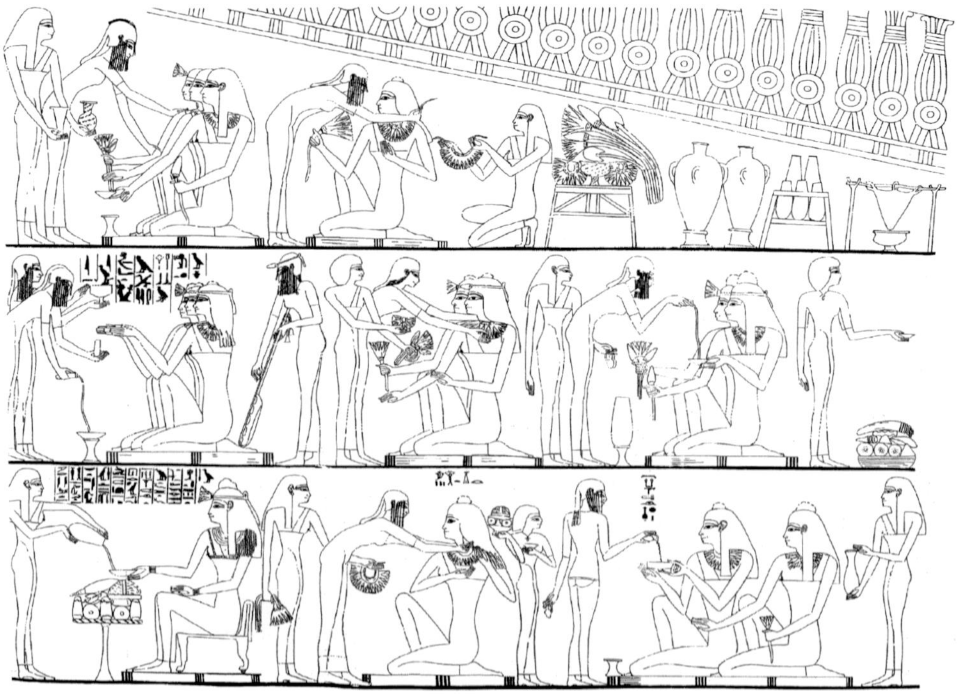

Figure 44: Banquet scene (detail), tomb of Rekhmire (TT 100). After Davies 1948: pl. lxiv.

are rarely shown eating,[74] yet aside from the Amarna period,[75] the consumption of food is usually assumed rather than explicitly illustrated. The mortuary banquet is deliberately timeless – situated simultaneously in the worlds of the living and the dead: all participants are youthful and idealised. The living and dead are not readily distinguished: some individuals (including musicians) are labelled *maa-kheru*,[76] while others, such as Rekhmire's mother have separate offering tables (Figure 44).

Since Siegfried Scott linked the great feast of Amun, Mut and Khonsu (known as the 'Beautiful Festival of the Wadi' or the 'Valley Festival'),[77] to the banquet (Figure 45), it has often been assumed that this is what banquet scenes represent: the gathering of the family to celebrate this annual event with the dead. This specific festival is in fact rarely mentioned in

---

[74] E.g. Manniche 2003: 44.

[75] The tomb of Mose dated to the Amarna period (TT 254: Strudwick and Strudwick 1998: pls xxviii, xxxi) may be unique for the New Kingdom in its depiction of food and drink consumption.

[76] For musicians captioned as *maa-kheru*, see e.g. TT 17 (Nebamun): Säve-Söderburgh 1957: pl. xxi.

[77] Schott 1953: 857. One Theban tomb example that specifically mentions the presence of Amun at Djeserakhet (Deir el-Bahri) is that of Menkheperreseneb, TT 86: (Schott 1953: 115, 111; cf. TT 39, Puyemre: Schott 1953: 110). Schott (1953: 28–9, 89–90) was forced to explain away the phrase being festive 'every day' in the context of banquet scenes, which is unnecessary if one accepts that general feast days are depicted rather than the Wadi Festival alone.

Figure 45: Banquet scene: the Festival of the Wadi is mentioned in text above the priest. Tomb of Userhet (TT 56), Sheikh Abd el-Qurna, 18th Dynasty.

relation to banquet scenes,[78] and the presentation of a 'bouquet of life' (not necessarily the Bouquet of Amun; Figure 46)[79] to the tomb owner was probably a regular occurrence. The floral arrangement was presented to a god by temple priests and then carried to the tomb to be offered to the deceased,[80] whereupon the life and blessings present in the bouquet would be transferred to the image of tomb owner.

The presence of Hathor, maternal protector of the deceased and goddess of the necropolis, seems to have been invoked by various means.[81] With her role as mistress of dancing, music,

[78] Tombs that mention the Wadi Festival or the Bouquet of Amun in conjunction with a banquet scene include TT 129 (name lost), TT 93 (Kenamun), TT 56 (Userhet), TT 247 (Simut), TT 112 and TT 86 (Menkheperreseneb), TT 84 (Amunedjeh), TT 49 (Neferhotep), TT 147 (name lost): Schott 1953: 122, 121, 123, 118, 109, 101, 99. Porter and Moss 1960: 244, 190, 111–12, 333, 229–30, 175, 168, 92–3, 258.

[79] Dittmar 1986: 125; Muhammed 1966: 96–8.

[80] In some cases the temple at which the bouquet was blessed is specifically named: in the tomb of Menkheperreseneb (TT 86), for example, bouquets are presented to the deceased from the mortuary temple of Thutmose III, the chapel of Hathor at Deir el-Bahri, and the temple of Hatshepsut and Thutmose III at Medinet Habu (Schott 1953: 118; Davies 1933: pl. xvii).

[81] Dorothea Arnold (2008: 4) suggests that in the cattle fording scenes in Old Kingdom tombs, the

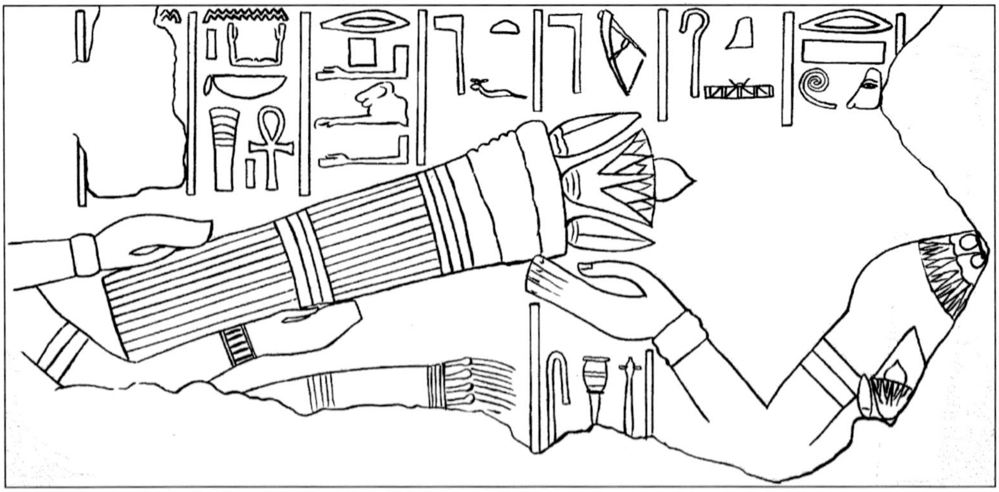

Figure 46: Bouquet of Amun. Tomb of Hekerneheh (TT 64), Sheikh Abd el-Qurna, 18th Dynasty. Davies MSS 10.22.8. Courtesy of the Griffith Institute.

garlands, incense, rejoicing, and harpists,[82] she might be considered as the goddess of banquets and festivities. The musicians are often shown as a distinct group separated from the rest of the banquet, sometimes on different sub-registers. This segregation is enhanced by the full-face rendering of some female musicians, which indicates that they are seated in a circle (Figure 47)[83] and could provide an iconographic link with the goddesses Nut or Hathor, the principal deities whose faces are shown frontally.[84] Hathor is also evoked through the presence of *menats* and *sistra* offered to the tomb owner in these or adjacent scenes (Figure 48).[85]

Hathor was also the Mistress of Drunkenness,[86] for whom festivals were held from the 18th Dynasty.[87] Her title is clearly appropriate to the banquet scenes (Figure 49) and to the concept of 'celebrating the holiday':[88]

> *For your ka*
> *Drink, be happily drunk (swri tḫ nfr),*
> *Celebrate the holiday (iri hrw nfr)!*
> ...

presence of Hathor is invoked by the 'mother cow', with associations of motherhood, feeding and the concept of rebirth.

82 Schott 1953: 77–8; 1950: 78. She may also be linked with the blue lily (Pinch 1993: 284).

83 E.g. Nebamun TT 90: Davies 1923: pl. xxiii; BM Nebamun: Parkinson 2008: 78, fig. 88.

84 Volokhine 2000: 37, 64–5.

85 E.g. Rekhmire, TT 100; Davies 1943: pl. lxiii. Compare the presentation of *menat* and *sistrum* by Isis in the Temple of Sety I at Abydos (Davis 1973: 41).

86 Pinch 1993: 132, 284.

87 Sheikholeslami 2011. Hartwig (2004) seeks to conflate festivals for Hathor with the Beautiful Festival of the Wadi, but is is likely that they were separate events.

88 Tomb of User (TT 21): Schott 1953: 82, no. 123; 1950: 127, no. 80; Davies 1913: pls xxv, xxvi.

Figure 47: Musicians and dancers at a banquet. Painted plaster fragment from the lost tomb chapel of Nebamun. British Museum, EA 37981. © Trustees of the British Museum.

O dignitary who loves wine
And is the favourite of frankincense (ḥsy n ʿntyw),[89]
May you never be lacking
Concerning satisfying your desire
Inside your beautiful house [of eternity].

The use of narcotic substances in conjunction with alcohol to assist in dissolving the barriers between the living and the dead and enable them to communicate directly has been suggested.[90] While it is possible that opiates or alkaloids were employed for the purpose of facilitating contact, the evidence for this is far from conclusive at present.

New Kingdom 'love songs' contain a great deal of imagery similar to that found in banquet scenes. The deities referred to in these poetic texts are the same as those whose presence is symbolically implied at banquets: Amun and Hathor. In the songs they are said to give lovers to one another, inferring that those chosen by the gods are destined to be together.[91] The components of banquet scenes, from white linen to oil, mandrakes, and alcohol are all replicated in the poems. Like the harpers' songs, they may have originated as oral recitations, and some express the same exhortations to lead a contented life. The example quoted here is thought to refer to a

89 Davies 1913: 26, n. 7: i.e. who is never without wine and incense.
90 E.g. by Merrillees 1962: 292; Harer 1985: 52. See further Harrington 2012.
91 Landgráfová and Navrátilová 2009: 103, 112, 117, 151, 166.

Figure 48: Banquet scene, tomb of Nebamun and Ipuky (TT 181). After Davies 1925a: pl. v.

holiday, with young lovers relaxing in the garden, though much of the imagery is reminiscent of festivals held in tomb courtyards (Figure 50).[92]

> *The little sycamore tree,*[93] *which she planted with her own hand,*
> *Opened her mouth to speak ...*
> *Her leaves are like turquoise,*[94]

---

[92] Landgráfová and Navrátilová 2009: 202 (P. Turin 1996: 3).

[93] The sycamore was associated with Hathor, and the tree goddess (sometimes identified as Nut) who is illustrated on mortuary monuments provisioning the dead. Sycamore trees were depicted set up in the mortuary garden area of the tomb forecourt; the tomb owner in both *akh* and *ba* form is shown in the shade of the tree drinking water from the pool beneath.

[94] Hathor was worshipped as Mistress of Faience and Mistress of Turquoise, particularly at the mines of Serabit el-Khadim (Friedman 1998: 15).

Figure 49: Banquet scene and festival depiction, tomb of Neferhotep (TT 49). After Davies 1933: pl. xviii.

Figure 50: Banquet scene in the courtyard, tomb of Tetiky (TT 15). After Davies 1925b: pl. iv.

Coloured like faience ...
A festival booth and tent are under me ...[95]
Have your servants brought in front of me
Equipped with their instruments.[96]

---

[95] Some funeral scenes depict temporary reed booths set up along the processional route to the tomb with a couple apparently erected near to the tomb entrance (e.g. TT 181, Nebamun and Ipuky: Davies 1925: pl. xix). The men who stand within these shelters burn incense and break pots as the cortege passes, perhaps to dispel any evil forces (see Chapter 3). It is possible that similar booths were constructed for use during festivals in tomb courtyards to protect participants from the sun. Festival booths were also set up on the banks of the Nile during celebrations including the Opet Festival procession at Luxor temple (Darnell 1995: 59). Reeds, as marsh flora, were associated with Hathor (Pinch 1993: 284).

[96] Hathor was mistress of music and musicians, particularly harpists (Schott 1953: 77).

People get drunk (just) by running to me,
Although they did not drink.[97]
Listen to me,
Make them come, carrying their supplies,
So that they bring beer of various kinds,
Bread of all sorts,
Numerous vegetables, yesterday's and today's,
All fruits for enjoyment,
Come and spend a beautiful day (mi iri p3 hrw nfr),
Morning after morning, three (full) days,[98]
While you are seated in my shadow.
Her companion is on her right,
While she is making him drunk ...
The house of beer is confused with drunkenness,
(Yet) she remains with her beloved ...

The songs that accompany images of musicians in banquet scenes display a more cynical approach to death and the afterlife than one might expect from Egyptian sources. The fear of death and the unknown has always haunted mankind, but rarely finds expression in ancient Egyptian texts, and even then it is tempered by encouragement to enjoy life despite its brevity. The most well known song is that of Antef, which notes that no-one has returned from the afterlife and that tombs crumble to dust so one should take pleasure in festivities while time allows.[99] Another example, from the 18th Dynasty tomb of Neferhotep, states:[100]

Celebrate the holiday (iri ḫrw nfr), o god's father!
Put incense and fine oil
Together to your nostrils
And garlands of water lilies and
Mandrakes on your breast,
While your sister whom you love
Sits at your side.
Put song and music before you.
Ignore all evil, recall for yourself joy,
Until that day of landing comes
At the land that loves silence.

It is possible that such songs were intended to remind festival and banquet attendees (including the tomb owner) of the importance of maximizing their time on earth and of enjoying the company of their family and friends, both living and dead.

---

[97] People were said to become intoxicated in the presence of divinities, including Hathor and Amun (e.g. Szkapowska 2003a: 230; Gardiner 1928: pl. 5, II. 7–8).

[98] This is the approximate duration of certain Theban festivals, for example the Feast of Amenhotep I was said to last for four consecutive days (O. Cairo 25234: Hagen and Koefoed 2005: 19; Černý 1927: 183–4), and the Festival of the Wadi was celebrated for two days (Hartwig 2004: 11).

[99] Lichtheim 1975: 194–7; Fox 1977: 403–12.

[100] TT 50, song I: Hari 1985: pl. iv.

Conclusions

Memory and mourning are both processes which involve deeply personal, often instinctive reactions to death, yet they are also largely shaped by collective cultural expectations.[101] Funerals allowed grief to manifest itself in ways that seem uncharacteristic for ancient Egypt, through laments that reflect the fear and pain of loss, and by the uninhibited actions of mourners. Both lack of inhibition and cynicism feature in banquets for the dead as well, with celebrants becoming inebriated to the point of sickness, and musicians singing of the need to enjoy the present, for 'to you will come that day of mourning, … and … weeping will not rescue a man's heart from the tomb … there is no-one who has gone who will come [back] again'.[102] The placement of such songs in tombs seems ironic, since they appear to mock the purpose of mortuary preparation including the construction of the buildings on which they are inscribed. This is another facet of the ambivalence that the Egyptians felt towards death and the dead, a theme that is explored further in the next chapter.

101 Huskinson 2011: 113.

102 Song of Antef. After Lichtheim 1975: 197.

Chapter 5

Attitudes to the dead

Although there is a vast amount of information regarding mortuary practices and the belief in an afterlife in ancient Egyptian society, there is comparatively little textual evidence relating directly to the attitudes of the living towards death and the dead.[1] In this chapter, manifestations of the Egyptians' ambivalence towards the dead are considered,[2] beginning with a discussion of commemoration and remembering and forgetting as active processes. Acts against the deceased, including tomb robbery, vandalism, and threat formulae, as well as fear of the dead, tomb graffiti, and the burial of children and infants are also examined.

Commemoration of ancestors and the maintenance of cults: ideals and realities

Definitions of remembrance

Remembering can be defined as 'a means of extending life beyond the limitations of biological existence',[3] and be politically manipulated and used as a tool for providing societal cohesion, or for legitimizing social hierarchies by affirming that a society 'consisting of rulers and ruled was proper and long-lasting'.[4] Jan Assmann distinguishes instances of commemorative practice (short-term memory and performance) from cultural memory (long-term memorialisation).[5] The long term in relation to elite mortuary practices seems to have generally covered only two generations at most[6] – the approximate limits of living memory – and in non-elite contexts such as the graves of Amarna South Tombs Cemetery was probably considerably less given the apparent scarcity of individual monuments or other mnemonic strategies. The fallibility of memory is widely recognised, with only one or two hundred years effectively separating memory from myth.[7]
It is easiest for archaeologists to access the inscribed, material end of the spectrum of memory practices, and despite the fact that embodied, performative, incorporated practices are more

1 Baines and Lacovara 2002: 6.

2 Ambivalence towards death itself is discussed in Chapter 4, with particular reference to harpers' songs.

3 Mack 2003: 85. For a discussion of the definition and meaning of memory, see Hope 2011: xii–xiv.

4 Schwartz 2007: 46.

5 1991a: 20–21; 1997. See also Meskell 2003: 34; Laneri 2007: 8, Van Dyke and Alcock 2003: 4.

6 At Deir el-Medina at least: McDowell 1992: 107. There are several exceptions, some of which are given below.

7 Bradley 2003: 221; see also e.g. Mbiti (1969: 25–6) on the importance of active memory and the status of the deceased.

difficult to study, 'footprints' left by these activities are traceable in the archaeological record.[8] In ancient Egypt such footprints take the form of physical remnants of cult practices, such as the offering trays and stelae discussed in Chapter 2, and the remains of objects relating to festive activities found in the vicinity of tombs mentioned in Chapter 4. Tomb scenes are more akin to fleeting shadows, wherein glimpses into idealistic worlds were conjured for an ideal eternity.

Remembering and forgetting as active processes

Tombs, stelae, statues and busts served as mnemonic devices, along with rituals and, to a lesser extent, texts; people needed to be reminded of the past and their place in relation to it as a means of maintaining social cohesion.[9] The transformation of Egyptian temples and tombs into places of Christian worship[10] constitutes an example of the active confrontation of the past,[11] and a means of rendering potentially dangerous places harmless:[12]

> *What lay beyond the known – in this case, Christian – world was perceived as heathen, barbaric, chaotic and demonic. It had to be purified and incorporated through ritual activities which would order the chaotic, and civilise, purify and domesticate the wilderness, Christianizing it. Indigenous spiritual beings were often incorporated into Christian iconography by recasting them as devils and demons.*

Thus the ambivalent *akh* (pl. *akhu*) becomes 'demon' in Coptic. Robert Demarée distinguishes between *akhu* 'deceased' and *akhu* 'demon-like entities',[13] but this may reflect ambivalence towards the dead: the deceased may behave in a demon-like manner if wronged in some way.

In most cases Egyptians seem to have actively reduced the burden of the past[14] by only including the names of their closest relatives in their tombs. There are exceptions, notably Paheri (Tomb 3 at Elkab; early 18th Dynasty), who incorporated five generations of his extended family in his tomb decoration. Besides his wife, children and grandchildren, his parents, siblings, mother's brothers, wife's father and mother, wife's sisters and brothers, and his wife's cousin are represented, while the adjacent tomb of his grandfather, Ahmose son of Ibana (Tomb 5), provides details of two further generations of the family.[15] Inherkhau's 20th Dynasty tomb at Deir el-Medina (TT 359) also records five generations of the owner's family, from his great-grandfather to his son.[16] In an act of commemoration, a priest of Amun-Re listed thirteen generations of his family at the temple of Thutmose III at Deir el-Bahri.[17] Listing or depicting

---

8 Van Dyke and Alcock 2003: 4.

9 Cf. Hope 2003: 136.

10 E.g. the conversion of the tomb of Panehsy at Amarna into a church: Jones 1991: 130–5; Pyke 2007.

11 Bradley 2003: 225.

12 Corbey 2003: 13.

13 Demarée 1983: 194, 233.

14 For this concept, see Baines and Lacovara 2002: 27; Joyce 2003: 105; Cummings 2003: 34. Van Dyke and Alcock (2003: 3) note that 'Obliteration of the past rather than connection to it may be involved [in the construction of social memory], as pasts may be subsumed and dominated, conquered and dismantled'.

15 Whale 1989: 70–1.

16 McDowell 1992: 107.

17 New Kingdom: Sadek 1984a: 85–6. Family members could also be commemorated on monuments some distance from the burial site. For example Aametiu and his family were depicted on a rock-cut shrine at Gebel el-Silsila, but were buried in Western Thebes (TT 83, 18th Dynasty): Dorman 2003: 37.

non-immediate family members may be considered as a form of ancestor worship, ensuring that their names were not forgotten, but it also served as an indicator of the social position and background of the scribe or tomb owner.

Active remembrance in cultic form was not necessarily altruistic. Aside from fear of the dead, cult officiants, usually family members, benefited from reversion of offerings and the cult endowment.[18] They were also depicted on stelae and might be interred in the dedicatee's tomb; as David Jeffreys notes:[19] 'The observation of the cult was thus strengthened and might assure the post-mortem future of the entire household.' The benefits of participation in cultic activities for the dead or the gods accrued mainly after death,[20] but for those responsible for the burial of the deceased some rewards were more immediate: according to P. Bulaq X (recto, lines 10–11), the possessions of the dead were to be given to 'him who buries'.[21] Thus those who claim to have buried people with no immediate kin[22] may not have been as philanthropic as they seem. Rubie Watson finds a similar relationship between property and the treatment of the dead in Southeastern China:[23]

> *The deceased's chances of 'survival' are greatly increased if he has left enough property to form an estate (tsu) in his name. With an estate the ancestor's continued 'existence' no longer depends so completely on the vagaries of human memory or emotion. There is little doubt that the wealthy have a better chance of attaining immortality than do the poor.*

Acts of burial and memorialisation were also a means of distancing society from the dead, providing a context for disposing of a corpse and preserving only selective memories of an individual. The transformation of a social person into a non-living entity involves the distillation of living people's memories through a complex process of remembering and forgetting.[24] A similar policy of 'active forgetting' was employed in medieval England, where those who were denied prime locations within the sacred space of a churchyard were 'rapidly incorporated into strategies of forgetting that emphasized the communal dead.'[25] Andrew Jones states that monuments by their material presence are repositories of memory,[26] but these memories discriminate actively, depicting the tomb owner as a pillar of society,[27] or, in cases of *damnatio memoriae* (see below), preserving a record of unrest and personal grievances.

The need to be commemorated at certain sites regardless of burial place is also evident at Abydos, where communal chapels for families or work colleagues were built to contain statues, offering tables and stelae from the 12th Dynasty onwards (Bourriau 1991: 8).

[18] The exchange of goods on ancestor's death days (Toivari-Viitala 2001: 225) may have also been a 'commercial' activity that simultaneously served to commemorate the dead. For a discussion of the reversion of offerings in relation to cult statues of the 26th Dynasty to the Ptolemaic Period, see Rizzo 2004.

[19] 2003: 199.

[20] Hays 2009: 23, 27.

[21] Janssen and Pestman 1968: 140, 144.

[22] E.g. the case of a man named Hormose who died in the house of Horemheb: O. DM 126, 19th Dynasty: Kitchen 2000: 372; Wente 1990: 143.

[23] 1988: 209.

[24] Chesson 2007: 109.

[25] Williams 2003: 231.

[26] 2003: 67.

[27] Cf. Hope 2003: 119, 136.

Tomb robbery, the desecration of human remains, *damnatio memoriae*, and fear of the deceased: conflicts between the living and the dead

Papyrus Leopold-Amherst, from Year 16 of Ramesses IX, indicates that tomb robbers included a cross-section of society, from field labourers, boatmen and water-pourers to craftsmen and priests. The stonemason Amenpanefer testified that thefts were commonplace,[28] and Papyrus Abbott, dating to the same period, graphically describes the state in which the corpses of the elite were left:[29]

> *The tombs (mꜥḥꜥwt) and burial chambers (isw) in which the blessed ones of old (ḥsyw ḏrtyw), the citizenesses (ꜥnḫw n niwt) and the men of the land rest on the West of Thebes: (It was) found that the thieves had violated them all, having turned their owners out of their inner (wtw) and outer (ḏbꜣwt) coffins, (so that) they were cast out on the desert, [the robbers] having stolen their funerary equipment which had been given over to them, along with the gold, silver, and adornments which had been in their inner coffins.*

The papyrus reveals that although some royal tombs were discovered intact, all elite tombs had been violated.[30] This may suggest that those responsible for sealing the tombs after burial were often the ones who later robbed them.[31] The robbers' disregard for the dead in the South Tombs Cemetery at Amarna is apparent from the manner in which the bodies were disarticulated and dumped:[32] 'usually leaving the lower body parts within the grave and dragging the upper body parts out, but leaving them in a pile on top of the interment.'

During robberies, gilded coffins were either broken and burnt in situ, as with those from the tomb of Sobekemsaf II described in P. Leopold-Amherst,[33] or taken from the tomb and set alight elsewhere with the intention of removing the molten metal.[34] While gold, silver and bronze were particularly valuable and portable in the form of jewellery and vessels,[35] luxury goods such as perfumed oils were also a target for thieves. In the tomb of Tutankhamun (KV 62) the robbers appear to have been well organised with the unguent being scooped out of vases and presumably transferred to other containers; the heavy and less valuable travertine vessels were left behind, complete with the raiders' finger marks.[36] A graffito dating to the reign of Horemheb in the tomb of Thutmose IV states that the royal scribe and necropolis official Maya was 'entrusted to renew the burial (*wḥm ḳrs*)' of the king following the robbery of the

---

[28] Capart *et al.* 1936: 172; Peden 1994: 250.

[29] P. BM EA 10221: Peden 1994: 233.

[30] Peet 1930: 37–42.

[31] Cf. Engelbach 1915: 21–2; Taylor 2001: 179–80.

[32] Stevens 2009b: 15.

[33] Peden 1994: 251; cf. Smith 1992: 194. Alternatively the gold bands could be scraped off, as with the coffins in TT 99 (Senneferi, 18th Dynasty: Strudwick 2006). At TT 233 (Saroy, 19th Dynasty) thieves stripped the metal from burial equipment in the tomb courtyard, as indicated by traces of a fire containing charred remains and tiny gold fragments (Ockinga 2007: 146).

[34] Capart *et al.* 1936: 180, n. 2, 16; 181, n. 3, 13.

[35] These metals are specifically mentioned in tomb robbery papyri P. Mayer A and B (Peet 1915a, b: 177; 205–6).

[36] Cairo JE 62127, JE 62121; Carter nos. 435, 420; Burton photograph nos. P 1653, P 1655: www.griffith.ox.ac.uk/gri/carter/gallery/p1653.html, www.griffith.ox.ac.uk/gri/carter/gallery/p1655.html.

tomb.[37] It was broken into again in the late 20th Dynasty: a graffito in KV 9 of Ramesses V/VI indicates that the tomb was ransacked within 20 years of being sealed following the burial of Ramesses VI.[38] By the 21st Dynasty tomb robbery was a phenomenon common enough to require officials whose specific task was to rebury the 'desecrated dead,' including 18th Dynasty elites as well as royalty.[39] According to Darnell, inscriptions in the area of the Wadi of Amenemhat in Thebes indicate that during the reign of Ramesses XI, the systematic looting of tombs was sanctioned by the state to fund war:[40] 'Continuing through the Twentieth Dynasty, workmen whose ancestors had buried the royal dead became government sponsored ghouls, removing valuables, rewrapping and transferring bodies.'

The motivations for tomb robbery are generally thought to be based on desperation brought about by financial hardship. Capart *et al.*[41] consider the economic crisis under Ramesses IX, the result of a succession of weak kings and political unrest, to have been the main contributory factor in the apparent rise in criminal activity on the West Bank. This may have been the case, but the dismantling and robbery of tombs was clearly not just a late New Kingdom development. Anna Stevens also considers hardship to have been a catalyst for robbery:[42] 'The scale of the damage [to the South Tombs cemetery at Amarna] might reflect a certain desperation on the part of the tomb robbers, perhaps in a time of broad civil unrest, such as that which may have prevailed towards the close of the New Kingdom.' There is evidence that necropolis officials cleared debris from around tombs following such robberies: for example, damaged items from ransacked tombs, the remnants of offerings, and the remains of meals held in the necropolis were buried in pits within courtyards at Thebes.[43]

Threat formulae

Fear of the dead returning in vengeance against the living is apparent in appeals to the living and in threat formulae inscribed in the tomb or on an image of the deceased. A rare 18th Dynasty example of the threat formula was inscribed on the group statue of the official Wersu and his wife Satre:[44]

> *As for anyone who shall violate my corpse in the Necropolis, or who shall damage my image in my chamber: ... The* ka *of Re shall abhor him. He shall not bequeath his goods to his children, nor shall he be restful in life, nor shall he receive water in the Necropolis. His* ba *shall be destroyed forever, as this land is wide without limit.*

---

37 Peden 2001: 143.

38 Reeves 1990: 34–8; Peden 2001: 205. For a discussion of royal tomb robberies and mummy caches, see Reeves 1990: 183 ff.

39 Dodson 1991.

40 2008: 55. The involvement in such a policy by rulers and officials in the 21st Dynasty (as noted by Taylor 2001: 182, for example) is disputed by Niwinski (2003: 417), because it is in direct opposition to the strongly-held concept of *Maat*.

41 1936: 185.

42 2009b: 15–16.

43 E.g. Theban Tombs 50, 23, 67, 68, 21, 43: Collins 1976: 32–9

44 Originally from his tomb in Koptos, now in a private collection: Morschauser 1991: 179; Sethe 1905: 1491; Griffith 1915: 5–6, pls ii, iii.

According to Morchauser, the formula of condemnation 'suggests that the crimes mentioned – especially the references to the violation of the burial chamber and the destruction of the corpse – were considered to have been acts of sacrilege' that led to the perpetrator becoming 'a criminal (*ẖbd*) against Re'.[45]

Threat formulae illustrate the Egyptians' awareness of the dangers posed to mortuary monuments and their contents by robbers and vandals. The tomb was so vulnerable to the threat of impurity alone that some tomb owners recorded the steps they had to take in order to protect it. An inscription in the 6th Dynasty tomb of Hesy at Saqqara, for example, states:[46] 'Never did those who hated (*msḏw*) entering it (or) being associated with it work for me in order that it would be pure for me.' Hezy also explicitly outlines states considered impure in a mortuary context: 'As for any man who will enter this tomb after he has eaten the abominations (*bwwt*) which an *akh* abominates (*bwt ꜣḫ*) and after he has had sexual relations with a woman, I will be judged with him in the council of the great god.' The First Intermediate Period tomb of Ankhtifi at Mo'alla bears an inscription asserting that any damage to the tomb or coffin it contained would result in the perpetrator's arm being severed during the festival of the local god Hemen.[47]

Curses and threats indicate the most feared punishments, and hence the most fundamentally important aspects of death, burial, cult, and memorialisation. Being burned alive was not only a horrific punishment and deterrent against criminal activity, but it also destroyed the body and thus any possibility of an afterlife existence. Death by immolation was threatened to tomb robbers particularly in the Middle Kingdom; an entrance inscription in Asyut Tomb IV, for instance, states that:[48] 'his name will not exist, he will not be buried in the desert, he will be cooked (*iw.f r pst*) together with the criminals (*ẖbntyw*) whom god has cursed.' In a similar context, the 22nd Dynasty Chronicle of Osorkon describes how those accused of transgressions against a Theban temple were burned alive 'at the place of [their] crime.'[49] The treatment of the men in the Tomb Robbery papyri suggests that such threats may have been carried out, though evidently they were insufficient deterrents. In the early New Kingdom the emphasis of threat formulae was on the annihilation of the enemy, who would be hated by the gods and removed from office.[50] An inscription from the 18th Dynasty tomb chapel of Tjawy appears to be a threat against any artisan who might redesign ('usurp') his tomb:[51]

> *As for any men, any overseers of work, and any necropolis workers who shall undertake any work [in this tomb ...] to make a tomb for another man, he shall not be buried in the West, and he shall be in the displeasure of the gods ... Khenty-amentiu and Wennofre shall [abandon] him.*

---

45 1991: 176–9; Baines 2010, personal communication.

46 Silverman 2000: 13, 11.

47 Willems 1990: 29.

48 Willems 1990: 37; Edel 1984: 120–7, fig. 15, lines 79–80.

49 Willems 1990: 50; Caminos 1958: 48–51; Epigraphic Survey 1954: pl. 20, lines 35–6.

50 Morschauser 1991: 263.

51 Boston Museum 1972.651: Simpson 1972: 78.

By the Ramesside period the gods were called on to punish the living,[52] suggesting that civil action was no longer considered effective enough to protect mortuary monuments.[53] Assmann states that the tomb owner was forced into presenting himself as a terrifying force because secular justice was insufficient to protect the tomb from certain acts of desecration, such as 'secret criminality' where visitors entered in impure states.[54]

Damnatio Memoriae

Cases of *damnatio memoriae* – destroying an individual's name and image, literally condemning their memory – show how both forgetting and remembering can be deliberate processes. As in ancient Rome, the damage to Egyptian tomb statues, reliefs, and inscriptions (Chapter 2) ensured that the individual thus symbolically destroyed became 'infamous rather than completely forgotten; a damned memory is still a memory.'[55] Thus the irony of *damnatio memoriae*, particularly on durable monuments, is that the destruction of the name or image makes it more noticeable than it would otherwise have been: one is constantly being reminded to forget something.[56]

The violent desecration of tombs probably had counterparts in actions among the living,[57] the damage being a permanent reminder of transient feuds. It may be that acts involving the deliberate defacing of an image were accompanied by some form of oral recitation,[58] intended to enhance the dramatic performance and add to its efficacy. Annette Kjølby states:[59] 'To the ancient Egyptians statues materialized the essence and presence of the individual depicted ... The terms chosen for the making of a statue surely indicate that the image was perceived as a life-extender, a physical manifestation of a living being, hosting or giving form to such a being.' Deliberate damage to a statue thus amounted to a direct assault on the person it represented, and a ritual attempt to destroy the essence/*ka* of the deceased that inhabited it, and the *akh* that it depicted.[60]

Fear of the dead and of premature death

The malevolent dead, discussed in Chapter 1, presented a menace to all through 'hauntings', causing crop failure, and inflicting disease, but were a particular threat to the vulnerable

---

52 E.g. graffiti at Deir el-Bahri (Sadek 1984b: 69), and the 20th Dynasty statue of Herihor: Morschauser 1991: 193; Kitchen 1983b: 351.15–352.2. Those who failed to report criminal activity were also condemned and threatened with the vengeance of Osiris in the Nauri Decree of Sety I: Morschauser 1991: 185–6; Kitchen 1975: 58, 1–7.

53 In contrast to the Old Kingdom, when threats for damaging tombs and their furniture included being disinherited by order of the king and the inability to join the blessed dead in the necropolis (Koptos R decree, issued by King Demdjibtawy in favour of Idi: Bolshakov 1991: 211). A similar inscription, without the emphasis on royal intervention, is found in the Middle Kingdom necropolis of Assiut (Asyut): Assmann 1992: 154; Edel 1984: 25–37.

54 1992: 151–2.

55 Hope 2003: 115.

56 Winthrop-Young 2005: 116.

57 Baines 1991: 139, n. 45.

58 Bochi 1999: 83.

59 2009: 36–7.

60 Cf. Hope 2011: 179f. For discussions of the *ka* and *akh*, see Chapter 1.

including pregnant women, young children, and the recently deceased. Propitiation of the dead through offerings to discourage unwanted behaviour is common in a range of societies both ancient and modern.[61] According to Willems, Coffin Texts Spells 38–41 were aimed at appeasing the deceased 'who might adopt a hostile attitude to his surviving relatives. He is accused of endangering his household, but ultimately also himself.'[62] In Spell 38, a hierarchy in the netherworld is indicated when a son asks his father to prevent his death since it would involve the father having to yield his place to his son, thereby pushing the older deceased man into the realm of the more remote ancestors.[63]

Any dead person who left the tomb to 'go forth by day' was a potentially malevolent entity. Coffin Texts Spell 38, for example, is an incantation to 'cause the heart of a dweller in the necropolis to be friendly to a man',[64] with the implication that he may otherwise not be, and The Book of Good and Bad Days specifically mentions a day when the 'dead walk about in the necropolis ... in order to spread fear' among the living.[65] CT 39 deals with the fear of being summoned by a dead relative before completing one's life on earth, while CT 40 expresses anxiety regarding dying before reaching old age, as well as mentioning the fear of attack by the dead.[66] Fear of premature death is also mentioned in Book of the Dead Spell 175,[67] and may be alluded to in the Middle Kingdom text known as the Dialogue Between a Man and His *Ba*.[68] Execration rituals as a means of warding off malicious spirits from both the living and dead are discussed in Chapter 1.

Placing the dead within the landscape

The placement of the remains of the deceased is a 'conscious and carefully thought out activity by which the dead are both remembered and forgotten, and through which we reaffirm and construct our attitudes to death and the dead and, through these, to place and identity.'[69] Mike Parker Pearson notes cases where the dead are physically separated from the living by being buried on the opposite side of the stream from a settlement, or tombs built with different alignments to the cardinal points from houses:[70] 'By examining how these juxtapositions changed through time, we may be able to examine some of the ways in which the dead were conceived of by the living and how much influence they were considered to exert'. On the basis of such an analysis, it could be argued that at Deir el-Medina in the 19th and 20th Dynasties the dead

61 E.g. Baines 1991: 152; Demarée 1983: 273 (ancient Egypt); Lewis 1989: 31; Scurlock 2006: 9 (Mesopotamia); Schwartz 2007: 45 (ancient Syria); Mbiti 1969: 27, 84; Chukuwere 1981: 62 (Africa).

62 2001: 360.

63 De Buck 1950: 82. For the antagonistic relationship between father and son, see Donnat 2003: 78–98, and for an analysis of CT 38, see de Jong 1994.

64 Willems 2001: 323–4; Faulkner 1962b: 36–7; 1973: 30.

65 3rd month of Peret, day 2; Leitz 1994: 279.

66 Willems 2001: 330–31, 334, 336; De Buck 1938: 173, h–i; 176, i.

67 De Buck 1950: 80.

68 Williams 1962: 53. For a discussion of this text, see Parkinson 2002: 216–26.

69 Parker Pearson 1999: 125; cf. 1993: 206–7. Tombs formed part of the 'identity and social memory of local communities' according to Chapman 2009: 72.

70 1999: 125.

Figure 51: View of the western tombs at Deir el-Medina from one of the village houses.

were thought to exert a significant degree of influence on the lives of the villagers. Not only was the settlement flanked by tombs to the west and earlier burial pits to the east, but the elite necropolis was visible to the north (Figures 51, 52, 53). The creation of enduring monuments aided in the demarcation of the settlement's boundaries, establishing the identities and claims of the society within, and providing a sense of permanence and stability.[71]

The decision about where to place memorials in the landscape involved envisaging them as accessible cult places in years to come and is an expression of the importance of the dead to society. In this way, the landscape may be an integral part of the monuments rather than a neutral backdrop for them.[72] It is possible that in planned settlements such as Deir el-Medina the occupants' desire for stone memorials developed from a need to create fixed commemorative spaces having left any ancestral monuments and burials behind. Tombs with clearly defined superstructures[73] were a link to both the communal past and the individual dead. Such a connection between tombs and the establishment of societies can be seen in ancient Jordan:[74] 'in creating enduring, visible monuments to the dead, the Early Bronze Age people literally inscribed their histories, identities, claims and rights across the very fields, hills, and river valleys in which they worked, played and lived.'

[71] Chesson 2007: 115; Meskell 2003: 48.

[72] Cummings 2003: 29.

[73] *mꜥḥꜥt* as opposed to *ḫr*; see Černý 1973: 14.

[74] Chesson 2007: 115.

Proximity to sacred space was probably the main factor that influenced the location of the Theban necropolis and encouraged its reuse over several centuries. The pylons of Karnak temple are visible from Dra Abu el-Naga, for example,[75] and many tombs were built beside or within sight of the processional route of the Beautiful Festival of the Wadi.[76] The desire to be close to the gods and participate in festivals is also seen at Abydos,[77] where statues and stelae were erected by processional routes, and which was a place of 'pilgrimage' both in life and after death.[78]

One of the greatest problems in discussing Egyptian burial practices is the near-absence of non-elite cemeteries. One of the most promising sites for the investigation of lower status burials in the New Kingdom is the South Tombs Cemetery at Amarna. Fourteen stelae have been discovered at the site so far, with rough cairns created from local boulders being the main means of demarcating graves.[79] The excavator suggests that the unusual pointed stelae found in the cemetery recall a mountainous landscape and were intended to 'combine a memorial representation of the deceased with a model of a rock-cut tomb, and therein a self-contained body-tomb substitute'. She also notes that, unlike round-topped stelae, pointed stelae are not found in Amarna houses because 'their role was largely that of landscape modifiers within a funerary context.'[80] Aside from the inscribed stelae, the absence of names in association with the majority of graves may reflect illiteracy, and would probably have meant that those buried in the cemetery would have been forgotten within a generation or two.[81] In her analysis of Roman burial practices, Hope[82] suggests that the funeral itself may have been the chief form of commemoration for some members of society, with simple grave markers erected as a focus for the bereaved.

Reuse of tombs, cemeteries, and funerary equipment: prioritising the living over the dead?

The Instruction for King Merikare, which dates to the Middle Kingdom, states clearly that tombs should not be constructed from the ruins of others:[83]

> *Do not destroy the monuments of another;*
> *You should quarry stone in Tura!*
> *Do not build your tomb-chamber (is.k) from ruins (s̱hnyt),*
> *For what is done will be what will be done.*

---

75 Ockinga 2007: 139.

76 E.g. TT 39, Puimre: Arrache 2008: 15.

77 Strudwick 2010: 259; Taylor 2001: 183–4.

78 Snape 1994: 305; Assmann 2005: 306.

79 Stevens 2009b: 18–20, fig. 9; 2010.

80 2009b: 20, although stelae with pointed tops are known from Deir el-Medina and other sites, including ancestor (*akh iqer*) stelae that are usually associated with domestic rather than mortuary contexts, e.g. Taylor 2001: 185, fig. 130; Bierbrier 1982: 94, fig. 68. In the 2010 season, a limestone stela in a pointed limestone frame (obj. 39938) was found in the South Tombs Cemetery (lower site) in association with a large quantity of pottery suggesting that this small monument may have been the focal point for some form of mortuary cult (Kemp 2010: 15).

81 Cf. Nubia: Kennedy 1978: 232.

82 2003: 121.

83 Parkinson 1998: 222; Lorton 1968: 51.

Figure 52: View across the village from the western tombs towards the Theban necropolis. The hill of Qurnet Mourrai (Eastern Necropolis) is on the right.

Figure 53: View across the Theban necropolis towards the village and the cemetery of Deir el-Medina with the tombs of Sheikh Abd el-Qurna in the foreground and Qurnet Mourrai to the right. The colourful Qurna houses have since been demolished.

Despite admonitions such as this, which acknowledge the trend of reusing old monuments to create new ones, tomb-reuse was common. Hope[84] notes a similar phenomenon in Rome, where gravestones were frequently salvaged as building material; and at Karnak New Kingdom private temple statues were re-carved for subsequent owners.[85] Saqqara exhibits a cycle of reuse that may have been paralleled at other multi-period sites: Old Kingdom blocks were incorporated into 18th and 19th Dynasty tombs (such as Horemheb, Maya, Tia and Tia),[86] Ramesside temples were built with old royal and non-royal masonry, and these temples in turn were dismantled for use in Medieval Cairo.[87] The expansion of the village of Deir el-Medina saw tombs used as cellars,[88] while cemeteries in the late Hyksos period at Tell el-Daba were covered by houses as the town expanded, the tombs being incorporated into the courtyards of houses or within the houses themselves.[89] At Sheikh Abd el-Qurna a number of tombs exhibit evidence of reuse with the later reworking of reliefs (e.g. TT 188, Parennefer),[90] or in places where plaster has fallen away to reveal the earlier decoration beneath. Other examples of reuse include TT 81 (Ineni), which began as an 11th Dynasty *saff*-tomb but was appropriated and extended by Ineni in the 18th Dynasty, the multi-period Cemetery Y at Diospolis Parva, and Roman adaptations in the Theban necropolis, for example TT 32 (Djehutymose).[91] The 18th Dynasty tomb of Nebamun (TT 65) also bears evidence of at least two phases of reuse, as a tomb in the 20th Dynasty and as part of the Coptic Monastery of Cyriacus.[92]

John Mack suggests that in some cases tomb reuse in Egypt was not necessarily an act of usurpation, but rather a means of 'recharging the cult with a new association', and thus indirectly benefiting the deceased former owner.[93] Hans Goedicke[94] also proposed that reuse was not necessarily an act of disrespect, while Longden,[95] argues that, at least in terms of artefacts, reuse can forge a link between the present and the past, could be motivated by the apotropaic functions that old objects were thought to possess, and may not necessarily have carried negative connotations. It may be that those buried in 'usurped' tombs hoped to benefit from the sanctity such buildings were thought to possess.[96] David Jeffreys rejects the term 'usurpation' on the grounds that it implies unlawful acquisition;[97] it is indeed clear that at least some tombs were officially re-assigned many years after the original owner's burial.[98] Tombs were sometimes

[84] 2003: 122.

[85] Kjølby 2007: 72.

[86] Blocks from these three tombs were found in the tomb of Ipay at Dahshur dating to the end of the Amarna period which was itself reused for a Ramesside burial that was subsequently robbed: Hasegawa 2003: 230. For the Old Kingdom blocks used in Maya's tomb, see Harpur 2009.

[87] Malek 1992: 60–1.

[88] Bruyère 1939: 275, 311; Chapter 2.

[89] Bietak 1996: 49

[90] Hawass 2009: 251.

[91] Dziobek 1987: 76–7; Bourriau 2009: 56, 56–60; Riggs 2005: 184; Porter and Moss 1960: 49–50.

[92] Vértes 2008: 264–5; Porter and Moss 1960: 129–32.

[93] 2003: 96, 91. See also Polz 1990.

[94] 1971: 6–7.

[95] 2003: 172; Eckhardt and Williams 2003: 165.

[96] Strudwick 2010: 251.

[97] 2003: 203.

[98] E.g. O. Madrid 16234: McDowell 1999: 71, no. 43; Kitchen 1989: 335–6. O. BM EA 5624: McDowell 1999: 68, no. 39; Blackman 1926: 176–85, pls xxxiv–xlii; Kitchen 1983: 475–6. P. BM EA 10375: Wente

used as depositories for important documents,[99] and ruined tombs were investigated and sealed after inventories of their contents had been made.[100]

Nigel Strudwick suggests that family connections and commemoration were the motivating factors behind New Kingdom tomb reuse within a short time of their original occupation,[101] and there is evidence that Theban tombs were reopened to permit the burial of several family members within them:[102] Sennedjem's burial chamber, for instance, contained 20 individuals.[103] Much later, other tombs at Deir el-Medina were reopened and used to deposit numerous bodies by a group of Ptolemaic mortuary workers known as 'choachytes.'[104] An elite Roman family ('the Pebos family burials') were interred in the cellar of a house at the site. The burial (no. 1407) contained five vaulted coffins, one re-used Third Intermediate Period coffin and two mummies,[105] and those responsible for the burial evidently considered the village to be a sacred place. It is not clear from 21st Dynasty graffiti in the 18th Dynasty tomb of Kheruef (TT 192) whether the visitors entered the tomb to look at the reliefs or for the benefit of those interred there in the Third Intermediate Period.[106] During the latter epoch, Middle and New Kingdom tombs were regularly reused, with new shafts sunk into the courtyards,[107] and it is likely that the proliferation of amulets on mummies during this period is directly linked to the reuse of older tombs and fear of attack by the spirits of the original tomb owners.[108]

The way in which the market for reused funerary equipment operated is not apparent,[109] but there is evidence for the reassignment of mortuary furniture throughout Egyptian history, with the practice of coffin theft and re-inscription becoming particularly common in Thebes during the 21st Dynasty.[110] Tomb 1386 in the 18th Dynasty Eastern Cemetery at Deir el-Medina contained a coffin that showed repeated re-use, which according to Bruyère was indicative of poverty.[111] The foot end of the coffin had been removed because the child was too tall for it, a further indicator of the low status of those responsible for the burial. With regard to the reuse of coffins in ancient Egypt, Cooney states:[112] 'at the base of usurpation was a negotiation between theft and re-association, essentially an innovative conciliation between the principles of *mꜣꜥt* (or truth) and the need for materiality'. She sees this need to possess equipment for the afterlife as the driving factor behind 're-commoditization':[113] social inequality created a crisis, from which acts of theft and reuse were the inevitable consequences. 'De-sacralisation' of tombs may have been carried out by family members responsible for maintaining the owner's

1967: 61.

99 P. BM 10326: Wente 1967: 38.

100 O. Vienna I, O. IFAO 628; McDowell 1999: 69–71, no. 41; Zonhoven 1979.

101 2010: 254.

102 Valbelle 1985: 288.

103 TT 1: McDowell 1999: 13; cf. TT 148, Ockinga 2007: 142; see also Dorman 2003.

104 Meskell 2003: 51; Taylor 2001: 177.

105 Riggs 2005: 206–11.

106 Peden 2001: 275.

107 Taylor 2010: 228.

108 Pinch 2003: 446.

109 Bleiberg 2010: 43.

110 Taylor 2001: 181.

111 1937: 188; Zillhardt 2009: 25.

112 2007: 274.

113 2007: 278, 280–3.

cult after a sufficient amount of (post-burial) time had elapsed: David Jeffreys[114] suggests that officiants with legitimate access to a tomb may also have been granted the use and disposal of its contents, providing opportunities for funerary goods to be re-used in daily life and/or form part of another set of burial equipment many years after the original interment.[115]

Tomb graffiti: form and function

One aspect of visitors' graffiti (*Besucherinschriften*)[116] particularly pertinent to the maintenance of cults is their location within tombs, because this provides information about the accessibility of tomb chambers. Wildung[117] noted that in some cases graffiti was written approximately fifty centimetres from the base of the wall, indicating that the tombs were not choked with debris at the time when they were inscribed. Unless the graffiti in Theban tombs were written during festivals or tomb inspections, their presence may intimate that the chapel was no longer sealed or used for cultic purposes.[118] Evidence for the presence of doorframes and doors[119] in Theban tombs implies that they were intended to be inaccessible unless in use as a place of funeral ceremonies, cultic activity or festivity. The likelihood that tombs were not generally accessible is further suggested by texts such as one accompanying three singers in the tomb of Menna (TT 69, *temp*. Thutmose IV):[120]

> *[Spend a] beautiful day! The mountain is open, the seal is broken.*
> *The door of your house is open.*
> *The incense reaches heaven.*
> *You are blessed. The door is open...*

In some cases the tombs may have provided respite from the sun, with the graffiti an afterthought in the same way that other west Theban graffiti are located in shaded rock shelters.[121]

Hana Navrátilová comments that scribes might have 'liked to use the walls of a venerated building in the necropolis for a message similar to those left in tomb inscriptions.'[122] Several groups of graffiti, such as those in the South Chapel of Djoser at Saqqara, take the form of

---

[114] 2003: 207.

[115] Peden (2001: 207) notes in relation to KV 34 (Thutmose IV) that tomb robberies could result in remaining valuables being appropriated by necropolis officials.

[116] Navrátilová (2009: 4) notes that the term *Besucherinschriften* suggests an established genre that may have represented 'a type of communication with the world of the dead and in some cases perhaps a kind of response to the "[Appeals] to the Living"'. For discussions and translations of visitors' graffiti, see also Negm 1998; Peden 2001: 290; cf. Wildung 1969: 69–72; Fischer-Elfert 2003: 132; Davies 1925: 18 (TT 15).

[117] 1977b: 65–6. A similar situation may be seen at Memphis: Hana Navrátilová, personal communication 2011.

[118] 19th Dynasty tombs containing graffiti include TT 51, 93, 112, 178, 311 (Peden 2001: 103–5).

[119] Kampp 1996: 72–4. Both the entrance and the burial chamber were sealed with doors, such as that from the tomb of Sennedjem (TT 1: Saleh and Sourouzian 1987: cat. no. 215). External doors are shown in many depictions of tomb chapels; Davies (1938: 38–9) noted that yellow paint was used to indicate wood.

[120] Schott 1953: 106, no. 61.

[121] Peden 2001: 153.

[122] 2007: 141.

such inscriptions, including sentences such as:[123] ‘your legs are given to you to dwell among the exalted spirits (*ꜣḫw ꜥꜣ.i*)’, and use of the *hetep di nesu* offering-formula. It may be that individuals buried in the Memphite necropolis were commemorated in these texts rather than the scribes themselves. At Thebes, a text of ‘incense for Re-Horakhty when he rises in the eastern horizon’ in the tomb of Nakht, is ambiguous in that it could be intended for the benefit of the writer or the tomb owner,[124] whereas Graffito 4 is expressly on behalf of the deceased and refers to purifying the offering table. According to Stephen Quirke,[125] the text ‘may reflect a specific need to purify the cult objects after a period of neglect or even desecration,’ and it seems that despite Amarna period damage, the tomb was restored by the end of the 18th Dynasty.

Another graffito in the tomb of Nakht (TT 161, no. 5) dates to the season of the Festival of the Wadi (Chapter 4), which suggests that the scribe was visiting the tomb to celebrate and commemorated the event with his inscription.[126] Navrátilová notes that:[127] ‘many graffiti were made at special occasions which brought people to places they would usually either not be allowed to or had no reason or entitlement to be in’. Other festivals were probably similarly celebrated, as implied by a 19th Dynasty inscription in the Pyramid of Khendjer at Saqqara that mentions the festival of Ptah when his cult image was seen outside the temple.[128] Evidently occasions such as the Festival of the Wadi attracted visitors from beyond Thebes,[129] since Memphis – and presumably other cities – did not have an equivalent festival.[130] Navrátilová sees the visitors’ graffiti as part of the ‘visitor cult’, addressing the wishes of the tomb owner and being part of social communication between the living and the dead.[131] In his discussion of the graffiti at Saqqara, Alexander Peden[132] states that most of the authors were ordinary scribes who visited monuments to inspect them, to offer prayers to the gods of Western Memphis, and to honour deified kings and ask for their favour. He does not mention the worship of deceased elites/ancestors, but this was probably a motivating factor in at least some of the visits.

The 19th and 20th Dynasty graffiti in the temple of Thutmose III at Deir el-Bahri are instructive with regard to the range of reasons given for visiting the monument and the concerns expressed in the texts.[133] Along with inscriptions relating to offerings,[134] curses, prayers for sexual potency,[135] and standard phrases,[136] are prayers for the dead. In DB 1, for

---

123 Navrátilová 2007: 114, 128.

124 Graffito 2 in TT 161: Quirke 1986: 80. Cf. an ink inscription in TT 63 (Sobekhotep; *temp.* Thutmose IV): Peden 2001: 69; Burkard 1990: 88–91.

125 Quirke 1986: 83, 85.

126 Quirke 1986: 87.

127 2009: 22.

128 Negm 1998: 119; Peden 2001: 99.

129 DB 4, 74, 90: Sadek 1984a: 77–8; 1984b: 74, 77.

130 Navrátilová 2009: 17.

131 2009: 6.

132 2001: 96.

133 Marciniak 1974.

134 Including DB 31 (Sadek 1984a: 89), which was written during the Festival of the Wadi, and DB 29 (Sadek 1984a: 88).

135 DB 6, lines 5–7 (Sadek 1984a: 78). For phallic objects found at Deir el-Bahri, primarily associated with the cult of Hathor, see Pinch 1993: 235–45.

136 E.g. ‘fill his stomach, clothe his back, let his mouth not speak evil’ (Sadek 1984a: 83). See also DB

instance, inscribed during a festival procession (*ḫꜥ*) of Hathor, the dedicator asks that the gods 'grant bread, breezes, water, wine, libations (and) incense to the Osiris, Chantress (of) Amun-Re, King of the Gods, Henutmehyt. Made by her son who perpetuates her name, the scribe Nesamun.'[137] Other graffiti are requests for the visitor's name to be remembered, and for the author to receive love and respect from their community.[138] A number of texts relate specifically to the remembrance of the visitor's name, and to its protection by the gods.[139]

Although it is not clear whether graffiti was pre-planned, the content of several Theban examples indicates they were intended as prayers for the deceased, being introduced by *r*, used to designate texts that are meant to be recited in ritual contexts.[140] Mack[141] states that memory in the context of texts such as Papyrus Chester Beatty IV is associated with speaking and hearing, not just reading and inwardly acknowledging, and that in a society with low literacy levels memorialising would have been particularly meaningful in an oral or narrative form. This might be relevant to graffiti dedicated to gods or the deceased, which may have been read aloud to enhance its efficacy or for the benefit of other people present.

The death and burial of children:[142] an example of attitudes towards those on the fringes of society

In many cultures the treatment of dead children and the locations for disposal of their remains differs from those of adults, often corresponding to the position of the deceased within a society based upon their age and stage of life. For example, premature and still-born infants may not be considered fully human and therefore will not be eligible for burial.[143] In Egypt and Nubia this distinction seems not to be complete because buried and even mummified foetuses have been found.[144] Ancient societies experienced high infant mortality rates[145] as well as an elevated risk

---

2, 15, 16, (Sadek 1984a: 77, 83), 37, 46, 47, 53 (Sadek 1984b: 65, 68, 70).

137 Sadek 1984a: 71; cf. DB 5, line 5 (Sadek 1984a: 78). Compare the reasons given by Peden (2001: 154–5) for graffiti inscribed in the Valleys of the Kings and Queens.

138 E.g. DB 6, lines 3–4: Sadek 1984a: 79: 'grant him love in the sight of every man and every woman'. Compare DB 38, line 3, and DB 41, line 5: Sadek 1984b: 66–7; also DB 11, line 4: Sadek 1984a: 81. Similar wishes are expressed in mortuary contexts, for example the Northampton Stela of Djehuty from TT 11 (Sethe 1905: 430).

139 E.g. Sadek 1984b: 69, 73, 84.

140 Quirke 1986: 81; Ogdon 1998: 137.

141 2003: 95. See Parkinson 1991: 149–50: 'Doors [of tomb chapels] were made: they have fallen, their funerary priests leaving, while their stelae are covered with earth, their chambers forgotten. (Yet) their names are (still) pronounced over their rolls which they made ... A man has perished, his corpse is dust ... it is a book which makes him remembered in the mouth of a speaker.'

142 For a summary of definitions of childhood or subadulthood, see Halcrow and Tayles 2011: 335–6; Kamp 2001: 3 (childhood as a cultural construct).

143 Whittlesey and Reid 2001: 75. See also Wileman 2005: 75, 77.

144 Filer 1998: 393–5; Meskell 2000: 429, with references, see also Stevens 2009: 11–12.

145 E.g. the cemetery at Mirgissa, where 50% of the skeletons belonged to children less than two years old (Baines and Lacovara 2002: 14). In the children's cemetery at Gurob 50% of children were under two, at Matmar 48%, and at Mostagedda 31% (Robins 1994–5: 28). It has been estimated that at least 20% of all infants died within their first year (Filer 1998: 391; cf. Halcrow and Tayles 2011: 339). In the Old

of death through childbirth.[146] In a study of reproductive health of women conducted in the 20th century in the Giza governorate,[147] early marriage, lack of education, and poor socioeconomic conditions were found to have a profound effect on female morbidity and mortality. A survey of 462 women revealed an extremely high death rate for young children, with 249 miscarriages, 41 stillbirths, and 497 child deaths, of which 58% occurred in the first year of life and 37% before the age of five.[148] In ancient Egypt, where gynaecological issues were not fully understood,[149] the concern to prevent miscarriage and the recognition that bleeding is one of its major symptoms is recorded in medical texts.[150] Miscarriage was one of the many physical traumas blamed on the intervention of the dead (*mwt*): for example, two knots of linen were used to 'repel [the] (evil) activity (?) of a dead person or a god [by] the magic power of Anubis.'[151]

Death as a result of complications during childbirth, such as haemorrhage, sepsis, and hypertensive diseases (toxaemia and eclampsia), must have been fairly common, as in modern rural Egypt where many births still take place in the house with the assistance of a traditional birth attendant or *daya*.[152] Miscarriages, stillborns and children that die immediately after birth are buried directly in the sand or under the wall of houses, stables, or the local mosque.[153] Burial of infants less than one year old within houses is known from all periods of ancient Egypt: sites include Nubian forts (Middle Kingdom), Elephantine (Middle Kingdom and Second Intermediate Period), Deir el-Medina, Hermopolis, Tell Basta, and Amarna (New Kingdom).[154] The reason for sub-floor interments is not clear; while in some cases it could be for the cultic benefit and protection of the child who would not have been weaned[155] and whose defencelessness would have made it particularly vulnerable to attack from malevolent forces, at Elephantine neonates were buried in unoccupied houses.[156] Suggestions for similar burials among other cultures include the domestication of death, emotional comfort for the bereaved by the proximity of

---

Kingdom cemetery of Balat in the Dakhla Oasis, 39% of burials were found to contain neonates, infants and children (Verlinden 2008: 263). See also Ronika Power's PhD thesis: From the cradle to the grave: child and infant burials in the Egyptian archaeological record. Macquarie University, 2012.

146 Filer 1998: 398.

147 Khattab *et al.* 1999: 4.

148 Khattab *et al.* 1999: 40.

149 See e.g. Ritner 1984: 212.

150 London Medical Papyrus (BM EA 10059): Incantations 27–30, Leitz 1999: 68–70. In parts of rural Egypt such as Giza where 80% of women are illiterate, bleeding during pregnancy is one of the few abnormal symptoms acknowledged as serious whereas many other potentially fatal problems are overlooked or misunderstood (El-Mouelhy *et al.* 1994: 28–9, 32). For gynaecologically-related morbidities see Khattab *et al.* 1999: 42–3.

151 Leitz 1999: 70; pl. 34, 14, Incantation 30.

152 Kane *et al.* 1992: 45, 52; El-Mouelhy *et al.* 1994: 29, 32.

153 Zillhardt 2009: 70.

154 Zillhardt 2009: 27, 58–65, 68–9. Peet and Woolley 1923: 17, 85, pl. xx, fig.1, no. 22/83. In the easternmost room of house T.35.4 at Amarna, Frankfort and Pendlebury (1933: 43) found a 'meat-jar' containing the bones of a child *c.* six months old. For infant burials in settlements in the First Intermediate Period at Abydos and Middle Kingdom Elephantine, see von Pilgrim 1996. Similar burials are known from a range of archaeological and ethnographic contexts: Wileman 2005: 77, 79.

155 Weaning seems to have taken place around the age of three. See e.g. the Instruction of Any: Lichtheim 1976: 141.

156 Zillhardt 2009: 58ff. For cultural beliefs related to appropriate ages for weaning, see Kamp 2001: 11.

the dead within the house, conceptual links to the continuity of a settlement, or the retaining of the soul within the walls so that the young could be reborn:[157] if an infant died in a Coptic Christian family prior to baptism in the early 20th century, for example, it was buried beneath the floor of the house to ensure that the mother would have another child.[158]

The Eastern Cemetery at Deir el-Medina was divided into age-related sectors: infants were buried at the base of the hill, with adolescents and adults in the slope above.[159] Maternal mortality may have been responsible for the discrepancy between the number of males and females interred in this cemetery. Meskell[160] suggests that more women were buried there because they could not afford to build western necropolis-style sepulchres, though given the general scarcity of tombs built exclusively for women, one might expect them to be incorporated into the burial place of their husband or family (unless they predeceased them). If, as Pierrat-Bonnefois contends,[161] the Eastern Cemetery was not intended for the burials of individuals from the village itself, but rather represents an overspill of other local burial grounds, then the location of the necropolis for the majority of 18th Dynasty workmen and their families has yet to be found.

In the 18th Dynasty at Deir el-Medina infants were buried in amphorae, baskets, boxes, and plain coffins, sometimes accompanied by grave goods.[162] There seems to have been no workshop or individual artisans responsible for producing containers specifically for dead juveniles. Ceramic vessels, amphorae, wooden boxes and baskets were all made initially for domestic use: in some cases the baskets were too small for the body of the child, so the end of the container was cut to allow the legs of the corpse to protrude.[163] The presence of food, pottery and jewellery suggests that the children were considered to be full social persons, an interpretation supported by the use of anthropoid coffins for some infants elsewhere in Egypt and Nubia (such as the Ramesside example of Paneferneb from Aniba),[164] as continued to be the case in the Greco-Roman period.[165] As with adult burials, the interment of the young was most likely determined by the family's means – thus the burial of children of similar ages in coffins or baskets may be economically rather than symbolically based.

Although it is often assumed that vessels and objects interred with the deceased indicate a belief in an afterlife, it is also possible that at least some items were deposited in graves to remove them from circulation due to negative associations.[166] This may be true of the flints used to cut the umbilical cord found in some infant burials:[167] the fact that the child came into

---

157 Wileman 2005: 79.

158 Blackman 1927: 101.

159 Andreu 2002c: 22; Pierrat-Bonnefois 2003: 51.

160 2000c: 429.

161 2003: 51, following Bruyère 1937: 110. Pierrat-Bonnefois objects to both the Western and Eastern cemeteries being considered as part of Deir el-Medina, proposing instead that the eastern necropolis should be named 'the cemetery to the west of Qurnet Mourrai' (2003: 63, n. 36). She notes that the eastern necropolis is an artificial archaeological construct, which ignores the ancient limits of the original extension to the centre and west of the valley (2003: 51).

162 Meskell 2000: 429; Bruyère 1937: 12–13. Cf. the infant burials with juglets at Tell el-Daba in the late 13th or 14th Dynasty (Bietak 1996: pl. 19c).

163 Zillhardt 2009: 11.

164 D'Auria 1988: no. 112.

165 Spieser 2007: 521–6; Dunand 2004.

166 For alternative meanings and uses of objects buried with or near the dead, see Pinch 2003: 445.

167 Zillhardt 2009: 10. Bloody cloths and placentas were also disposed of by burial in the cemetery

Figure 54: Deceased child, named Taia, justified, beneath an adult's chair. Her youth is indicated by the sidelock, although her dress suggests that she was adolescent; in contrast, young children in this tomb are shown naked. Tomb of Sennedjem (TT 1), Deir el-Medina, 19th Dynasty.

contact with the knife and subsequently died may have meant that it was considered unsuitable for further use.[168] The lack of toys but inclusion of protective amulets suggest that in death children were treated as and experienced the same journey to the next world as their parents and siblings and that they were equally (if not more) vulnerable to its dangers.

In the 19th Dynasty children were interred in the Western Cemetery at Deir el-Medina where they were given quite meagre burials. In general anthropoid coffins seem to have been limited to the offspring of the highest elite and royalty,[169] including the foetuses from the tomb of Tutankhamun (KV 62), the son of Amenhotep II from KV 32, three infants from KV 43

(*ibid.*).

168 The act of breaking or burying objects that were deemed to have been polluted by death or the corpse itself is part of the process of separating the dead from the world of living and is common in many cultures (e.g. Parker Pearson 1993: 203–4).

169 Exceptions include two children buried in anthropoid coffins in Tomb 1372 at Deir el-Medina (Bruyère 1937: 161–4).

Figure 55: Mortuary stela depicting a deceased couple and child ('her daughter, Irynefert (i), justified' as recipients of offerings from their family. Tomb chapel of May (Maia), Deir el Medina, 18th Dynasty. Turin 1579. © Fondazione Museo Antichità Egizie di Torino – used with permission.

(Thutmose IV), and Prince Ahmose-Pairy from the Deir el-Bahri cachette.[170] A 19th Dynasty anthropoid coffin with scenes of 'daily life' belonging to Tairitsekheru[171] contained the mummy of a very young child who was titled 'the Osiris',[172] which indicates that she was considered to be a blessed member of the afterlife community.

It would seem that ailing children were cared for in life and buried with dignity, at least at the Eastern Cemetery in the 18th Dynasty. One of the best-provisioned graves in the necropolis was that of a four year old girl with hydrocephalus (tomb no. 1375). The child was buried in a sycamore wood coffin, and interred with stone, bronze, and ceramic vessels, amphorae, lamps, jewellery, a wig, cloth, oil, food and beer.[173] Other tombs for disabled or diseased children include 1373 (a four year old boy with scoliosis),[174] 1372b, c (four and six year old children with dwarfism/achondroplasty), and 1390 (a severely deformed three year old boy named Iriky). Malnutrition and parasitic infections such as schistosomiasis resulted in a weakened immune system and greater susceptibility to disorders (scurvy, inflammation, ulcers, anaemia), as evidenced in Middle Kingdom burials at Elephantine.[175] Kamp[176] points out that little scholarly attention has been paid to the consequences of ill health for the children themselves or for the society of which they were a part, but the careful burial of sick and disabled children in Thebes implies that they were not rejected or treated differently to those without obvious signs of ill-health.

Other than Prince Ahmose-Sipair,[177] no mortuary cult of children or adolescents is known, though a faience ancestor-style bust with the hairstyle of a child now in the Petrie Museum[178] may have been one of many. Beyond these limited examples, it seems that young children in general were not intended to be individually remembered. Bruyère did not mention any constructed masonry or external monuments marking the locations of graves in the Eastern Cemetery,[179] nor did he find offerings or evidence of funerary or mortuary rituals conducted in their vicinity. Thus, while young children were buried with dignity, they were not accorded any form of permanent memorial or cult comparable to that of elite adults, except when they were depicted in tombs or on stelae where they could be remembered with their parents (Figures 54 and 55).

---

170 Spieser 2007: 512.

171 Spieser 2007: 514–5, fig. 10. The coffin probably derived from Deir el-Medina.

172 'The Osiris, the royal son, Siamun, justified' is an 18th Dynasty example (Spieser 2007: 514). See Smith 2006 for a discussion of Osiris as an epithet of the deceased. Cooney (2008: 18–19) suggests that anthropoid coffins may depict the deceased in *akh*-form: if this is the case it implies that at least in some cases children were thought to undergo the same process of transfiguration as adults.

173 Zillhardt 2009: 27–8; Bruyère 1937: 166f.

174 Zillhardt 2009: 22, 15–16, 26; Bruyère 1937: 164, 202; Meskell 1999: 171. See also Fischer-Elfert's 2005 study of outsiders and those with illnesses or physical defects.

175 Zillhardt 2009: 60–1.

176 2001: 10.

177 17th Dynasty: Demarée 1983: 46, pl. 37, 2; Vandersleyen 2005.

178 UC 1236: Harrington 2007: 59, fig. 13.

179 Pierrat-Bonnefois 2003: 51, 53. In contrast, the intact grave of a child at the South Tombs Cemetery at Amarna (Ind. 133, grave pit 13123) was covered with a row of unworked stones in a linear arrangement, which would probably have been visible on the surface (Kemp 2010: 6–7).

Conclusions

As Valerie Hope notes in her discussion of memory and funerary monuments in ancient Rome:[180]

> *In the end all these attempts to stimulate the public to remember reflect [the fact] that human memory is a weak and fickle thing; most people forget as easily as they remember and what they remember is subjective and open to manipulation. The very fact that some individuals went to such lengths to be remembered suggests that they were all too aware of how quickly people both forget and are forgotten.*

Equally, however, it could be argued that while the individual may be forgotten, mortuary monuments still function as reminders of the collective dead and of the omnipresence of death itself.[181] Curses are a testament to the fact that the Egyptians recognised that vandalism, theft, desecration of corpses, and reuse of tombs and artefacts occurred and was largely beyond the scope of terrestrial law. These concerns are reflected in other societies, including the Romans who sought to 'gain protection against the wanton forgetfulness and destructive nature of the living', some by making their tombs a focal point for visits, banquets and entertainment and providing money for their maintenance, while others built shared tombs so that future generations would have an interest in preserving them.[182] Ultimately these tactics were as unsuccessful as the threats inscribed in Egyptian tombs.

Deceased children may not have received the same level of mortuary provision as adults but they were nonetheless buried in ways indicative of their importance to their families and the community of which they were a part. The division of cemeteries into age-related sectors has been interpreted as the rejection of juveniles from society,[183] but the fact that infants and neonates were given individual burials, sometimes with grave goods, rather than being discarded or placed together in pits implies that they were not thought of as sub-human.

Egyptian attitudes to the dead may be best described as ambivalent. As powerful ancestors the deceased could intercede between petitioners and the gods, restore fertility and protect the home. Equally, as malevolent spirits they could cause disease and death, destroy crops, and disrupt the household.[184] Yet neither respect nor fear were sufficient to prevent tomb robbery, the desecration of corpses, or the reuse of funerary equipment. Ironically, the emphasis on the need for material objects in securing a place in the afterlife may have been partly responsible for the theft and 'usurpation' of artefacts and monuments. For those interred with grave goods, particularly the elite, inequality in life led to greater vulnerability in death.

---

180 2003: 120.

181 Cf. Parker Pearson 1999: 193.

182 Hope 2003: 122–3.

183 E.g. Lillehammer 2002: 78ff.

184 See Chapter 1.

Chapter 6

Conclusions: Living with the dead in ancient Egypt

Strange is it not? that of the myriads who
Before us pass'd the door of Darkness through
Not one returns to tell us of the Road,
Which to discover we must travel too.[1]

The recently deceased and the distant dead were viewed differently. Both could behave malevolently, but only the recently deceased seemed to be in direct communication with the living and to be responsive to requests for help. Their names, characters and relationships with the living were common knowledge, whereas the distant ancestors – whether *akhu* or *mwt* – whose names were forgotten, represented the unknown and might therefore be expected to behave in a manner that was inherently more chaotic and disruptive.

As in many cultures, ancient and modern, cults of individual ancestors in Egypt had a finite existence. Once those who remembered the deceased died and there was no direct link to the past, the cults were abandoned and artefacts associated with them were discarded or reused. The deceased passed into the realm of the collective dead and as part of this community they could be blamed for illness (including possessing the victim), death,[2] crop failure, infertility, and other inexplicable disasters. This was also the case in Mesopotamia, where texts deal specifically with ghost-induced illnesses.[3] The malevolent dead could be male or female.[4] There were differences between the gender manifestations of the dead, and perhaps between the manners in which they affected the living. Medico-magical texts often list antagonistic beings in a specific, perhaps hierarchical, order: male and female *akhs*, dead men and women, male and female adversaries, and demons.[5] According to Donnat,[6] the dead were the principal adversaries of the living, but demons, deities, snakes, and scorpions too were responsible for various afflictions. The Egyptians dealt with malevolent entities through execration rituals, intended to separate the living from the dead (smashing pots, for example), or to annihilate them altogether.[7]

---

[1] E. Clodd 1906: 87. Cf. Song of Antef (after Lichtheim 1973: 196): 'No one has come back from there,/ that he might tell of their condition,/ that he might calm our hearts/ until we go to the place they have gone.'

[2] Cf. Wickett 2010: 232.

[3] Scurlock 2006.

[4] E.g. O. Gardiner 363: Ritner 1990: 25–6.

[5] E.g. P. Leiden I, 348 v. 2: Szpakowska 2003a: 168; P. Edwin Smith, Spell 5: Allen 2005: 109, v. 2, 2–14.

[6] 2003: 323.

[7] By burning wax effigies, for instance; see Chapter 1.

The deceased, once buried, could exist without the assistance of the living, since the magically effective tomb decoration would provide for their needs.[8] Equally the living could survive without intervention from the deceased, since they had the gods and human society to support them. The situation, however, was far more complicated. Not only were doubts expressed about the efficacy of preparations for the next world (for example in the harpers' songs), but the dead were vulnerable to neglect as much as by attacks from vandals and robbers. The living turned to their deceased kin for help in times of emergency, for fertility issues, protection from malevolent entities, or with family disputes (as recorded in letters to the dead), and provided offerings not just out of duty or respect but from fear of the consequences should the dead become hostile. Alan Gardiner concluded that the Egyptians felt no great fear of their ancestors,[9] given the 'extreme prevalence of tomb-robbery'. The two attitudes need not have been mutually exclusive: practicality may well have overridden concerns regarding retribution by the deceased. In Papyrus Leopold-Amherst, dating to Year 16 of Ramesses IX,[10] craftsmen and priests are named among the robbers: poverty-stricken farmers were not the only ones to supplement their income by stealing from the dead.

The popular conception that the ancient Egyptians were obsessed with death and mortuary provision is unsurprising given the weight of evidence for burial preparation and the costs involved. However, Howard Williams[11] suggests that in prehistory generally, death was probably more visible, and that there was little sanitising of its reality. The visibility and effects of death may have been amplified at specialist villages given their comparative isolation from other settlement sites, and at Deir el-Medina in particular, with its proximity to the cemeteries on its east and west. This village, which provides the majority of New Kingdom information regarding 'daily life', is unlikely to be representative of the many communities that were not planned and first occupied for the purpose of creating and furnishing tombs. Thus while the dead were presumably commemorated in some manner in outlying regions, this may not have taken the form of the cults and rituals found at the artisans' village, where access to texts, skilled labour and materials facilitated the production of artefacts and monuments that formed the focus of cult practices and the memorialisation of the deceased.

According to Howard Williams:[12]

> *Some might regard [the] current obsession [in contemporary archaeology] with death in ancient societies as merely ghoulish and voyeuristic, perhaps replicating the contemporary media's fascination with every intimate detail of people's lives and (particularly violent) deaths. But it might be suggested that the popular interest with tombs, mummies and graves has a deeper psychological and social significance which archaeology has encouraged and mediated. Such a view is supported by the consideration that we are in a society in which death, in its mundane and common forms, is hidden from view, medicalised, privatised and sanitised.*

It could indeed be argued that there is a need to look beyond Western concepts and practices associated with death and burial in order to approach those of ancient cultures, and here ethnographic material is particularly valuable. This is especially true for ancient Egypt since,

---

8 Taylor 2001: 97.

9 1935: 33.

10 Peden 1994: 249.

11 2003b: 90; cf. Chesson 2007: 121.

12 2003a: 10.

as Baines and Lacovara point out:[13] 'Relatively little textual evidence relates directly to the attitudes of living society towards death and the dead themselves.' An additional benefit of incorporating anthropological research is the parallels it offers for sensory aspects of ancient life that might otherwise be overlooked, such as the audibility of grief – the chanting of laments, the weeping for the deceased, and the shrieking and wailing that accompany the announcement of a death.[14]

Throughout this book I have relied heavily on material from elite sources because there is so little comparable evidence for the burials and beliefs of the poorer classes. In the absence of written documents and undisturbed graves it is very difficult to reconstruct the eschatological concerns of the majority of the populace. Did the religion of officials and literate artisans filter down through the social hierarchy, or were non-elite concepts and rituals associated with death, burial, and the afterlife entirely different? The excavations at the South Tombs Cemetery at Amarna are proving instructive, insofar as there seems to have been some provision for the dead at burial and possibly a form of mortuary cult. The act of burying in reed matting in itself, rather than mass inhumation, speaks of respect for the dead,[15] but the apparent general lack of permanent grave markers suggests that long term memorialisation was not intended.

John Taylor states:[16] 'After the New Kingdom, the role of the tomb as the chief focus of the mortuary cult diminished. The tombs themselves were less conspicuous and relatively few possessed a dedicated cult place.' It could be argued, however, that during the New Kingdom, notably at sites such as Deir el-Medina, the house formed an equally important venue for interaction with the dead. The desire to communicate with ancestors within the domestic space indicates the close-knit nature of the family unit. A similar belief that the relationship between the living and the dead is intrinsic to the survival of the entire family operates today in parts of Upper Egypt.[17] At Deir el-Medina, the deceased could enter via doorways, through the media of busts, statuettes or stelae, or by means of false doors that linked the house to the tomb. The desire of the dead to return to their homes is expressed in mortuary texts, where their role as protectors of their kin, particularly their children, is clearly stated.[18] Ancestor worship was not, however, confined to the house:[19] chapels, shrines, temples, and 'pilgrimage' sites such as Abydos, were all places of potential interaction between the living and the dead.

If stelae from the Theban area can be taken at face value, then women were much involved in local cults and participated to a greater extent than men in interaction with ancestors, since only females are shown in the presence of busts. Literacy would not have been a barrier, because requests could be made orally; as with laments,[20] rituals may have been passed from one generation to another. Votive stelae dedicated by or on behalf of women depict them worshipping

---

13 2002: 6.

14 Wickett 2010: 101.

15 Taylor (2010: 230) makes a similar point with regard to graves at 22nd–25th Dynasty Matmar.

16 2010: 233.

17 Wickett 2010: 239.

18 E.g. Assmann 2005: 216, 219, 220, 451 n. 36.

19 Schulman 1986: 315.

20 Compare modern Egyptian lamenters, who are illiterate: 'How do women learn laments? I asked one woman. She replied: *kutr al-huzn y'allim al-buka*: 'a surfeit of sadness teaches one how to weep'' (Wickett 2010: 75).

various gods including statues of deified kings.[21] At Deir el-Bahri several stelae and votive cloths were dedicated by mothers and daughters.[22] Women as ancestors were themselves the focus of cult, as is shown by *akh iqer* stelae,[23] female *akhs* mentioned in medico-magical texts, and probably in the form of anthropoid busts. The separation of women and men in images of funerals, and to a lesser extent, in banquet scenes, may reflect on gender divisions in everyday life, which might be comparable, for instance, with the Kota in the Nilgiri Hills of South India: 'In the funeral procession, at the feast, and in all other ceremonies the 'normal' order of rank is maintained. Thus men come before women, elders before the young men, etc. In this way the funeral ceremony highlights the central motifs of the culture.'[24]

Social aspects of the relationship of the living with the dead include the manner in which men and women deal with bereavement, or at least how they are depicted as doing so, since texts generally do not record peoples' responses to death. The focus is on the bereaved and on the corpse but never on the dying,[25] explicit causes for individual deaths are rarely mentioned,[26] and the process of dying is never depicted. In funeral scenes, women are shown in states of distress that vary from one tomb to another. Aside from weeping and raising their arms, other typical actions include throwing dust onto their dishevelled hair, as is paralleled in modern Luxor, and rending their clothes.[27] These images may represent socially acceptable performance enhanced by the presence of professional mourners, genuine, unpremeditated reactions to loss, or artisans' renderings of standard mourning behaviour. The laments that accompany these scenes may be deliberately ambiguous – partly conventional expressions of grief but combined with a counter-cultural questioning of the prevalent beliefs regarding death and the afterlife. Funeral scenes themselves combine control and chaos. Formal lines of offering bringers contrast with hysterical mourners, while the solemn professionalism of the priests responsible for the Opening of the Mouth ritual outside the tomb entrance is at variance with the weeping widow crumpled on the ground clinging to her husband's coffin or mummy. They are pictures of extremes.

The funerary banquet with its formal representations of seated guests contrasts with the mortuary banquets of the 18th Dynasty.[28] In the latter, the apparent atmosphere of solemnity and duty present in the former is replaced by one of relaxed entertainment. The fear, chaos, and formality of funerary scenes is no longer present. This difference is perhaps due to the control the living now have over the dead, who were encouraged to come at the voice for offerings and invited to participate in banquets, or to listen and respond to requests for assistance – they were not expected to be present unless called upon. The breaking of barriers during

[21] E.g. Holden 1982: 298–9; Jørgensen 1998: 116–7.

[22] Pinch 1993: fig. 10b, pls 16a, 18b.

[23] E.g. Bruyère 1939: 317–18, figs 186, 187.

[24] Palgi and Abramovitch 1984: 395.

[25] Palgi and Abramovitch 1984: 385.

[26] Toivari-Viitala 2001: 220.

[27] Wickett 2010: 74. Palgi and Abramovitch note in relation to general behaviour at funerals (1984: 399): '... if there are sex differences in emotions during bereavement, it is the women who tend to cry and self-mutilate more than men, who tend to direct anger and aggression away from self', and: 'Women ... may not experience death more strongly; they may only be used (and allow themselves to be used) as the person who symbolizes publicly, in burdensome or self-injuring ways, the loss that all have experienced' (*ibid.*: 400).

[28] For the distinction, see Harrington 2012.

communication with the dead was thus done largely at the behest of the living and on their terms. This relationship is also apparent in modern rural Egypt, where 'much effort is normally undertaken to dissuade the soul of the departed to return to the land of the living except for specific feast days and for specific feasts.'[29]

The relationship between the living and the dead in New Kingdom Egypt was based on principles of reciprocity, yet was at the same time highly complex. Part of the reason for this may have be the multifaceted nature of the deceased, discussed in Chapter 1. Ambivalence of the dead toward the living as well of *vice versa* is apparent in medico-magical and didactic texts and other sources such as letters to the dead, where it is clear that fear and the need to appease (*sḥtp*) the deceased were factors behind some aspects of mortuary cults. The tomb was not the only location where interaction with ancestors took place. Equally important were installations in the house, while chapels and temples, festivals and banquets were other potential focal points for communication with and rites involving the dead (Chapters 3 and 4). Objects related to mortuary cults including statues, stelae, and offering tables (Chapter 2), were a tangible, durable media simultaneously foci for ritual activities and memorials to the dead. Long-term memorialisation was evidently recognised as an unattainable goal (Chapter 5), and yet investment in tombs and funerary equipment continued. Perhaps it was sufficient to prepare for burial and arrange a mortuary cult.[30] By doing so one was both complying with cultural norms and guaranteeing, as far as possible, a place in the afterlife, regardless of the inevitable robbery, reuse, and decay that would follow the sealing of the burial chamber.

29 Wickett 2010: 130.

30 Baines and Lacovara 2002: 26; Cooney 2007: 274.

Bibliography

Abdalaal, A. M. (2005), The Egyptian Museum stela of *ḥnwt*. *Bulletin of the Egyptian Museum* 2. 17–20.

Abdalla, A. (1992), The cenotaph of the Sekwaskhet family from Saqqara. *Journal of Egyptian Archaeology* 78. 93–111.

Abu-Lughod, L. (1986), *Veiled sentiments: honor and poetry in a Bedouin society*. Berkeley, University of California Press.

Adams, C. (2007), Shades of meaning: the significance of manifestations of the dead as evidenced in texts from the Old Kingdom to the Coptic period. In M. Cannata (ed.) *Current Research in Egyptology 2006: proceedings of the seventh annual symposium*. Oxford, Oxbow Books. 1–20.

Allen, J. P. (1988), Funerary texts and their meaning. In S. D'Auria, P. Lacovara and C. H. Roehrig (eds), *Mummies and magic: the funerary arts of ancient Egypt*. Boston, Museum of Fine Arts. 38–49.

Allen, J. P. (2005a), *The ancient Egyptian Pyramid Texts*. Atlanta, Society of Biblical Literature.

Allen, J. P. (2005b), *The art of medicine in ancient Egypt*. New York and New Haven, Metropolitan Museum of Art; Yale University Press.

Allen, J. P. (2011), *The Debate Between a Man and his Soul: a masterpiece of ancient Egyptian literature*. Leiden, Brill.

Allen, S. J. (2003), Tutankhamun's embalming cache reconsidered. In Z. Hawass and L. Pinch Brock (eds), *Egyptology at the dawn of the Twenty-first century: Proceedings of the Eighth International Congress of Egyptologists, Volume 1: Archaeology*. Cairo, American University in Cairo Press. 23–9.

Allen, T. G. (1974), *The Book of the Dead, or, Going Forth by Day: ideas of the ancient Egyptians concerning the hereafter as expressed in their own terms*. Chicago, Oriental Institute of the University of Chicago.

Altenmüller, H. (1978), Zur Bedeutung der Harfnerlieder des Alten Reiches. *Studien zur Altägyptischen Kultur* 6. 1–24.

Altenmüller, H. (1990), Einleitung. In B. Schmitz (ed.), *Suche nach Unsterblichkeit: Totenkult und Jenseitsglaube im Alten Ägypten*. Hildesheim and Mainz, Pelizaeus-Museum; Philipp von Zabern. 6–25.

Altenmüller, H. (1994), Das Graffito 551 aus der thebanischen Nekropole. *Studien zur Altägyptischen Kultur* 21. 19–28.

Anderson, R. (2002), Kill or cure: Athenian judicial curses and the body in fear. In P. A. Baker and G. Carr (eds), *Practitioners, practices and patients: new approaches to medical archaeology and anthropology*. Oxford, Oxbow Books. 221–37.

Andreu, G. (1997), Ostracon: an order for windows. In G. Andreu, M.–H. Rutschowscaya and C. Ziegler (eds) *Ancient Egypt at the Louvre*. Paris, Hachette. 153–4.

Andreu, G. (2002a), Linteau d'une niche destinée aux cultes domestiques (no. 2). In G. Andreu (ed.), *Les artistes de pharaon: Deir el–Médineh et la Vallée des Rois*. Paris, Turnhout, Reunion des Musées Nationaux/Brepols. 74–5.

Andreu, G. (2002b), Stèle familiale de Mésou et Apy; Stèle familiale d'Arinéfer (nos. 57, 58). In G. Andreu (ed.), *Les artistes de Pharaon: Deir el–Médineh et la Vallée des Rois.* Paris, Turnhout, Reunion des Musées Nationaux/Brepols. 116–7.

Andreu, G. (2002c), «Artistes» de Pharaon. In G. Andreu (ed.), *Les artistes de Pharaon: Deir el–Médineh et la Vallée des Rois*. Paris, Reunion des Musées Nationaux. 15–41.

Andrews, C. (1994), *Amulets of ancient Egypt*. London, British Museum Press.

Anthes, R. (1943), Die deutschen Grabungen auf der Westseite von Theben in den Jahren 1911 und 1913. *Mitteilungen des Deutschen Instituts für Ägyptische Altertumskunde in Kairo* 12. 1–68.

Anthes, R. (1954), The Original Meaning of *mꜣꜥ ḫrw*. *Journal of Near Eastern Studies* 13. 21–51.

Arnold, D. (2003), *The encyclopaedia of ancient Egyptian architecture*, trans. S. H. Gardiner, H. Strudwick and N. Strudwick. London, I. B. Tauris.

Arnold, Do. (2008), Egyptian art – a performing art? In S. H. D'Auria (ed.), *Servant of Mut: Studies in Honor of Richard A. Fazzini*. Leiden, Boston, Brill. 1–18.

Arnst, C.-B. (1991), Relieffragment aus dem Grab des Ptahemhat. In K.-H. Priese (ed.), *Ägyptisches Museum*. Mainz, Philipp von Zabern. 136–8.

Arrache, G. (2008), Theban Tomb 39, Puimra, tomb or funerary temple? *Tenth International Congress of Egyptologists.* Rhodes, University of the Aegean. www.rhodes.aegean.gr/tms/XICE%20Abstract%20book.pdf. 15.

Assmann, J. (1970), *Der König als Sonnenpriester: ein kosmographischer Begleittext zur kultischen Sonnenhymnik*. Glückstadt, J. J. Augustin.

Assmann, J. (1977), Fest des Augenblicks im Verheissung der Dauer: die Kontroverse der Ägyptischen Harfnerlieder. In J. Assmann, E. Feucht and R. Grieshammer (eds), *Fragen an die altägyptische Literatur: Studien zum Gedenken an Eberhard Otto*. Wiesbaden, Dr. Ludwig Reichert. 55–84.

Assmann, J. (1979), Zwei Blöcke aus dem verschollenen Grab des Bürgermeisters Amenemhēt (Theben nr. 163) im Britischen Museum. *Journal of Egyptian Archaeology* 65. 54–77.

Assmann, J. (1983), *Sonnenhymnen in thebanischen Gräbern*. Mainz, Philipp von Zabern.

Assmann, J. (1986), Verklärung. In C. Meyer (ed.), *Lexikon der Ägyptologie*. Wiesbaden, Harrassowitz. 998–1006.

Assmann, J. (1989), Death and initiation in the funerary religion of ancient Egypt. In J. P. Allen (ed.), *Religion and philosophy in ancient Egypt*. New Haven, Yale Egyptological Seminar, Yale University. 135–59.

Assmann, J. (1990), Egyptian mortuary liturgies. In S. Israelit-Groll (ed.), *Studies in Egyptology presented to Miriam Lichtheim, I*. Jerusalem, Hebrew University. 1–45.

Assmann, J. (1991a), Der zweidimensionale Mensch: Das Fest als Medium des kollektiven Gedächtnisses. In J. Assmann and T. Sundermeier (eds), *Das Fest und das Heilige: religiöse Kontrapunkte zur Alltagswelt*. Gütersloh, Gerd Mohn. 13–30.

Assmann, J. (1991b), Das ägyptische Prozessionsfest. In J. Assmann and T. Sundermeier (eds), *Das Fest und das Heilige: religiöse Kontrapunkte zur Alltagswelt*. Gütersloh, Gerd Mohn. 105–22.

Assmann, J. (1991c), *Das Grab des Amenemope (TT 41)*. Mainz, Philipp von Zabern.

Assmann, J. (1992), When justice fails: Jurisdiction and imprecation in ancient Egypt and the Near East. *Journal of Egyptian Archaeology* 78. 149–62.

Assmann, J. (1994), Ocular desire in a time of darkness: Urban festivals and divine visibility in Ancient Egypt. In A. R. E. Agus and J. Assmann (eds), *Ocular desire, Sehnsucht des Auges*. Berlin, Akademie-Verlag. 13–29.

Assmann, J. (1995), *Egyptian solar religion in the New Kingdom: Re, Amun and the crisis of polytheism*, trans. A. Alcock. London and New York, Kegan Paul International.
Assmann, J. (1997), *Das kulturelle Gedächtnis: Schrift, Erinnerung und politische Identität in Frühen Hochkulturen*. Munich, Beck.
Assmann, J. (2001), *The search for god in ancient Egypt*, trans. D. Warburton. Ithaca and London, Cornell University Press.
Assmann, J. (2002), *The mind of Egypt: history and meaning in the time of the pharaohs*, trans. A. Jenkins. New York, Metropolitan Books.
Assmann, J. (2003a), The Ramesside tomb of Nebsumenu (TT 183) and the ritual of Opening the Mouth. In N. Strudwick and J. H. Taylor (eds), *The Theban Necropolis: Past, present and future.* London, British Museum Press. 53–60.
Assmann, J. (2003b), The Ramesside tomb and the construction of sacred space. In N. Strudwick and J. H. Taylor (eds), *The Theban Necropolis: past, present and future.* London, British Museum Press. 46–52.
Assmann, J. (2005), *Death and salvation in ancient Egypt*, trans. D. Lorton. Ithaca and London, Cornell University Press.
Aston, B., Harrell, J. and Shaw, I. (2000), Stone. In P. T. Nicholson and I. Shaw (eds), *Ancient Egyptian materials and technology.* Cambridge, Cambridge University Press. 5–77.
Baines, J. (1973), The destruction of the pyramid temple of Sahure‘. *Göttinger Miszellen* 4. 9–14.
Baines, J. (1987), Practical religion and piety. *Journal of Egyptian Archaeology* 73. 79–98.
Baines, J. (1991), Society, morality, and religious practice. In B. E. Shafer (ed.), *Religion in ancient Egypt: gods, myths, and personal practice.* Ithaca and London, Cornell University Press. 123–200.
Baines, J. (2007), *Visual and written culture in ancient Egypt*. Oxford, Oxford University Press.
Baines, J. (2009), The stelae of Amenisonbe from Abydos and Middle Kingdom display of personal religion. In D. Magee, J. Bourriau and S. Quirke (eds), *Sitting beside Lepsius: studies in honour of Jaromir Malek at the Griffith Institute*. Leuven, Peeters. 1–22.
Baines, J. and Frood, E. (2011), Piety, change and display in the New Kingdom. In M. Collier and S. Snape (eds), *Ramesside Studies in honour of K. A. Kitchen*. Liverpool, Rutherford Press. 1–18.
Baines, J. and Lacovara, P. (2002), Burial and the dead in ancient Egyptian society: respect, formalism, neglect. *Journal of Social Archaeology* 2. 5–36.
Baines, J. and Malek, J. (2000), *Cultural atlas of ancient Egypt*. New York, Facts on File.
Bakir, A. E-M. (1966), *The Cairo Calendar no. 86637*. Cairo, General Organisation for Government Printing Offices.
Barbotin, C. (2002), Linteau avec la vache Hathor protégeant Ramsès II (no. 184). In G. Andreu (ed.), *Les artistes de Pharaon: Deir el-Médineh et la Vallée des Rois.* Paris, Turnhout, Reunion des Musées Nationaux/Brepols. 229.
Barley, N. (1997), *Grave matters: A lively history of death around the world*. New York, Henry Holt.
Bavay, L. (2002), Autel portatif. In G. Andreu (ed.), *Les artistes de pharaon: Deir el-Médineh et la Vallée des Rois.* Paris, Turnhout, Reunion des Musées Nationaux/Brepols. 248.
Becker, E. (1973), *The denial of death*. New York, The Free Press.
Beinlich-Seeber, C. and Shedid, A. G. (1987), *Das Grab des Userhet (TT 56)*. Mainz, Philipp von Zabern.
Bell, L. (1997), The New Kingdom ‘divine’ temple: the example of Luxor. In B. E. Shafer (ed.), *Temples of ancient Egypt.* London and New York, I. B. Tauris. 127–84.

Berlandini, J. (1977), Varia Memphitica II (II–III). *Bulletin de l'Institut Français d'Archéologie* 77. 29–44.

Berman, L. M. (1999), *Catalogue of Egyptian art in the Cleveland Museum of Art.* New York, Hudson Hills Press.

Bernhauer, E. (2002), Der Bittgestus in der Privatplastik. *Göttinger Miszellen* 186. 17–26.

Bierbrier, M. L. (1982a), *The tomb-builders of the pharaohs*. London, British Museum Publications.

Bierbrier, M. L. (1982b), *Hieroglyphic texts from Egyptian stelae etc.* 10. London, British Museum Publications.

Bierbrier, M. L. and Parkinson, R. B. (1993), *Hieroglyphic texts from Egyptian stelae etc.* 12. London, British Museum Press.

Bietak, M. (1979), Urban archaeology and the 'town problem' in ancient Egypt. In K. Weeks (ed.), *Egyptology and the social sciences.* Cairo, American University in Cairo Press. 97–144.

Bietak, M. (1996), *Avaris, the capital of the Hyksos: recent excavations at Tell el-Dab'a*. London, British Museum Press.

Bisset, N. G., Bruhn, J. G., Curto, S., Holmstedt, B., Nyman, U. and Zenk, M. H. (1994), Was opium known in 18th Dynasty ancient Egypt? An examination of materials from the tomb of the chief royal architect Kha. *Journal of Ethnopharmacology* 41. 99–114.

Bjerke, S. (1965), Remarks on the Egyptian ritual of 'Opening the Mouth' and its interpretation. *Numen* 12. 201–16.

Blackman, A. M. (1916), Libations to the dead in modern Nubia and ancient Egypt. *Journal of Egyptian Archaeology* 3. 31–4.

Blackman, A. M. (1920), On the name of an unguent used for ceremonial purposes. *Journal of Egyptian Archaeology* 6, 1. 58–60.

Blackman, A. M. (1924), The rite of the Opening the Mouth in Ancient Egypt and Babylonia. *Journal of Egyptian Archaeology* 10. 47–59.

Blackman, A. M. (1925a), Oracles in ancient Egypt. *Journal of Egyptian Archaeology* 11. 249–55.

Blackman, A. M. (1925b), Osiris or the sun god? A reply to Mr Perry. *Journal of Egyptian Archaeology* 11. 201–9.

Blackman, A. M. (1926), Oracles in ancient Egypt II. *Journal of Egyptian Archaeology* 12. 176–85.

Blackman, W. S. (1927), *The Fellāhīn of Upper Egypt*. London, George G. Harrap & Company Ltd.

Blake, E. (2003), The familiar honeycomb: Byzantine era reuse of Sicily's prehistoric rock–cut tombs. In R. M. Van Dyke and S. E. Alcock (eds), *Archaeologies of memory.* Malden, MA, Blackwell. 203–20.

Bloch, M. and Parry, J. (1982), *Death and the regeneration of life*. Cambridge, Cambridge University Press.

Bloch-Smith, E. (1992a), *Judahite burial practices and beliefs about the dead*. Sheffield, Sheffield Academic Press.

Bloch-Smith, E. (1992b), The cult of the dead in Judah: interpreting the material remains. *Journal of Biblical Literature* 111. 213–24.

Blumenthal, E. (2000), *Kuhgöttin und Gottkönig: Frömmigkeit und Staatstreue auf der Stele Leipzig Ägyptisches Museum 5141*. Leipzig, Ägyptisches Museum der Universität.

Bochi, P. A. (1998), Gender and genre in ancient Egyptian poetry: the rhetoric of performance in the Harpers' songs. *Journal of the American Research Center in Egypt* 35. 89–95.

Bochi, P. A. (1999), Death by drama: the ritual of *damnatio memoriae* in ancient Egypt. *Göttinger Miszellen* 171. 73–86.
Bogoslovsky, E. S. (1980), Hundred Egyptian draughtsmen. *Zeitschrift für Ägyptische Sprache und Altertumskunde* 107. 89–116.
Bohleke, B. (1997), An oracular amuletic decree of Khonsu in the Cleveland Museum of Art. *Journal of Egyptian Archaeology* 83. 155–67.
Bolshakov, A. O. (1991), The moment of the establishment of the tomb-cult in ancient Egypt *Altorientalische Forschungen* 18. 204–18.
Bolshakov, A. O. (2002), Ka. In D. B. Redford (ed.), *The Oxford encyclopaedia of ancient Egypt II.* New York, Oxford University Press. 215–17.
Bomann, A. H. (1991), *The private chapel in ancient Egypt: a study of the chapels in the workmen's village at el Amarna with special reference to Deir el Medina and other sites.* London, Kegan Paul International.
Bonnet, C. and Valbelle, D. (1976), Le village de Deir el-Médineh: Étude archéologique. *Bulletin de l'Institut Français d'Archéologie Orientale* 76. 317–42.
Borchardt, L. (1929), Bilder des 'Zerbrechens der Krüge'. *Zeitschrift für Ägyptische Sprache und Altertumskunde* 64. 12–6.
Borchardt, L. and Ricke, H. (1980), *Die Wohnhäuser in Tell el-Amarna.* Berlin, Gebrüder Mann.
Borghouts, J. F. (1971), *The magical texts of Papyrus Leiden I 348.* Leiden, E. J. Brill.
Borghouts, J. F. (1982), Divine intervention in ancient Egypt and its manifestation (*b3w*). In R. J. Demarée and J. J. Janssen (eds), *Gleanings from Deir el-Medina.* Leiden, Nederlands Instituut voor het Nabije Oosten. 1–70.
Bosse-Griffiths, K. (1980), Two lute-players of the Amarna era. *Journal of Egyptian Archaeology* 66. 70–82.
Bothmer, B. V. (1987), Ancestral bust. In E. Swan-Hall (ed.), *Antiquities from the collection of Christos G. Bastis.* Mainz, Philipp von Zabern. 24–9.
Botti, G. (1932), Il cofano N 1969 del Museo Civico di Bologna. In *Studies presented to F. Ll. Griffith.* London, Egypt Exploration Society and Oxford University Press. 263–66.
Bouquillon, A., Caubert, A., Kaczmarczyk, A. and Pierrat-Bonnefois, G. (2005), Introduction – les matières vitreuses dans l'antiquité. In A. Caubert and G. Pierrat-Bonnefois (eds), *Faïences: faïences de l'antiquité – de l'Egypte a l'Iran.* Paris, Musée du Louvre/5 Continents Editions. 13–18.
Bourriau, J. (1988), *Pharaohs and mortals: Egyptian art in the Middle Kingdom.* Cambridge, Cambridge University Press.
Bourriau, J. (1991), Patterns of change in burial customs during the Middle Kingdom. In S. Quirke (ed.), *Middle Kingdom studies.* New Malden (England), SIA. 3–20.
Bourriau, J. (2009), Mace's Cemetery Y at Diospolis Parva. In D. Magee, J. Bourriau and S. Quirke (eds), *Sitting beside Lepsius: studies in honour of Jaromir Malek at the Griffith Institute.* Leuven, Peeters. 39–98.
Bovot, J.-L. (2003), Les chaouabtis du Musée du Louvre: Une collection exceptionelle. *Les chaouabtis: Serviteurs d'éternité: Dossiers d'Archéologie:* 9. 4–19.
Bowie, A. (1993), Oil in ancient Greece and Rome. In M. Dudley and G. Rowell (eds), *The oil of gladness: Anointing in the Christian tradition.* London, Society for Promoting Christian Knowledge. 26–34.
Brack, A. and Brack, A. (1977), *Das Grab des Tjanuni: Theben Nr. 74.* Mainz, Philipp von Zabern.
Brack, A. and Brack, A. (1980), *Das Grab des Haremheb: Theben Nr. 78.* Mainz, Philipp von Zabern.

Bradley, R. (2003), The translation of time. In R. M. Van Dyke and S. E. Alcock (eds), *Archaeologies of memory.* Malden, MA, Blackwell. 221–27.

Breasted, J. H. (1930), *The Edwin Smith surgical papyrus*. Chicago, University of Chicago Press.

Bröckelmann, D. (2006), Die „Schiffsfahrten" im Grab Sarenputs I. auf der Qubbet el-Hawa: ein früher Hinweis auf Prozessionsfeste der Anuket? *Göttinger Miszellen* 209. 6–31.

Brovarski, E. J. (1982), Chalices. In E. J. Brovarski, S. K. Doll and R. E. Freed (eds), *Egypt's golden age: the art of living in the New Kingdom 1558–1085 B.C.* Boston, Museum of Fine Arts. 145–47.

Broze, M. (1989), *La princesse de Bakhtan: essai d'analyse stylistique*. Brussels, Fondation Égyptologique Reine Élisabeth.

Brunner, H. (1954), Die theologische Bedeutung der Trunkenheit. *Zeitschrift für Ägyptische Sprache und Altertumskunde* 79. 81–83.

Brunner–Traut, E. (1955), Die Wochenlaube. *Mitteilungen des Instituts für Orientforschung* 3. 11–30.

Bruyère, B. (1923), Un fragment de fresque de Deir el Médineh. *Bulletin de l'Institut Français d'Archéologie Orientale* 22. 121–33.

Bruyère, B. (1925), *Rapport sur les fouilles de Deir el Médineh (1923–1924)*. Cairo, Institut Français d'Archéologie Orientale.

Bruyère, B. (1926), *Rapport sur les fouilles de Deir el Médineh (1924–1925)*. Cairo, Institut Français d'Archéologie Orientale.

Bruyère, B. (1929), *Rapport sur les fouilles de Deir el Médineh (1928)*. Cairo, Institut Français d'Archéologie Orientale.

Bruyère, B. (1930), *Rapport sur les fouilles de Deir el Médineh (1929)*. Cairo, Institut Français d'Archéologie Orientale.

Bruyère, B. (1933), *Rapport sur les fouilles de Deir el Médineh (1930)*. Cairo, Institut Français d'Archéologie Orientale.

Bruyère, B. (1934), *Rapport sur les fouilles de Deir el Médineh (1931–1932)*. Cairo, Institut Français d'Archéologie Orientale.

Bruyère, B. (1937), *Rapport sur les fouilles de Deir el Médineh (1934–1935): Deuxième Partie: La Nécropole de l'Est*. Cairo, Institut Français d'Archéologie Orientale.

Bruyère, B. (1939), *Rapport sur les fouilles de Deir el Médineh (1934–1935)*. Cairo, Institut Français d'Archéologie Orientale.

Bruyère, B. (1953), *Rapport sur les fouilles de Deir el Médineh (1948–1951)*. Cairo, Institut Français d'Archéologie Orientale.

Bruyère, B. (1959), *La tombe no. 1 de Sen-nedjem à Deir el Médineh*. Cairo, Institut Français d'Archéologie Orientale.

Bryan, B. (1985), Evidence for female literacy from Theban tombs of the New Kingdom. *Bulletin of the Egyptological Seminar* 6. 17–32.

Bryce, T. (2002), *Life and society in the Hittite world*. Oxford, Oxford University Press.

Buchberger, H. (1991), *ḥtp* an *'Ipw–rs.ti* – Der Brief auf dem Gefäss München ÄS 4313. *Studien zur Altägyptischen Kultur* 18. 49–87.

Budge, E. A. W. (1909), *The British Museum: a guide to the Egyptian galleries (sculpture)*. London, British Museum Press.

Budge, E. A. W. (1923), *Hieratic papyri in the British Museum*. London, British Museum Press.

Budge, E. A. W. (1924), *British Museum: a guide to the First, Second and Third Egyptian Rooms (third edition)*. London, Harrison and Sons Ltd.

Budka, J. (2001), *Der König an der Haustür: die Rolle des ägyptischen Herrschers an dekorierten Türgewänden von Beamten im Neuen Reich*.Vienna, Afro-Pub.

Burkard, G. (1990), in E. Dziobek and M. A. Raziq (eds). *Das Grab des Sobekhotep: Theban Nr. 63*. Mainz, Philipp von Zabern. 88-91.

Burn, L. (2002), Ostracon figuré: dessin d'une porte de chapelle, profils et hiéroglyphes. In G. Andreu (ed.), *Les artistes de Pharaon: Deir el-Médineh et la Vallée des Rois*. Paris, Turnhout, Reunion des Musées Nationaux/Brepols. 171.

Burnett, D. (2000), *World of the spirits: a Christian perspective on traditional and folk religions*. Oxford, Monarch Books.

Butler, G. and Hope, T. (2007), *Manage your mind: the mental fitness guide* (second edition). Oxford, Oxford University Press.

Cabrol, A. (2002), Stele anonyme aux deux chats (no. 219). In G. Andreu (ed.), *Les artistes de pharaon: Deir el-Médineh et la Vallée des Rois*. Paris, Turnhout, Reunion des Musées Nationaux/Brepols. 270.

Caminos, R. A. (1954), *Late-Egyptian Miscellanies*. London, Geoffrey Cumberlege, Oxford University Press.

Caminos, R. A. (1958), *The chronicle of Prince Osorkon*. Rome, Pontificium Institutum Biblicum.

Centrone, M. C. (2005), Behind the corn-mummies. In K. Piquette and S. Love (eds), *Current Research in Egyptology 2003: Proceedings of the Fourth Annual Symposium, University College London 2003*. Oxford, Oxbow Books. 11–28.

Centrone, M. C. (2006), Choosing the burial place for corn-mummies: a random selection? In R. J. Dann (ed.), *Current Research in Egyptology 2004: Proceedings of the Fifth Annual Symposium, University of Durham 2004*. Oxford, Oxbow Books. 20–33.

Capart, J., Gardiner, A. H. and van der Walle, B. (1936), New light on the Ramesside tomb robberies. *Journal of Egyptian Archaeology* 22. 169–93.

Capel, A. K. (1996), Female figurine with model bed (no. 16b). In A. K. Capel and G. E. Markoe (eds), *Mistress of the house, mistress of heaven: women in ancient Egypt*. New York, Hudson Hills Press and Cincinnati Art Museum. 66–7.

Carter, H. (1972) [1923], *The tomb of Tutankhamen*. [Abridged.] London, Sphere Books Limited.

Castel, G. and Meeks, D. (1970), *Deir el-Médineh 1970, fascicule II: Gournet Mar'eï Sud*. Cairo, Institut Français d'Archéologie Orientale.

Cátedra, M. (2004) [1992], Kinds of death and the house. In A. C. G. M. Robben (ed.), *This world, other worlds: sickness, suicide, death and the afterlife among the Vaqueiros de Alzada of Spain* [extract in *Death, mourning, and burial: a cross–cultural reader*]. Malden MA, Blackwell. 77–90.

Černý, J. (1927), Le culte d'Amenophis Ier chez les ouvriers de la nécropole thébaine. *Bulletin de l'Institut Français d'Archéologie Orientale* 27. 159–203.

Černý, J. (1945), The will of Naunakhte and the related documents. *Journal of Egyptian Archaeology* 31. 29–53.

Černý, J. (1954), Prices and wages in Egypt in the Ramesside period. *Cahiers d'histoire mondiale* 4. 903–21.

Černý, J. (1958), *Egyptian stelae in the Bankes collection*. Oxford, Griffith Institute.

Černý, J. (1973), *A community of workmen at Thebes in the Ramesside period*. Cairo, Institut Français d'Archéologie Orientale.

Černý, J. and Gardiner, A. H. (1957), *Hieratic ostraca I*. Oxford, Oxford University Press for the Griffith Institute.

Champdor, A. (1963), *Le Livre des Morts: Papyrus d'Ani, de Hunefer, d'Anhaï, du British Museum*. Paris, Albin Michel.
Chapman, J. (1994), The living, the dead and the ancestors: time, life cycles and the mortuary domain in later European prehistory. In J. Davies (ed.), *Ritual and remembrance: responses to death in human societies*. Sheffield, Sheffield Academic Press. 40–85.
Chauvet, V. (2008), Decoration and architecture: the definition of private tomb environment. In S. H. D'Auria (ed.), *Servant of Mut: Studies in Honor of Richard A. Fazzini*. Leiden, Boston, Brill. 44–52.
Chauvet, V. (2010), *Entrance porticoes: liminal and ritual space in Old Kingdom private tombs*. Seminar presented to the Faculty of Oriental Studies, University of Oxford.
Cherpion, N. (1994), Le 'cône d'onguent', gage de survie. *Bulletin de l'Institut Français d'Archéologie Orientale* 94. 79–106.
Cherpion, N. (1999), *Deux tombes de la XVIIIe dynastie à Deir el-Medina*. Cairo, Institut Français d'Archéologie Orientale.
Chesson, M. S. (2007), Remembering and forgetting in early Bronze Age mortuary practices on the Southeastern Dead Sea Plain, Jordan. In N. Laneri (ed.), *Performing death: social analyses of funerary traditions in the ancient Near East and Mediterranean*. Chicago, The Oriental Institute of the University of Chicago. 109–39.
Chukwukere, I. (1981), A coffin for 'The Loved One': the structure of Fante death rituals. *Current Anthropology* 22. 61–8.
Chung, A. (2000), Paper offerings. In A. Sheridan (ed.), *Heaven and Hell and other worlds of the dead*. Edinburgh, NMS Publishing. 48.
Clère, J. J. (1995), *Les chauves d'Hathor*. Leuven, Peeters.
Clodd, E. (1918), *Animism: the seed of religion*. London, Constable.
Cooney, K. M. (2007), *The cost of death: the social and economic value of ancient Egyptian funerary art in the Ramesside period*. Leiden, Nederlands Instituut voor het Nabije Oosten.
Cooney, K. M. (2007), The problem of female rebirth in New Kingdom Egypt: the fragmentation of the female individual in her funerary equipment. In C. Graves-Brown (ed.), *Sex and gender in ancient Egypt*. Swansea, Classical Press of Wales. 1–25.
Corbey, R. (2003), Destroying the graven image: Religious iconoclasm on the Christian frontier. *Anthropology Today* 19, 4. 10–14.
Crocker, P. T. (1985), Status symbols in the architecture of el-'Amarna. *Journal of Egyptian Archaeology* 71. 52–65.
Cummings, V. (2003), Building from memory: remembering the past at Neolithic monuments in western Britain. In H. Williams (ed.), *Archaeologies of remembrance: death and memory in past societies*. New York, Springer. 25–43.
Curto, S. (1984), *L'antico Egitto nel Museo Egizio di Torino*. Turin, Tipografia Torinese Editrice.
D'Amicone, E. (1993), Lavoro e produzione. In A. M. Donadoni *et al.*, *Il Museo Egizio di Torino: Guida alla lettura una civiltà* (second edition). Novara, DeAgostini. 114–15.
Dakin, A. N. (1938), The stela of the sculpture Sirē' at Oxford. *Journal of Egyptian Archaeology* 24. 190–97.
Dalley, S. (1993), Anointing in ancient Mesopotamia. In M. Dudley and G. Rowell (eds), *The oil of gladness: anointing in the Christian tradition*. London, Society for Promoting Christian Knowledge. 19–25.
Darnell, J. C. (1995), Hathor returns to Medamûd. *Studien zur Altägyptischen Kultur* 22. 47–94.

Darnell, J. C. (2008), The Valley of Amenemhat and the end of the Ramesside Period. *Tenth International Congress of Egyptologists*. Rhodes, University of the Aegean. www.rhodes.aegean.gr/tms/XICE%20Abstract%20book.pdf. 55–6.

David, A. R. (1973), *Religious ritual at Abydos (*c. *1300 BC)*. Warminster, Aris & Phillips.

Davies, J. (1994), One hundred billion dead: A general theology of death. In J. Davies (ed.), *Ritual and remembrance: Responses to death in human societies*. Sheffield, Sheffield Academic Press. 24–39.

Davies, N. de G. (1903), *The rock tombs of el Amarna I: The tomb of Meryra*. London, Egypt Exploration Fund.

Davies, N. de G. (1905), *The rock tombs of el Amarna II: The tombs of Panehesy and Meryra II*. London, Egypt Exploration Fund.

Davies, N. de G. (1906), *The rock tombs of el Amarna III: the tombs of Huya and Ahmes*. London, Egypt Exploration Fund.

Davies, N. de G. (1908), *The rock tombs of el Amarna VI: the tombs of Parennefer, Tutu and Ay*. London, Egypt Exploration Fund.

Davies, N. de G. (1913), *Five Theban tombs*. London, Egypt Exploration Fund.

Davies, N. de G. (1917), *The tomb of Nakht at Thebes*. New York, Metropolitan Museum of Art.

Davies, N. de G. (1923), *The tombs of two officials of Tuthmosis the Fourth (nos. 75 and 90)*. London, Egypt Exploration Society.

Davies, N. de G. (1925a), *The tomb of two sculptors at Thebes (no. 181)*. New York, Metropolitan Museum of Art.

Davies, N. de G. (1925b), The tomb of Tetaky at Thebes (No. 15). *Journal of Egyptian Archaeology* 11. 10–18.

Davies, N. de G. (1927), *Two Ramesside tombs at Thebes*. New York, Metropolitan Museum of Art.

Davies, N. de G. (1929), The town house in ancient Egypt. *Metropolitan Museum Studies* 1. 233–55.

Davies, N. de G. (1930), *The tomb of Ḳen-Amun at Thebes*. New York, Metropolitan Museum of Art.

Davies, N. de G. (1932), Tehuti: owner of Tomb 110 at Thebes. In *Studies presented to F. Ll. Griffith*. London, Egypt Exploration Society and Oxford University Press. 279–90.

Davies, N. de G. (1933a), *The tomb of Nefer-hotep at Thebes*. New York: Metropolitan Museum of Art.

Davies, N. de G. (1933b), *The tombs of Menkheperresoneb, Amenmose, and another (nos. 86, 112, 42, 226)*. London, Egypt Exploration Fund.

Davies, N. de G. (1943), *The tomb of Rekh-mi-Re' at Thebes*. New York, Metropolitan Museum of Art.

Davies, N. de G. and Gardiner, A. H. (1948), *Seven private tombs at Ḳurnah*. London, Egypt Exploration Society.

Davies, N. M. (1938), Some representations of tombs from the Theban Necropolis. *Journal of Egyptian Archaeology* 24. 25–40.

Davies, N. M. (1958), *Egyptian tomb paintings from originals, mainly of the 18th Dynasty, in the British Museum and the Bankes Collection*. London, Faber and Faber.

Davies, N. M. (1963), *Scenes from some Theban tombs (nos. 38, 66, 162, with excerpts from 81)*. Oxford, Griffith Institute.

Davies, N. M. and Gardiner, A. H. (1936), *Ancient Egyptian paintings* (3 volumes). Chicago, University of Chicago Press.

Davies, W. V. and O'Connell, E. R. (2011), British Museum Expedition to Elkab and Hagr Edfu 2011. *British Museum Studies in Ancient Egypt and Sudan* 17. 1–29.

Davis, V. L. (1980), Remarks on Michael V. Fox's "The Cairo Love Songs". *Journal of the American Oriental Society* 100, 2. 111–14.

Dawson, W. R. (1933), Studies in the Egyptian medical texts II (continued). *Journal of Egyptian Archaeology* 19. 133–37.

De Buck, A. (1935), *The ancient Egyptian Coffin Texts I: Texts of Spells 1–75*. Chicago, University of Chicago Press.

De Buck, A. (1938), *The ancient Egyptian Coffin Texts II: Texts of Spells 76–163*. Chicago, University of Chicago Press.

De Buck, A. (1947), *The ancient Egyptian Coffin Texts III: Texts of Spells 164–267*. Chicago, University of Chicago Press.

De Buck, A. (1950), The fear of premature death in ancient Egypt. In W. J. Kooiman and J. M. Van Veen (eds), *Pro regno pro sanctuario. Een bundel studies en bijdragen van vrienden en vereerders bij de zestigste verjaardag van Prof. Dr. G. van der Leeuw.* Nijkerk, Callenbach. 79–85.

De Buck, A. (1953), *The ancient Egyptian Coffin Texts IV: Texts of Spells 268–354*. Chicago, University of Chicago Press.

De Buck, A. (1954), *The ancient Egyptian Coffin Texts V: Texts of Spells 355–471*. Chicago, University of Chicago Press.

De Buck, A. (1956), *The ancient Egyptian Coffin Texts VI: Texts of Spells 472–786*. Chicago, University of Chicago Press.

De Buck, A. (1961), *The ancient Egyptian Coffin Texts VII: Texts of Spells 787–1185*. Chicago, University of Chicago Press.

De Buck, A. (1963), *Egyptian readingbook: exercises and Middle Egyptian texts* (second edition). Leiden, Nederlands Instituut voor het Nabije Oosten.

De Jong, A. (1994), Coffin Texts Spell 38: The case of the father and the son. *Studien zur Altägyptischen Kultur* 21. 141–57.

Demarée, R. J. (1982), 'Remove your stela'. In R. J. Demarée and J. J. Janssen (eds), *Gleanings from Deir el–Medina.* Leiden, Nederlands Instituut voor het Nabije Oosten. 101–7.

Demarée, R. J. (1983), *The ꜣḫ iḳr n rꜥ stelae: On ancestor worship in ancient Egypt*. Leiden, Nederlands Instituut voor het Nabije Oosten.

Demarée, R. J. (1986), More *ꜣḫ iḳr n rꜥ* stelae. *Bibliotheca Orientalis* 43. 348–51.

Demarée, R. J. (2002), Bassin à libations (no. 83). In G. Andreu (ed.), *Les artistes de pharaon: Deir el–Médineh et la Vallée des Rois.* Paris, Turnhout, Reunion des Musées Nationaux/Brepols. 140.

Demarée, R. J. (2006), *The Bankes Late Ramesside Papyri*. London, British Museum Press.

Derchain, P. (1975), Le lotus, la mandragore et le perséa. *Chronique d'Egypte* 50. 65–86.

Derchain, P. (1976), Symbols and metaphors in literature and representations of private life. *Royal Anthropological Institute News* 15. 7–10.

Derriks, C. (2001), *Les miroirs cariatides Egyptiens en bronze: typologie, chronologie et symbolique.* Mainz, Philipp von Zabern.

Desroches-Noblecourt, C. (1938), Un modèle de maison citadine du Nouvel Empire. *Revue d'Égyptologie* 3. 17–25.

Desroches-Noblecourt, C. (1963), *Tutankhamen: life and death of a pharaoh*. London, The Connoisseur and Michael Joseph.

Desroches-Noblecourt, C. (1990), Le message de la grotte sacrée. *Egypte: Vallee des Reines, Vallee des Rois, Vallee des Nobles: Dossiers d'Archéologié* 149–150. 4–21.

Dewey, W. (1999), Headrest (no. 3.25). In T. Phillips (ed.), *Africa: the art of a continent.* Munich, Prestel. 208.

Dick, M. B. and Walker, C. (1999), The induction of the cult image in ancient Mesopotamia: the Mesopotamian *mīs pî* ritual. In M. B. Dick (ed.), *Born in heaven, made on earth: the making of the cult image in the ancient Near East.* Winona Lake, IN, Eisenbrauns. 55–121.

Dittmar, J. (1986), *Blumen und Blumensträusse als Opfergabe im alten Ägypten*. Munich, Deutscher Kunstverlag.

Dodson, A. (1991), A Twenty-first Dynasty private reburial at Thebes. *Journal of Egyptian Archaeology* 77. 180–2.

Donadoni, A. M., Leospo, E., D'Amicone, E., Roccati, A. and Donadoni, S. (1996), *Il Museo Egizio di Torino: Guida alla lettura di una civiltà*. Novara, DeAgostini.

Dondelinger, E. (1987), *Das Totenbuch des Schreibers Ani*. Graz, Adeva.

Donnat, S. (2002), Le bol comme support de la lettre au mort: Vers la mise en évidence d'un rituel magique. *La magie en Égypte: à la recherche d'une définition, cycle de conférences, musée du Louvre 2000.* Paris, Musée du Louvre. 209–36.

Donnat, S. (2003), *La peur du mort: Nature et structures des relations entre les vivants et les morts dans l'Egypte pharaonique*. Départément d'histoire de l'art et d'archéologie. Montpellier, Université Paul Valéry – Montpellier III. Unpublished doctoral thesis.

Donnat, S. (2007a), Beschriftete Objekte: Totenbrief? No. 328. In E. Graefe (ed.), *Die Doppelgrabanlage "M" aus dem Mittleren Reich unter TT 196 im Tal el–Asasif in Theben–West.* Aachen, Shaker. 136–41.

Donnat, S. (2007b), Contacts with the dead in pharaonic Egypt: ritual relationships and dead classification. Formerly at: www.uni–koeln.de/phil–fak/afrikanistik/down/insvisible/Donnat%Sylvie_Contacts.pdf.

Dorman, P. F. (1988), *The monuments of Senenmut: problems in historical methodology*. London and New York, Kegan Paul International.

Dorman, P. F. (1995), Two tombs and one owner. In J. Assmann *et al.* (eds), *Thebanische Beamtennekropolen: Neue Perspektiven archäologischer Forschung, Internationales Symposion.* Heidelberg, Heidelberger Orientverlag. 141–54.

Dorman, P. F. (2003), Family burial and commemoration in the Theban necropolis. In N. Strudwick and J. H. Taylor (eds), *The Theban necropolis: past, present and future.* London, British Museum Press. 30–41.

Dornan, J. L. (2004), Beyond belief: religious experience, ritual, and cultural neuro–phenomenology in the interpretation of past religious systems. *Cambridge Archaeological Journal* 14.1. 25–36.

Drioton, É, (1927), *Rapport sur les fouilles de Médamoud (1926): Les inscriptions*. Cairo, Institut Français d'Archéologie Orientale.

Duchesne-Guillemin, M. (1981), Music in ancient Mesopotamia and Egypt. *World Archaeology* 12, 3. 287–97.

Dunand, F. (2004), Les enfants et la mort en Egypte. In V. Dasen (ed.), *Naissance et petite enfance dans l'Antiquité: Actes du colloque de Fribourg 2001*. Göttingen, Vandenhoeck and Ruprecht. 13–32.

Duquesne, T. (2007), *Anubis, Upwawet, and other deities: personal worship and official religion in ancient Egypt*. Cairo, The Egyptian Museum/Supreme Council of Antiquities.

Dziobek, E. (1992), *Das Grab des Ineni, Theban Nr. 81*. Mainz, Philipp von Zabern.

Dziobek, E. (1995), Theban tombs as a source for historical and biographical evaluation: the case of User–Amun. In J. Assmann *et al.* (eds), *Thebanische Beamtennekropolen: Neue Perspektiven archäologischer Forschung, Internationales Symposion.* Heidelberg, Heidelberger Orientverlag. 129–40.

Eaton-Krauss, M. (1982), Broad collar, no. 308. In E. J. Brovarski, S. K. Doll and R. E. Freed, (eds), *Egypt's golden age: the art of living in the New Kingdom 1558–1085 B.C.* Boston, Museum of Fine Arts. 234–5.

Eaton-Krauss, M. (1984), *The representations of statuary in private tombs of the Old Kingdom.* Wiesbaden, Otto Harrassowitz.

Eaton-Krauss, M. and Graefe, E. (1985), *The small golden shrine from the tomb of Tutankhamun.* Oxford, Griffith Institute.

Eckhardt, H. and Williams, H. (2003), Objects without a past? The use of Roman objects in early Anglo–Saxon graves. In H. Williams (ed.), *Archaeologies of remembrance: death and memory in past societies.* New York, Springer. 141–70.

Edel, E. (1984), *Die Inschriften der Grabfronten der Siut–Gräber in Mittelägypten aus der Herakleopolitenzeit: Eine Wiederherstellung nach den Zeichnungen der Description de l'Egypte.* Opladen, Westdeutscher Verlag.

Edwards, I. E. S. (1960), *Oracular amuletic decrees of the late New Kingdom.* London, British Museum Press.

Effras, B. (2003), Memories of the early medieval past: grave artefacts in 19th century France and 20th century America. In H. Williams (ed.), *Archaeologies of remembrance: death and memory in past societies.* New York, Springer. 225–80.

El-Dalmaty, M. M. (1990), Squatting statues in the Cairo Museum. *Mitteilungen des Deutschen Archäologischen Instituts, Abteilung Kairo* 46. 1–13.

El-Leithy, H. (2003), Letters to the dead in ancient and modern Egypt. In Z. Hawass and L. Pinch Brock (eds), *Egyptology at the dawn of the Twenty-first Century: Proceedings of the Eighth International Congress of Egyptologists, Volume 3: Language, conservation, museology.* Cairo, American University in Cairo Press. 304–13.

El-Mouelhy, M., El-Helw, M., Younis, N., Khattab, H. and Zurayk, H. (1994), Women's understanding of pregnancy-related morbidity in rural Egypt. *Reproductive Health Matters* 2, 4. 27–34.

El-Noubi, M. (1998), A harper's song from the tomb of Roma-Roy at Thebes (TT 283). *Studien zur Altägyptischen Kultur* 25. 251–5.

El-Saady (1996), *The tomb of Amenemhab, no. 44 at Qurnah. The tomb-chapel of a priest carrying the shrine of Amun.* Warminster, Aris & Phillips.

El-Shimy, M. (2003), The preparation and use of perfumed substances in ancient Egypt. In Z. Hawass and L. Pinch Brock (eds), *Egyptology at the dawn of the Twenty-first Century: Proceedings from the Eighth International Congress of Egyptologists, Volume 3: Language, conservation, museology.* Cairo, American University in Cairo Press. 509–13.

El-Shohoumi, N. (2004), *Der Tod im Leben: eine vergleichende Analyse altägyptischer und rezenter ägyptischer Totenbräuche.* Vienna, Verlag der Österreischischen Akademie der Wissenschaften.

El-Shohoumi, N. (2006), 'Stay a while at my grave': Two modern Islamic tomb-inscriptions and the ancient Egyptian 'appeals to the living'. In E. Czerny *et al.* (eds), *Timelines: Studies in honour of Manfred Bietak, III.* Leuven, Peeters. 351–60.

Emboden, W. A. (1978), The sacred narcotic water lily of the Nile: Nymphaea Caerulea. *Economic Botany* 32, 4. 395–407.

Emboden, W. A. (1981), Transcultural use of narcotic water lilies in ancient Egypt and Maya drug ritual. *Journal of Ethnopharmacology* 3. 39–83.

Endruweit, A. (1998), Houses, cities, and palaces – ancient Egyptian lifestyles. In R. Schultz and M. Seidel (eds), *Egypt: the world of the pharaohs.* Cologne, Könemann. 386–97.

Englund, G. (1978), *Akh - une notion religieuse dans l'Egypte pharaonique*. Uppsala, Acta Universitatis Upsaliensis.

Engelbach, R. (1915), *Riqqeh and Memphis VI*. London, British School of Archaeology in Egypt.

Enmarch, R. (2008), The language of grief: reflections on the laments of Isis and Nephthys in some mortuary liturgies attested in the Coffin Texts. *Tenth International Congress of Egyptologists*. Rhodes, University of the Aegean. www.rhodes.aegean.gr/tms/XICE%20Abstract%20book.pdf. 80.

Epigraphic Survey (1954), *Reliefs and inscriptions at Karnak III: The Bubastite Portal*. Chicago, University of Chicago Press.

Etienne, M. (2000), *Heka: magie et envoûtement dans l'Egypte ancienne*. Paris, Réunion des Musées Nationaux.

Evans-Prichard, E. E. (1956), *Nuer religion*. Oxford, Oxford University Press.

Evans-Prichard, E. E. (1940), *The Nuer: a description of the modes of livelihood and political institutions of a Nilotic people*. Oxford, Oxford University Press.

Exell, K. (2008), Ancestor bust. In W. Wendrich (ed.), *UCLA Encyclopedia of Egyptology*. Los Angeles, UCLA. http://www.escholarship.org/uc/item/59k7832w.

Exell, K. (2006), The Senior Scribe Ramose (1) and the cult of the king: a social and historical reading of some private votive stelae from Deir el Medina in the reign of Ramesses II. In R. J. Dann (ed.), *Current Research in Egyptology 2004: Proceedings of the Fifth Annual Symposium, University of Durham, 2004*. Oxford, Oxbow Books. 51–67.

Eyre, C. J. (1987), Work and the organisation of work in the New Kingdom. In M. A. Powell (ed.), *Labor in the ancient Near East*. New Haven, American Oriental Society. 167–221.

Eyre, C. J. (1992), The adoption papyrus in social context. *Journal of Egyptian Archaeology* 78. 207–21.

Eyre, C. J. (2002), *The cannibal hymn: a cultural and literary study*. Liverpool, University of Liverpool Prcss.

Fairman, H. W. (1954), Worship and festivals in an Egyptian temple. *Bulletin of the John Rylands Library* 37. 165–203.

Fantechi, S. E. and Zingarelli, A. P. (2002), Singers and musicians in New Kingdom Egypt. *Göttinger Miszellen* 186. 27–35.

Faraone, C. A. (1991), Burying and binding the forces of evil: the defensive use of "voodoo dolls" in ancient Greece. *Classical Antiquity* 10, 2. 165–220.

Faulkner, R. O. (1936), The Bremner–Rhind Papyus: I. A. The songs of Isis and Nephthys. *Journal of Egyptian Archaeology* 22. 121–40.

Faulkner, R. O. (1962a), *A concise dictionary of Middle Egyptian*. Oxford, Griffith Institute.

Faulkner, R. O. (1962b), Spells 38–40 of the Coffin Texts. *Journal of Egyptian Archaeology* 48. 36–44.

Faulkner, R. O. (1969), *The ancient Egyptian Pyramid Texts*. Oxford, Clarendon Press.

Faulkner, R. O. (1973), *The ancient Egyptian Coffin Texts (Spells 1–354)*. Warminster, Aris & Phillips.

Faulkner, R. O. (1977), *The ancient Egyptian Coffin Texts (Spells 355–787)*. Warminster, Aris & Phillips.

Faulkner, R. O. (1978), *The ancient Egyptian Coffin Texts (Spells 788–1185)*. Warminster, Aris & Phillips.

Faulkner, R. O. (1985), *The ancient Egyptian Book of the Dead*. London, British Museum Publications.

Federn, W. (1946), The opening lines of the Antef song. *Journal of Near Eastern Studies* 5, 4. 259.

Ferguson, T. J., Dongoske, K. E. and Kuwanwisiwma, L. J. (2001), Hopi perspectives on Southwestern mortuary studies. In D. R. Mitchell and J. L. Brunson-Hadley (eds), *Ancient burial practices in the American Southwest: Archaeology, physical anthropology, and native American perspectives.* Albuquerque, University of New Mexico Press. 9–26.

Feucht, E. (1995), *Das Kind im alten Ägypten: Die Stellung des Kindes in Familie und Gesellschaft nach altägyptischen Texten und Darstellungen.* Frankfurt and New York, Campus.

Filer, J. (1998), Mother and baby burials. *Orientalia* 82. 391–399.

Finnestad, R. B. (1978), The meaning and purpose of Opening the Mouth in mortuary contexts. *Numen* 25. 118–34.

Finnestad, R. B. (1999), Enjoying the pleasures of sensation: reflections on a significant feature of Egyptian religion. In E. Teeter and J. A. Larson (eds), *Gold of praise: Studies on ancient Egypt in honor of Edward F. Wente.* Chicago, Oriental Institute of the University of Chicago. 111–19.

Fischer, H. G. (1963), Varia aegyptiaca. *Journal of the American Research Center in Egypt* 2. 17–51.

Fischer, H. G. (1972), Some emblematic uses of hieroglyphs with particular reference to an archaic ritual vessel. *Metropolitan Museum Journal* 5. 5–23.

Fischer, H. G. (1973), An eleventh dynasty couple holding the sign of life. *Zeitschrift für Ägyptische Sprache und Altertumskunde* 100. 16–28.

Fischer, H. G. (1975), An elusive shape within the fisted hands of Egyptian statues. *Metropolitan Museum Journal* 10. 143–55.

Fischer, H. G. (1976), More emblematic uses from ancient Egypt. *Metropolitan Museum Journal* 11. 125–28.

Fischer-Elfert, H.-W. (1998), *Die Vision von Statue in Stein: Studien zum altägyptischen Mundöffnungsritual.* Heidelberg, Carl Winter, Universitätsverlag.

Fischer-Elfert, H.-W. (2003), Representations of the past in New Kingdom literature. In W. J. Tait (ed.), *'Never had the like occurred': Egypt's view of its past.* London, UCL Press. 119–37.

Fischer-Elfert, H.-W. (2005), *Abseits von Ma'at. Fallstudien zu Außenseitern im Alten Ägypten.* Würzburg, Ergon.

Fitzenreiter, M. (1994), Zum Ahnenkult in Ägypten. *Göttinger Miszellen* 143. 51–72.

Fitzenreiter, M. (1995), Totenverehrung und soziale Repräsentation im thebanischen Beamtengrab der 18. Dynastie. *Studien zur Altägyptischen Kultur* 22. 95–130.

Fleischer, A. and Fleischer, Z. (1994), The fragrance of Biblical mandrake. *Economic Botany* 48, 3. 243–51.

Follmi, D., and Follmi, O. (2005), *African wisdom: 365 days.* London and New York, Thames and Hudson.

Fox, M. V. (1977), A study of Antef. *Orientalia* 46. 393–423.

Fox, M. V. (1985), *The Song of Songs and the ancient Egyptian love songs.* Madison and London, University of Wisconsin Press.

Frandsen, P. J. (1986), Tabu. In C. Meyer (ed.) *Lexikon der Ägyptologie.* Wiesbaden, Harrassowitz. 135–42.

Frandsen, P. J. (1992), The letter to Ikhtay's coffin: O. Louvre Inv. No. 698. In R. J. Demarée and A. Egberts (eds), *Village voices: proceedings of the symposium 'Texts from Deir el-Medîna and their interpretation', Leiden, May 31–June 1, 1991.* Leiden, Centre of Non–Western Studies. 31–49.

Frandsen, P. J. (1999), On fear of death and the three *bwts* connected with Hathor. In E. Teeter and J. A. Larson (eds), *Gold of praise: Studies in honor of Edward F. Wente.* Chicago, The Oriental Institute of the University of Chicago. 131–47.

Frandsen, P. J. (2007), The menstrual 'taboo' in ancient Egypt. *Journal of Near Eastern Studies* 66, 2. 81–106.

Franke, D. (1988), Die Hockerstatue des Sonbso-mei in Leiden und Statuen mit nach oben gerichteten Handflächen. *Oudheidkundige Mededelingen uit het Rijksmuseum van Oudheden te Leiden* 68. 59–76.

Frankfort, H. (1952), State festivals in Egypt and Mesopotamia. *Journal of the Warburg and Courtauld Institutes* 15. 1–12.

Frankfort, H. and Pendlebury, J. D. S. (1933), *The City of Akhenaten II: The Northern Suburb and the desert altars*. London, Egypt Exploration Society.

Frédéricq, M. (1927), The ointment spoons in the Egyptian section of the British Museum. *Journal of Egyptian Archaeology* 13. 7–13.

Freed, R. E. (1981), *Egypt's Golden Age: The art of living in the New Kingdom 1558–1085 B.C. (colour supplement)*. Boston, Museum of Fine Arts.

Freed, R. E. (1982), Cosmetic arts; cylindrical box, no. 237. In E. Brovarski, S. K. Doll and R. E. Freed (eds), *Egypt's Golden Age: The art of the living in the New Kingdom 1558–1085 B.C.* Boston, Museum of Fine Arts. 199–200, 203.

Friedman, F. D. (1982), Review of G. Englund *'Akh – une notion religieuse dans l'Egypte pharaonique.* Journal of the American Research Center in Egypt 19. 145–8.

Friedman, F. D. (1985), On the meaning of some anthropoid busts from Deir el–Medina. *Journal of Egyptian Archaeology* 71. 82–97.

Friedman, F. D. (1986), *ꜣḫ* in the Amarna period. *Journal of the American Research Center in Egypt* 23. 99–106.

Friedman, F. D. (1994), Aspects of domestic life and religion. In L. H. Lesko (ed.), *Pharaoh's workers: the villagers of Deir el Medina.* Ithaca and London, Cornell University Press. 95–117.

Friedman, F. D. (ed.), (1998), *Gifts of the Nile: Ancient Egyptian faience*. London, Thames and Hudson.

Friedman, F. D. (2001), Akh. In D. B. Redford (ed.), *The Oxford encyclopaedia of ancient Egypt I.* New York, Oxford University Press. 47–8.

Frood, E. (2007), *Biographical texts from Ramessid Egypt*. Atlanta, Society of Biblical Literature.

Frood, E. (in press), Sensuous experience, performance and presence in Third Intermediate Period biography. In R. Enmarch and V. Lepper (eds), *Ancient Egyptian literature: theory and practice*. London, British Academy. 86–108.

Fuscaldo, P. (2003), Tell al-Daba: Two execration pits and a foundation deposit. In Z. Hawass and L. Pinch Brock (eds), *Egyptology at the dawn of the Twenty-first Century: Proceedings of the Eighth International Congress of Egyptologists, Volume 1: Archaeology.* Cairo, American University in Cairo Press. 185–8.

Gaber, H. (2002), Différences thématiques dans la décoration des tombes thébaines polychromes et monochromes de Deir al-Médina. *Bulletin de l'Institut Français d'Archéologie Orientale* 102. 211–30.

Galán, J. M. (2003), Amenhotep Son of Hapu as intermediary between people and god. In Z. Hawass and L. Pinch Brock (eds), *Egyptology at the dawn of the Twenty–first Century: Proceedings of the Eighth International Congress of Egyptologists, Volume 2: History, religion.* Cairo, American University in Cairo Press. 221–9.

Galán, J. M. (2007), The tombs of Djehuty and Hery (TT 11–12) at Dra Abu el-Naga. In J.-C. Goyon and C. Cardin (eds), *Proceedings of the Ninth International Congress of Egyptologists 1.* Leuven, Peeters. 777–87.

Galán, J. M. (2009), Early investigations in the tomb-chapel of Djehuty (TT 11). In D. Magee, J. Bourriau and S. Quirke (eds), *Sitting beside Lepsius: studies in honour of Jaromir Malek at the Griffith Institute*. Leuven, Peeters. 155–81.

Galán, J. M. and Menéndez, G. (2011), The funerary banquet of Hery (TT 12), robbed and restored. *Journal of Egyptian Archaeology* 97. 143–166.

Gallorini, C. (1998), A reconstruction of Petrie's excavation at the Middle Kingdom settlement at Lahun. In S. Quirke (ed.), *Lahun studies*. Reigate, Sia Publishing. 42–59.

Galpaz-Feller, P. (2000), Pregnancy and birth in the Bible and ancient Egypt (comparative study). *Biblische Notizen* 102. 42–53.

Gardiner, A. H. (1913), The statue of Amenhotep. In W. M. F Petrie, G. A.Wainwright and A. H. Gardiner, *Tarkhan I and Memphis V*. London, Egypt Exploration Fund. 33–6.

Gardiner, A. H. (1928), The graffito from the tomb of Perē. *Journal of Egyptian Archaeology* 14. 10–1.

Gardiner, A. H. (1930), A new letter to the dead. *Journal of Egyptian Archaeology* 26. 18–22.

Gardiner, A. H. (1935a), *Hieratic papyri in the British Museum. Third series: Chester Beatty Gift*. London, British Museum.

Gardiner, A. H. (1935b), *The attitude of the ancient Egyptians to death and the dead*. Cambridge, Cambridge University Press.

Gardiner, A. H. (1946), The Instruction addressed to Kagemni and his brethren. *Journal of Egyptian Archaeology* 32. 71–4.

Gardiner, A. H. (1957), *Egyptian grammar: Being an introduction to the study of hieroglyphs*. Oxford, Griffith Institute.

Gardiner, A. H. and Davies, N. de G. (1915), *The tomb of Amenemhet (TT 82)*. London, Egypt Exploration Fund.

Gardiner, A. H. and Sethe, K. (1928), *Egyptian letters to the dead, mainly from the Old and Middle Kingdoms*. London, Egypt Exploration Society.

Gaston, A.-M. (1991), Dance and the Hindu woman: Bharatanātyam re-ritualized. In J. Leslie (ed.), *Roles and rituals for Hindu women*. London, Pinter Publishers. 149–71.

Gee, J. (2002), Oracle by image: Coffin Text 103 in context. In L. Ciraolo and J. Seidel (eds), *Magic and divination in the ancient world*. Leiden, Brill, Styx. 83–8.

Gee, J. (2003), *B3* sending and its implications. In Z. Hawass and L. P. Brock (eds), *Egyptology at the dawn of the Twenty-first Century: Proceedings of the Eighth International Congress of Egyptologists, Volume 2: History, religion*. Cairo and New York, American University in Cairo Press. 230–7.

Gee, J. (2009), A new look at the conception of the human being in ancient Egypt. In R. Nyord and A. Kjølby (eds), *'Being in ancient Egypt': Thoughts on agency, materiality and cognition, proceedings of the seminar held in Copenhagen, September 29–30, 2006*. Copenhagen, Archaeopress, Oxford. 1–14.

Germer, R. (1985), *Flora des pharaonischen Ägypten*. Mainz, Philipp von Zabern.

Germer, R. (1989), *Die Pflanzenmaterialien aus dem Grab des Tutanchamun*. Hildesheim, Gerstenberg.

Germer, R. (1990), Pflanzlicher Mumienschmuck und andere altägyptische Pflanzenreste im Ägyptischen Museum. *Forschungen und Berichte* 28. 7–15.

Giddy, L. L. (1999), *The survey of Memphis: Kom Rabi'a: the New Kingdom and post-New Kingdom objects*. London, Egypt Exploration Society.

Gilbert, P. (1949), *La poésie egyptienne*. Brussels. Fondation Égyptologique Reine Élisabeth.

Glazier, J. (1984), Mbeere ancestors and the domestication of death. *Journal of the Royal Anthropological Institute (Man)* 19. 133–47.

Gluckman, M. (1937), Mortuary customs and the belief in survival after death among the south-eastern Bantu. *Bantu Studies* 11. 117–36.

Goebs, K. (2008), *Crowns in Egyptian funerary literature: royalty, rebirth and destruction*. Oxford, Griffith Institute.

Goedicke, H. (1971), *Re-used blocks from the pyramid of Amenemhet I at Lisht*. New York, Metropolitan Museum of Art.

Goedicke, H. (1977), The date of the 'Antef Song'. In J. Assmann, E. Feucht and R. Grieshammer (eds), *Fragen on die altägyptische Literatur: Studien zum Gedenken an Eberhard Otto*. Wiesbaden, Dr. Ludwig Reichert. 185–96.

Goedicke, H. (1982), A 'new' relief showing a blind harpist. *Bulletin Société d'Égyptologie de Genève* 7. 33–8.

Gordon, A. (1982), House model (no. 1). In E. J. Brovarski, S. K. Doll and R. E. Freed (eds), *Egypt's Golden Age: the art of living in the New Kingdom 1558–1085 B.C.* Boston, Museum of Fine Arts. 34–5.

Gordon, A. H. (1996), The *k3* as an animating force. *Journal of the American Research Center in Egypt* 33. 31–5.

Gordon, A. H. and Schwabe, C. W. (1998), 'Live flesh' and 'Opening-of-the-Mouth:' Biomedical, ethnological, and Egyptological aspects. In C. J. Eyre (ed.), *Proceedings of the Seventh International Congress of Egyptologists, Cambridge 3-4th September 1995*. Leuven, Peeters. 461–9.

Goyon, J.-C. (2000), Rituels de l'embaumement et des funérailles. *Images et rites d'éternité en Egypte: Dossiers d'Archéologié* 257. 14–25.

Grandet, P. (2002), Ostracon: liste de mobilier (no. 3). In G. Andreu (ed.), *Les artistes de Pharaon: Deir el-Médineh et la Vallée des Rois*. Paris, Turnhout, Reunion des Musées Nationaux/ Brepols. 75.

Graves-Brown, C. A. (2005), The spitting goddess and the stony eye: Divinity and flint in pharaonic Egypt. In K. Piquette and S. Love (eds), *Current Research in Egyptology: Proceedings of the Fourth Annual Symposium, University College London, 2003*. Oxford, Oxbow Books. 57–70.

Graves-Brown, C. A. (2006), Emergent flints. In K. Szpakowska (ed.), *Through a glass darkly: magic, dreams and prophecy in ancient Egypt*. Swansea, Classical Press of Wales. 47–62.

Gray, P. H. K. and Slow, D. (1968), *Egyptian mummies in the City of Liverpool Museums*. Liverpool, Liverpool Corporation.

Greven, L. (1954), *Der Ka in Theologie und Königskult der Äegypter des Alten Reiches*. Glückstadt, Hamburg, New York, J. J. Augustin.

Grieshammer, R. (1975–6), Zur Formgeschichte der Sprüche 38–41 der Sargtexte. *Orientalia Lovaniensia Periodica* 6–7. 231–5.

Griffith, F. Fl. (1915), A new monument from Coptos. *Journal of Egyptian Archaeology* 2. 5–7.

Griffiths, J. G. (1971), Review of R. Grieshammer *Das Jenseitsgericht in den Sargtexten*. *Journal of Egyptian Archaeology* 57. 211.

Grinsell, L. V. (1960), The breaking of objects as a funerary rite. *Folklore* 71. 475–91.

Grinsell, L. V. (1975), *Barrow, pyramid and tomb: ancient burial customs in Egypt, the Mediterranean and the British Isles*. London, Thames and Hudson.

Guasch-Jané, M. R., Andrés-Lacueva, C., Jáuregui, O. and Lamuela-Raventós, R. M. (2006a), The origin of the ancient Egyptian drink *Shedeh* revealed using LC/MS/MS. *Journal of Archaeological Science* 33. 98–101.

Guasch-Jané, M. R., Andrés-Lacueva, C., Jáuregui, O. and Lamuela-Raventós, R. M. (2006b), First evidence of white wine from ancient Egypt from Tutankhamun's tomb. *Journal of Archaeological Science* 33. 1075–80.

Guksch, H. (1995), *Die Gräber des Nacht-Min und des Men-cheper-Ra-seneb: Theben Nr. 87 und 79*. Mainz, Philipp von Zabern.

Gunn, B. (1916), The religion of the poor in ancient Egypt. *Journal of Egyptian Archaeology* 3. 81–94.

Gunn, B. (1930), Review of A. H. Gardiner and K. Sethe; *Egyptian letters to the dead, mainly from the Old and Middle Kingdoms*. *Journal of Egyptian Archaeology* 26. 147–55.

Habachi, L. (1974), Three objects of unusual form. *Studia Aegyptiaca* 1. 137–50.

Habachi, L. (1976), The royal scribe Amenmose, son of Penzerti and Mutemonet: His monuments in Egypt and abroad. In J. H. Johnson and E. F. Wente (eds), *Studies in honor of George R. Hughes*. Chicago, Oriental Institute of the University of Chicago. 83–103.

Hackett, R. I. J. (1996), *Art and religion in Africa*. London, Cassell.

Haeny, G. (1979), New Kingdom architecture. In K. R. Weeks (ed.), *Egyptology and the social sciences*. Cairo, American University in Cairo Press. 85–94.

Hagen, F. and Koefoed, H. (2005), Private feasts at Deir el-Medina. Aspects of eating and drinking in an ancient Egyptian village. *Archaeological Review from Cambridge* 20.2. 6–31.

Haimov-Kochman, R., Sciaky-Tamir, Y. and Hurwitz, A. (2005), Reproduction concepts and practices in ancient Egypt mirrored by modern medicine. *European Journal of Obstetrics and Gynaecology and Reproductive Biology* 123. 3–8.

Halcrow, S. E. and Tayles, N. (2011), The bioarchaeological investigation of children and childhood. In S. C. Agarwal and B. A. Glencross (eds), *Social bioarchaeology*. Oxford, Blackwell. 333–59.

Hammond, P. B. (1978), *An introduction to cultural and social anthropology* (second edition). New York and London, Macmillan.

Harer, W. B. (1985), Pharmacological and biological properties of the Egyptian lotus. *Journal of the American Research Center in Egypt* 22. 49–54.

Hari, R. (1985), *La tombe thébaine du Père Divin Neferhotep (TT 50)*. Editions de Belles-Lettres, Geneva.

Haring, B. (2003), From oral practice to written record in Ramesside Deir el-Medina. *Journal of the Economic and Social History of the Orient* 46. 249–72.

Haring, B. (2003), Pratique écrite et pratique orale à Deir el-Médineh. In G. Andreu (ed.), *Deir el-Médineh et la Vallée des Rois: La vie en Égypte au temps des pharaons du Nouvel Empire*. Paris, Éditions Khéops, Musée du Louvre. 139–56.

Harpur, Y. (1987), *Decoration in Egyptian tombs of the Old Kingdom: studies in orientation and scene content*. London and New York, Kegan Paul International.

Harpur, Y. (2009), Re-used blocks in the Eighteenth Dynasty tomb of Maya at Saqqara: a preview of nine reliefs from an unpublished corpus. In D. Magee, J. Bourriau and S. Quirke (eds), *Sitting beside Lepsius: Studies in honour of Jaromir Malek at the Griffith Institute*. Leuven, Peeters. 203–25.

Harrington, N. (2005), From the cradle to the grave: Anthropoid busts and ancestor cults at Deir el Medina. In K. Piquette and S. Love (eds), *Current Research in Egyptology 2003: Proceedings of the Fourth Annual Symposium, University College London, 2003*. Oxford, Oxbow Books. 71–88.

Harrington, N. (2005/2007), A new approach to the small golden shrine of Tutankhamun. *Discussions in Egyptology* 63. 59–66.

Harrington, N. (2007), Children and the dead in New Kingdom Egypt. In R. Mairs and A. Stevenson (eds), *Current Research in Egyptology 2005: Proceedings of the Sixth Annual Symposium, University of Cambridge, 2005*. Oxford, Oxbow Books. 51–65.

Harrington, N. (2009), Funerary furniture made to order? UC 14228. In D. Magee, J. Bourriau, and S. Quirke (eds), *Sitting beside Lepsius: Studies in honour of Jaromir Malek at the Griffith Institute*. Leuven, Peeters. 227–36.

Harrington, N. (2013, in press), The 18th Dynasty banquet: ideals and realities. In C. Draycott (ed.), *Dining and Death: interdisciplinary perspectives on the 'Funerary Banquet' in ancient art, burial and belief.* Leuven, Peeters.

Harrington, N. (2013, forthcoming), Ancestor and ancestral ceremony/ancestor worship. In R. Segal and K. von Stuckrad (eds), *Vocabulary for the Study of Religion, Volume 1*. Leiden, Brill

Hartwig, M. (2004), *Tomb painting and identity in ancient Thebes, 1419–1372 BCE*. Turnhout, Fondation Égyptologique Reine Élisabeth; Brepols.

Hasegawa, S. (2003), The New Kingdom Necropolis at Dahshur. In Z. Hawass and L. Pinch–Brock (eds), *Egyptology at the dawn of the Twenty-first Century: Proceedings of the Eighth International Congress of Egyptologists, Volume 1: Archaeology.* Cairo and New York, American University in Cairo Press. 229–133.

Hassan, S. (1943), *Excavations at Giza, IV*. Oxford, Oxford University Press.

Hatem, M. (1987), Toward the study of the psychodynamics of mothering and gender in Egyptian families. *International Journal of Middle East Studies* 19, 3. 287–305.

Hawass, Z. (2009), *The lost tombs of Thebes*. London, New York, Thames and Hudson.

Hayes, W. C. (1939), *The burial chamber of the treasurer Sobk-mose from er-Rizeikat*. New York, Metropolitan Museum of Art.

Hayes, W. C. (1959), *The Scepter of Egypt II: The Hyksos Period and the New Kingdom*. New York, Metropolitan Museum of Art.

Hays, H. (2009), Between identity and agency in ancient Egyptian ritual. In R. Nyord and A. Kjølby (eds), *'Being in ancient Egypt': Thoughts on agency, materiality and cognition, proceedings of the seminar held in Copenhagen, September 29–30, 2006*. Oxford, Archaeopress. 15–30.

Hays, H. (2010), Funerary rituals (pharaonic period). In W. Wendrich and J. Dieleman (eds), *UCLA encyclopaedia of Egyptology.* Los Angeles. http://www.escholarship.org/uc/item/1r32g9zn.

Heiden, D. (2003), New aspects of the treatment of the cult statue in the daily temple ritual. In Z. Hawass and L. Pinch Brock (eds), *Egyptology at the dawn of the Twenty-first century: Proceedings of the Eighth International Congress of Egyptologists, Volume 2: History, religion.* Cairo, American University in Cairo Press. 308–15.

Helck, W. (1959), *Urkunden der 18. Dynastie Heft 22*. Berlin, Akademie–Verlag.

Helck, W. (ed.), (1985), *Nofret die Schöne: Die Frau im Alten Ägypten*. Hildesheim, Roemer und Pelizaeus Museum.

Hellinckx, B. R. (2001), The symbolic assimilation of head and sun as expressed by headrests. *Studien zur Altägyptischen Kultur* 29. 61–95.

Hema, R. H. (2005), *Group statues of private individuals in the New Kingdom*. Oxford, British Archaeological Reports.

Hentschel, K. (1987), *Ǧinn-Glaube, Zauber- und Heilwesen im heutigen Kairo*. Unpublished doctoral dissertation. University of Vienna.

Hepper, F. N. (2009), *Pharaoh's flowers: the botanical treasures of Tutankhamun* (second edition). Chicago, KWS Publishers/University of Chicago Press.

Herbin, F. R. (2000), Une brève histoire des textes funéraires égyptiens. *Images et rites d'éternité en Egypte: Dossiers d'Archéologié* 257. 4–13.

Hermann, A. (1940), *Die Stelen der thebanischen Felsgräber der 18. Dynastie*. Glückstadt and New York, J. J. Augustin.

Hildburgh, W. L. (1951), Psychology underlying the employment of amulets in Europe. *Folklore* 62, 1. 231–51.

Hobbs, J. J. (1998), Troubling fields: the opium poppy in Egypt. *Geographical Review* 88, 1. 64–85.

Hofmann, E. (1995a), *Das Grab des Neferrenpet gen. Kenro (TT 178)*. Mainz, Philipp von Zabern.

Hofmann, E. (1995b), Typen ramessidischer Plastik in thebanischen Privatgräbern. In J. Assmann *et al.* (eds), *Thebanische Beamtennekropolen: Neue Perspektiven archäologischer Forschung Internationales Symposion.* Heidelberg, Heidelberger Orientverlag. 271–9.

Hofmann, E. (2004), *Bilder im Wandel: Die Kunst der ramessidischen Privatgräber*. Mainz, Philipp von Zabern.

Holden, L. H. (1982), Votive stela (no. 408); Votive stela dedicated to Amen-Re (no. 410). In E. J. Brovarski, S. K. Doll and R. E. Freed (eds), *Egypt's golden age: the art of living in the New Kingdom 1558–1085 B.C.* Boston, Museum of Fine Arts. 298–301.

Hölzl, R. (2001), Zur Typologie der Opfertafeln und Kultbecken. *Göttinger Miszellen* 183. 53–69.

Hope, V. M. (2003), Remembering Rome: Memory, funerary monuments and the Roman soldier. In H. Williams (ed.), *Archaeologies of remembrance: death and memory in past societies.* New York, Springer. 113–40.

Hornung, E. (1967), *Das Amduat: die Schrift des verborgenen Raumes III: Die Kurzfassung; Nachträge*. Wiesbaden, Otto Harrassowitz.

Hornung, E. (1968), *Altägyptische Höllenvorstellungen*. Berlin, Akademie-Verlag.

Hornung, E. (1979), *Das Totenbuch der Ägypter*. Zurich, Artemis.

Hornung, E. (1982), *Conceptions of god in ancient Egypt: the one and the many*, trans. J. Baines. Ithaca, Cornell University Press.

Hornung, E. (1990), *The Valley of the Kings: Horizon of eternity*, trans. D. Warburton. New York, Timken.

Hornung, E. (1992), *Idea into image: Essays on ancient Egyptian thought*, trans. E. Bredeck. New York, Timken.

Hornung, E. (1999), *The ancient Egyptian books of the afterlife*, trans. D. Lorton. Ithaca and London, Cornell University Press.

Hornung, E. (2008), Some remarks on the inhabitants of the West. *Spotlight on Egyptian religion: study day*. Department of Zoology/Fitzwilliam Museum, University of Cambridge.

Hornung, E. and Abt, T. (2007), *The Egyptian Amduat: The Book of the Hidden Chamber*, trans. D. Warburton. Zurich, Living Human Heritage.

Hozumi, N. (1901), *Ancestor worship and Japanese law*. Tokyo, Z. P. Maruya.

Hunter, M. L. (1964), *Memory*. Harmondsworth, Pelican Books.

Ikram, S. (1989), Domestic shrines and the cult of the royal family at el-'Amarna. *Journal of Egyptian Archaeology* 75. 89–101.

Ikram, S. and Dodson, A. (1998), *The mummy in ancient Egypt: Equipping the dead for eternity*. London and New York, Thames and Hudson.

Irvine, F. R. and Trickett, R. S. (1953), Waterlilies as food. *Kew Bulletin* 8, 3. 363–70.

Iversen, E. (1979), The Chester Beatty Papyrus, No. I. *Journal of Egyptian Archaeology* 65. 78–88.

James, T. G. H. (1970), *Hieroglyphic texts from Egyptian stelae etc.* 9. London, British Museum Publications.

James, T. G. H. and Davies, W. V. (1983), *Egyptian sculpture*. London, British Museum Press.

Janák, J. (2006), *New light on the akh-bird*. Paper presented at the seventh Current Research in Egyptology Symposium. Oxford.

Janes, G. (2002), *Shabtis: A private view. Ancient Egyptian funerary statuettes in European private collections*. Paris, Cybele.

Janssen, J. J. (1975), *Commodity prices in the Ramessid Period: an economic study of the village of necropolis workmen at Thebes*. Leiden, E. J. Brill.

Janssen, J. J. (1980), Absence from work by the necropolis workmen of Thebes. *Studien zur Altägyptischen Kultur* 8. 127–52.

Janssen, J. J. (1990), *Late Ramesside letters and communications*. London, British Museum Press.

Janssen, J. J. and Janssen, R. (1996), *Getting old in ancient Egypt*. London, Rubicon Press.

Janssen, J. J. and Pestman, P. W. (1968), Burial and inheritance in the community of necropolis workmen at Thebes (Pap. Bulaq X and O. Petrie 16). *Journal of the Economic and Social History of the Orient* 11.2. 137–70.

Jeffreys, D. (2003), All in the family? Heirlooms in ancient Egypt. In W. J. Tait (ed.), *'Never had the like occurred': Egypt's view of its past*. London, UCL Press. 197–211.

Jeffreys, D. (2010), Regionality, cultural and cultic landscapes. In W. Wendrich (ed.), *Egyptian archaeology*. Chichester, Wiley-Blackwell. 102–18.

Jolles, F. (1998), Children of earth: Zulu clay dolls. In E. Dell (ed.), *Evocations of the child: Fertility figures of the southern African region*. Cape Town, Human and Rousseau. 99–109.

Jones, A. (2003), Technologies of remembrance: memory, materiality and identity in Early Bronze Age Scotland. In H. Williams (ed.), *Archaeologies of remembrance: death and memory in past societies*. New York, Springer. 65–88.

Jones, M. (1991), The early Christian sites at Tell el-Amarna and Sheikh Said. *Journal of Egyptian Archaeology* 77. 129–49.

Jørgensen, M. (1998), *Catalogue: Egypt II (1550-1080 B.C.), Ny Carlsberg Glyptotek*. Copenhagen, Ny Carlsberg Glyptotek.

Kaiser, W. (1990), Zür Büste als einer Darstellungsform ägyptischer Rundplastik. *Mitteilungen des Deutschen Archäologischen Instituts, Abteilung Kairo* 46. 269–85.

Kaiser, W., Andraschko, F., Aston, D. A., Jaritz, H., Krekeler, A., Nebe, I., Niederberger, W., Pigur, M. and von Pilgrim, C. (1990), Stadt und Tempel von Elephantine 17./18. Grabungsbericht. *Mitteilungen des Deutschen Archäologischen Instituts, Abteilung Kairo* 46. 185–249.

Kákosy, L. and Fábián, I. (1995), Harper's song in the tomb of Djehutimes (TT 32). *Studien zur Altägyptischen Kultur* 22. 211–25.

Kamp, K. A. (2001), Where have all the children gone? The archaeology of childhood. *Journal of Archaeological Method and Theory* 8, 1. 1–34.

Kampp, F. (1996), *Die thebanische Nekropole: zum Wandel des Grabgedankens von der XVIII. bis zur XX. Dynastie*. Mainz, Philipp von Zabern.

Kampp-Seyfried, F. (1998), Overcoming death: the private tombs of Thebes. In R. Schultz and M. Seidel (eds), *Egypt: the world of the pharaohs*. Cologne, Könemann. 248–263.

Kampp-Seyfried, F. (2003), The Theban necropolis: an overview of topography and tomb development from the Middle Kingdom to the Ramesside period. In N. Strudwick and J. H. Taylor (eds), *The Theban Necropolis: past, present and future*. London, British Museum Press. 2–10.

Kanawati, N. (1981), The living and the dead in Old Kingdom tomb scenes. *Studien zur Altägyptischen Kultur* 9. 213–25.

Kane, T. T., El-Kady, A. A., Saleh, S., Hage, M., Stanback, J. and Potter, L. (1992), Maternal mortality in Giza, Egypt: magnitude, causes, and prevention. *Studies in Family Planning* 23,1. 45–57.

Keimer, L. (1940), Jeux de la nature retouchés par la main de l'homme, provenant de Deir el-Médineh (Thèbes) et remontant du Nouvel-Empire. In L. Keimer (ed.), *Études d'Égyptologie, fascicule II*. Cairo, Institut Français d'Archéologie Orientale. 1–21.

Keith, J. L. (with contributions by S. Donnat, A. Stevens and N. Harrington) (2011), *Anthropoid busts of Deir el Medineh and other sites and collections: Analysis, catalogue raisonée, appendices*. Cairo, Institut Français d'Archéologie Orientale.

Keith-Bennett, J. (1981), Anthropoid busts II: Not from Deir el Medineh alone. *Bulletin of the Egyptological Seminar* 3. 43–71.

Keller, C. A. (1991), Royal painters: Deir el–Medina in Dynasty XIX. In E. Bleiberg and R. E. Freed (eds), *Fragments of a shattered visage: The proceedings of the International Symposium on Ramesses the Great*. Memphis, Memphis State University. 50–86.

Keller, C. A. (2008), Some thoughts on religious change at Deir el-Medina. In S. H. D'Auria (ed.), *Servant of Mut: Studies in Honor of Richard A. Fazzini*. Leiden, Boston, Brill. 149–54.

Kemp, B. J. (1977), The city of el-Amarna as a source for the study of urban society in ancient Egypt. *World Archaeology* 9.2. 123–39.

Kemp, B. J. (1979), Wall paintings from the Workmen's Village at el-Amarna. *Journal of Egyptian Archaeology* 65. 47–53.

Kemp, B. J. (1986), *Amarna Reports III*. London, Egypt Exploration Society.

Kemp, B. J. (1987), The Amarna workmen's village in retrospect. *Journal of Egyptian Archaeology* 73. 21–50.

Kemp, B. J. (1995a), How religious were the ancient Egyptians? *Cambridge Archaeological Journal* 5.1. 25–54.

Kemp, B. J. (ed.) (1995b), *Amarna Reports VI*. London, Egypt Exploration Society.

Kemp, B. J. (2007), Tell el-Amarna, 2006–7 [South Tombs Cemetery]. *Journal of Egyptian Archaeology* 93. 1–63 [11–35].

Kemp, B. J. (2009), A wall painting of Bes figures from Amarna. *Egyptian Archaeology* 34. 18–9.

Kemp, B. J. (2010), *Horizon: the Amarna Project and Amarna Trust Newsletter*. 7. www.amarnaproject.com/documents/pdf/horizon-newsletter-7.pdf.

Kendall, T. (1981), An unusual rock-cut tomb at Giza. In W. K. Simpson and W. M. Davis (eds), *Studies in ancient Egypt, the Aegean, and the Sudan: Essays in honour of Dows Dunham*. Boston, Museum of Fine Arts. 104–14.

Kendall, T. (1982), The house. In E. J. Brovarski, S. K. Doll and R. E. Freed (eds), *Egypt's golden age: the art of living in the New Kingdom 1558–1085 B.C.* Boston, Museum of Fine Arts. 25–34.

Kennedy, J. G. (1978), Mushāhara: a Nubian concept of supernatural danger and the theory of taboo; Nubian death ceremonies. In J. G. Kennedy (ed.), *Nubian ceremonial life*. Cairo, American University in Cairo Press. 125–50, 224–50.

Kessler, D. (2001), Die kultische Bindung der Ba-Konzeption 2. Teil: Die Ba-Zitate auf den Kultstelen und Ostraka des Neuen Reiches. *Studien zur Altägyptischen Kultur* 29. 139–86.

Keswani, P. (2004), *Mortuary ritual and society in Bronze Age Cyprus*. London and Oakville, Equinox.

Khattab, H., Younis, N. and Zurayk, H. (1999), *Women, reproduction, and health in rural Egypt: The Giza Study*. Cairo, American University in Cairo Press.

Kiernan, J. P. (1982), The 'problem of evil' in the context of ancestral intervention in the affairs of the living in Africa. *Man* 17. 287–301.

Killen, G. (1980), *Ancient Egyptian Furniture I*. Warminster, Aris & Phillips.

Killen, G. (1994a), *Egyptian woodworking and furniture*. Princes Risborough, Shire.

Killen, G. (1994b), *Ancient Egyptian Furniture, II*. Warminster, Aris & Phillips.

Kitchen, K. A. (1961), An unusual stela from Abydos. *Journal of Egyptian Archaeology* 47. 10–18.

Kitchen, K. A. (1975), *Ramesside inscriptions: historical and biographical. Volume I: Ramesses I, Sethos I and his contemporaries*. Oxford, B. H. Blackwell.

Kitchen, K. A. (1980), *Ramesside inscriptions: historical and biographical. Volume III: Ramesses II, his contemporaries*. Oxford, B. H. Blackwell.

Kitchen, K. A. (1982), *Ramesside inscriptions: historical and biographical. Volume IV: Merenptah and the late 19th Dynasty*. Oxford, B. H. Blackwell.

Kitchen, K. A. (1983a), *Ramesside inscriptions, historical and biographical: Setnakht, Ramesses III, his comtemporaries. Volume V*. Oxford, B. H. Blackwell.

Kitchen, K. A. (1983b), *Ramesside inscriptions, historical and biographical: Ramesses IV to XI, his comtemporaries. Volume VI*. Oxford, B. H. Blackwell.

Kitchen, K. A. (1989), *Addenda and indexes. Volume VII*. Oxford, B. H. Blackwell.

Kitchen, K. A. (1993), *Ramesside inscriptions, translated and annotated: Translations I; Ramesses I, Sethos I and contemporaries*. Oxford, B. H. Blackwell.

Kitchen, K. A. (2000), *Ramesside Inscriptions, translated and annotated: Translations III; Ramesses II, his contemporaries*. Oxford, B. H. Blackwell.

Kjølby, A. (2007), *New Kingdom private temple statues: a study of agency, decision-making and materiality*. Copenhagen, University of Copenhagen.

Kjølby, A. (2009), Material agency, attribution and experience of agency in ancient Egypt: The case of New Kingdom private temple statues. In R. Nyord and A. Kjølby (eds), *'Being in ancient Egypt': Thoughts on agency, materiality and cognition, proceedings of the seminar held in Copenhagen, September 29–30, 2006*. Oxford, Archaeopress. 31–46.

Knapp, S. (1989), Collective memory and the actual past. *Representations* 26. 123–49.

Koenig, Y. (1979), Un revenant inconvenant? (Papyrus Deir el-Médineh 37). *Bulletin de l'Institut Français d'Archéologie Orientale* 79. 103–19.

Koltsida, A. (2007), *Social aspects of ancient Egyptian domestic architecture*. Oxford, Archeopress.

Kousoulis, P. I. M. (2007), Dead entities in living bodies: The demonic influence of the dead in the medical texts. In J.-C. Goyon and C. Cardin (eds), *Proceedings of the Ninth International Congress of Egyptologists I*. Leuven, Peeters. 1043–50.

Krikorian, A. D. (1975), Were the opium poppy and opium known in the Ancient Near East? *Journal of the History of Biology* 8, 1. 95–114.

Kübler-Ross, E. (1970), *On death and dying*. London, New York, Routledge.

Lacau, P. (1909), *Stèles du Nouvel Empire*. Cairo, Institut Français d'Archéologie Orientale.

Lacovara, P. (1988), *Rishi* coffin, no. 64. In S. D'Auria, P. Lacovara and C. H. Roehrig (eds), *Mummies and magic: The funerary arts of ancient Egypt*. Boston, Museum of Fine Arts. 131.

Laing, G. (1921), The origin of the cult of the Lares. *Classical Philology* 16. 124–40.

Landgráfová, R. and Navrátilová, H. (2009), *Sex and the Golden Goddess I: ancient Egyptian love songs in context*. Prague, Agama.

Laneri, N. (2007), An archaeology of funerary rituals. In N. Laneri (ed.), *Performing death: social analyses of funerary traditions in the ancient Near East and Mediterranean*. Chicago, The Oriental Institute of the University of Chicago. 1–13.

Lansing, A. and Hayes, W. C. (1937), The Museum's excavations at Thebes. *The Metropolitan Museum of Art Bulletin* 32, 1, Part 2: The Egyptian expedition 1935–1936. 4–39.

Lau, G. F. (2002), Feasting and ancestor veneration at Chinchawas, North Highlands of Ancash, Peru. *Latin American Antiquity* 13. 279–304.

Lawergren, B. (1980), Reconstruction of a shoulder harp in the British Museum. *Journal of Egyptian Archaeology* 66. 165–8.

Lawergren, B. (2001), Music. In D. B. Redford (ed.), *The Oxford encyclopaedia of ancient Egypt II.* New York, Oxford University Press. 450–54.

Layton, R. (1989), Introduction: Who needs the past? In R. Layton (ed.), *Who needs the past? Indigenous values and archaeology*. London, Boston, Sydney, Wellington, Unwin Hyman. 1–20.

Leahy, A. (1984), Death by fire in ancient Egypt. *Journal of the Economic and Social History of the Orient* 27. 199–206.

Leibovitch, J. (1960), The statuette of an Egyptian harper and string-instruments in Egyptian statuary. *Journal of Egyptian Archaeology* 46. 53–9.

Leitz, C. (1994), *Tagewählerei: Das Buch ḥꜥt nḥḥ pḥ.wy ḏt und verwandte Texte*. Wiesbaden, Harrassowitz.

Leitz, C. (1999), *Magical and medical papyri of the New Kingdom*. London, British Museum Press.

Leospo, E. (1993), Espressioni religiose e funerarie. In A. M. Donadoni, E. Leospo, E. D'Amicone, A. Roccati and S. Donadoni, *Il Museo Egizio di Torino: Guida alla lettura una civiltà*. Second edition. Novara, DeAgostini. 59–99.

Lesko, L. H. (1991), Ancient Egyptian cosmogonies and cosmology. In B. E. Shafer (ed.), *Religion in ancient Egypt: Gods, myths, and personal practice.* Ithaca and London, Cornell University Press. 88–122.

Lewis, G. (1994), Magic, religion and the rationality of belief. In T. Ingold (ed.), *Companion encyclopaedia of anthropology.* London and New York, Routledge. 563–90.

Lewis, T. J. (1989), *Cults of the dead in ancient Israel and Ugarit*. Atlanta, Georgia, Scholars Press.

Lichtheim, M. (1945), The songs of the harpers. *Journal of Near Eastern Studies* 4. 178–212.

Lichtheim, M. (1973), *Ancient Egyptian Literature: A book of readings I: The Old and Middle Kingdoms*. Berkeley, Los Angeles and London, University of California Press.

Lichtheim, M. (1976), *Ancient Egyptian literature: A book of readings II: The New Kingdom.* Berkeley, Los Angeles, London, University of California Press.

Lichtheim, M. (1980), *Ancient Egyptian literature: A book of readings III: The Late period.* Berkeley, Los Angeles, London, University of California Press.

Limme, L. (1992), Le Livre des Morts de Neferrenpet. *Écritures de L'Égypte Ancienne.* Brussels, Musées Royaux d'Art et d'Histoire. 36–7.

Lines, D. (2001), A curious Middle Kingdom stela in Birmingham. *Journal of Egyptian Archaeology* 87. 41–54.

Lloyd, A. B. (1989), Psychology and society in the ancient Egyptian cult of the dead. In W. K. Simpson (ed.), *Religion and philosophy in ancient Egypt.* New Haven, Yale University. 117–33.

Longden, G. (2003), Iconoclasm, belief and memory in early medieval Wales. In H. Williams (ed.), *Archaeologies of remembrance: death and memory in past societies.* New York, Springer. 171–92.

Lopez-Grande, M. J. and Torrado De Gregorio, E. (2008), *Pottery vases from a votive deposit found at Dra Abu el-Naga (Djehuty Project Archaeological Excavations)*. Tenth International Congress of Egyptologists, Rhodes, Abstracts. University of the Aegean. www.rhodes.aegean.gr/tms/XICE%20Abstract%20book.pdf. 99–100.

Lorton, D. (1968), The expression *šms–ib*. *Journal of the American Research Center in Egypt* 7. 41–54.

Lorton, D. (1969–1970), A note on the expression *šms–ib*. *Journal of the American Research Center in Egypt* 8. 55–7.

Lorton, D. (1975), The expression *ỉrỉ ḥrw nfr*. *Journal of the American Research Center in Egypt* 12. 23–31.

Lorton, D. (1977), The treatment of criminals in ancient Egypt: through the New Kingdom. *Journal of the Economic and Social History of the Orient* 20, 1. 2–64.

Lorton, D. (1999), The theology of cult statues in ancient Egypt. In M. B. Dick (ed.), *Born in heaven, made on earth: the making of the cult image in the ancient Near East.* Winona Lake, IN, Eisenbraun. 123–211.

Lowenthal, D. (1975), Past time, present place: landscape and memory. *Geographical Review* 65, 1. 1–36.

Lucas, A. (1930), Perfumes and incense in ancient Egypt. *Journal of Egyptian Archaeology* 16. 41–53.

Lucas, A., revised by J. R. Harris (1962), *Ancient Egyptian materials and industries.* London, Edward Arnold.

Lüddeckens, E. (1943), Untersuchungen über religiösen Gehalt, Sprache und form der ägyptischen Totenklagen. *Mitteilungen des Deutschen Instituts für Ägyptische Altertumskunde in Kairo* 11.

Luiselli, M. M. (2009), *Die Suche nach Gottesnähe: untersuchungen zur persönliche frömmigkeit in ägypten von der ersten zwischenzeit bis zum ende des neuen reiches*. Wiesbaden, Harrassowitz.

Lustig, J. (1997), (ed.), *Anthropology and Egyptology: A developing dialogue*. Sheffield, Sheffield Academic Press.

MacDonald, W. L. (1992), Idionecrophanies: the social construction of perceived contact with the dead. *Journal for the Scientific Study of Religion* 31, 2. 215–23.

Mack, J. (2003), *The museum of the mind.* London, British Museum Press.

Maher-Taha, M. (2002), *Le tombeau de Menna (TT No. 69)*. Cairo, Conseil Suprême des Antiquités.

Mahmoud, A. (2002), Mummy bed of Sennedjem (cat. no. 66). In E. Hornung and B. M. Bryan (eds), *The quest for immortality: treasures of ancient Egypt.* Munich, London, New York, National Gallery of Art, Washington; United Exhibits Group, Copenhagen; Prestel Publishers. 149.

Malek, J. (1997), *The cat in ancient Egypt* (second edition). London, British Museum Press.

Malek, J. and Miles, E. (1989), Early squeezes made in the tomb of Khaemhet (TT 57). *Journal of Egyptian Archaeology* 75. 227–9.

Mandelbaum, D. G. (1965), Alcohol and culture. *Current Anthropology* 6, 3. 281–93.

Manniche, L. (1986), The tomb of Nakht, the gardener, at Thebes (no. 161) as copied by Robert Hay. *Journal of Egyptian Archaeology* 72. 55–78.

Manniche, L. (1987), *City of the dead: Thebes in Egypt*. London, British Museum Publications.

Manniche, L. (1988a), *Lost Tombs: a study of certain Eighteenth Dynasty monuments in the Theban Necropolis*. London and New York, KPI.

Manniche, L. (1988b), *The wall decoration of three Theban tombs (TT 77, 175, 249)*. Copenhagen, Carsten Niebuhr Institute of Ancient Near Eastern Studies, University of Copenhagen and Museum Tusculanum Press.

Manniche, L. (1989), *An ancient Egyptian herbal*. London, British Museum Press.

Manniche, L. (1997), Reflections on the banquet scene. In R. Tefnin (ed.), *La peinture Égyptienne ancienne: un monde de signes à préserver. Actes du Colloque International de Bruxelles, Avril 1994.* Brussels, Fondation Égyptologique Reine Élisabeth. 29–36.

Manniche, L. (1999), *Sacred luxuries: fragrance, aromatherapy and cosmetics in ancient Egypt*. Ithaca and London, Cornell University Press.

Manniche, L. (2009), Perfume. In W. Wendrich and J. Dieleman (eds), *UCLA encyclopaedia of Egyptology.* Los Angeles, http://escholarship.org/uc/item/7s07628w.
Mantellini, E. (2007), L'ombre pour les anciens Égyptiens. In J.-C. Goyon and C. Cardin (eds), *Ninth International Congress of Egyptologists, volume II.* Leuven, Paris, Dudley, MA, Peeters and Departement Oosterse Studies, Leuven. 1237–42.
Manuelian, P. D. (1982), Furniture. In E. J. Brovarski, S. K. Doll and R. E. Freed (eds), *Egypt's Golden Age: the art of living in the New Kingdom 1558–1085 B.C.* Boston, Museum of Fine Arts. 63–6.
Manuelian, P. D. (1998), A case of prefabrication at Giza? The false door of Inti. *Journal of the American Research Center in Egypt* 35. 115–27.
Manuelian, P. D. (1999), Semi-literacy in Egypt: some erasures from the Amarna Period. In E. Teeter and J. A. John Larson (eds), *Gold of Praise: studies on ancient Egypt in honor of Edward F. Wente.* Chicago, The Oriental Institute, University of Chicago. 285–98.
Marciniak, M. (1974), *Deir el-Bahri I: les inscriptions hiératiques du Temple de Thoutmosis III.* Warsaw, PWN–Editions scientifiques de Pologne.
Martin, G. T. (1985), *The tomb-chapels of Paser and Ra'ia at Saqqâra*. London, Egypt Exploration Society.
Martin, G. T. (1989a), *The Memphite tomb of Horemheb, Commander in Chief of Tutankhamun I: The reliefs, inscriptions, and commentary*. London, Egypt Exploration Society.
Martin, G. T. (1989b), *The royal tomb at el-'Amarna II*. London, Egypt Exploration Society.
Martin, G. T. (1991), *The hidden tombs of Memphis: new discoveries from the time of Tutankhamun and Ramesses the Great.* London, Thames and Hudson.
Martin, G. T. Van Dijk, J., Raven, M. J., Aston, B. G., Aston, D. A., Strouhal, E. and Horáčková, L. (2001), *The tombs of three Memphite officials: Ramose, Khay and Pabes*. London, Egypt Exploration Society.
Martin-Pardey, E. (1985), Damen beim fest (cat. 126). In W. Helck (ed.), *Nofret die Schöne: Die Frau im Alten Ägypten*. Hildesheim, Roemer und Pelizaeus Museum. 68-9.
Mathieu, B. (1996), *La poésie amoureuse de l'Egypte ancienne: recherches sur un genre littéraire au Nouvel Empire*. Cairo, Institut Français d'Archéologie Orientale.
Matsushima, E. (1993), Divine statues in ancient Mesopotamia: their fashioning and clothing and their interaction with society. In E. Matsushima (ed.), *Official cult and popular religion in the ancient Near East.* Heidelberg, Heidelberg Universitätsverlag. 209–19.
Mbiti, J. S. (1969), *African religions and philosophy*. London, Heinemann Educational Books Ltd.
McCarthy, H. L. (2002), The Osiris Nefertari: a case study of decorum, gender, and regeneration. *Journal of the American Research Center in Egypt* 39. 173-95.
McDonald, A. (2000), Tall tails: the Seth animal reconsidered. In A. McDonald and C. Riggs (eds), *Current research in Egyptology 2000.* Oxford, Archaeopress. 283–91.
McDonald, A. (2005), Glimpses of life in letters to the dead. *Egypt Exploration Society Study Day: 'Gossips and pedants': learning from ancient Egyptian texts.* School of Oriental and African Studies, London.
McDonald, J. K. (1982), Grill (no. 92). In E. J. Brovarski, S. K. Doll and R. E. Freed (eds), *Egypt's golden age: the art of living in the New Kingdom 1558–1085 B.C.* Boston, Museum of Fine Arts. 111.
McDowell, A. G. (1990), *Jurisdiction in the workmen's community at Deir el Medina*. Leiden, Nederlands Instituut voor het Nabije Oosten.
McDowell, A. G. (1992), Awareness of the past in Deir el-Medîna. In R. J. Demarée and A. Egberts (eds), *Village voices: proceedings of the symposium "Texts from Deir el-Medîna and their interpretation", Leiden, May 31–June 1, 1991.* Leiden, Centre of Non-Western Studies. 95–109.

McDowell, A. G. (1994), Contact with the outside world. In L. H. Lesko (ed.), *Pharaoh's workers: The villagers of Deir el Medina.* Ithaca and London, Cornell University Press. 41–59.

McDowell, A. G. (1999), *Village life in ancient Egypt: laundry lists and love songs*. Oxford, Oxford University Press.

McGovern, P. E. (1997), Wine of Egypt's Golden Age: an archaeochemical perspective. *Journal of Egyptian Archaeology* 83. 69–108.

McGuire, R. H. (2001), Ideologies of death and power in the Hohokam community of La Ciudad. In D. R. Mitchell and J. L. Brunson-Hadley (eds), *Ancient burial practices in the American Southwest: Archaeology, physical anthropology, and native American perspectives.* Albuquerque, University of New Mexico Press. 27–44.

Meader, J. and Demeter, B. (2004), The Egyptian blue water lily. *KMT* 15, 2. 57–63.

Meeks, D. (2002), Demons. In D. B. Redford (ed.), *The Oxford encyclopaedia of ancient Egypt I.* New York, Oxford University Press. 375–8.

Meeks, D. and Favard-Meeks, C. (1996), *Daily life of the Egyptian gods*, trans. G. M. Goshgarian. London, Pimlico.

Mekhitarian, A. (1978), *Egyptian painting*, trans. S. Gilbert. Geneva, Skira.

Mekhitarian, A. (1994), *La misère des tombes thébaines*. Brussels, Fondation Égyptologique Reine Élisabeth.

Merlin, M. D. (2003), Archaeological evidence for the tradition of psychoactive plant use in the Old World. *Economic Botany* 57, 3. 295–323.

Merrillees, R. S. (1962), Opium trade in the Bronze Age Levant. *Antiquity* 36. 287–292.

Merrillees, R. S. (1968), *The Cypriote Bronze Age pottery found in Egypt*. Lund, Carl Bloms Boktryckeri A–B.

Merrillees, R. S. (1974), *Trade and transcendence in the Bronze Age Levant: three studies*. Göteborg, Paul Åström.

Merrillees, R. S. and Winter, J. (1972), Bronze Age trade between the Aegean and Egypt: Minoan and Mycenaean pottery from Egypt in the Brooklyn Museum. *Miscellanea Wilbouriana* 1. 101–35.

Meskell, L. (1994), Deir el Medina in hyperreality: seeking the people of pharaonic Egypt. *Journal of Mediterranean Archaeology* 7. 193–216.

Meskell, L. (1998a), An archaeology of social relations in an Egyptian village. *Journal of Archaeological Method and Theory* 5. 209–43.

Meskell, L. (1998b), Intimate archaeologies: the case of Kha and Merit. *World Archaeology* 29. 363–79.

Meskell, L. (1999), *Archaeologies of social life: age, sex, class etc. in ancient Egypt*. Oxford, Blackwell.

Meskell, L. (2000a), Re-em(bed)ding sex: domesticity, sexuality, and ritual in New Kingdom Egypt. In R. A. Schmidt and B. L. Voss (eds), *Archaeologies of sexuality.* London, Routledge. 253–62.

Meskell, L. (2000b), Spatial analyses of the Deir el-Medina settlement and necropoleis. In R. J. Demarée and A. Egberts (eds), *Deir el-Medina in the Third Millennium AD: A tribute to Jac J. Janssen.* Leiden, Nederlands Instituut voor het Nabije Oosten. 259–75.

Meskell, L. (2000c), Cycles of life and death: Narrative homology and archaeological realities. *World Archaeology* 31, 3. 423–441.

Meskell, L. (2002), *Private life in New Kingdom Egypt*. Princeton, Princeton University Press.

Meskell, L. (2003), Memory's materiality: ancestral presence, commemorative practice and disjunctive locales. In R. M. Van Dyke and S. E. Alcock (eds), *Archaeologies of memory.* Malden, MA, Oxford, Melbourne, Berlin; Blackwell. 34–55.

Meskell, L. (2004), *Object worlds in ancient Egypt*. Oxford, Berg.
Meskell, L. and Joyce, R. A. (2003), *Embodied lives: figuring ancient Maya and Egyptian experience*. London, Routledge.
Metcalf, P. (1981), Meaning and materialism: the ritual economy of death. *Journal of the Royal Anthropological Institute (Man)* 16. 563–78.
Metcalf, P. and Huntington, R. (1991), *Celebrations of death, the anthropology of mortuary ritual, (second edition)*. Cambridge, Cambridge University Press.
Milde, H. (1991), *The vignettes of the Book of the Dead of Neferrenpet*. Leiden, Nederlands Instituut voor het Nabije Oosten.
Moreno Garcia, J. C. (2007), Oracles, ancestor cults and letters to the dead: the involvement of the dead in the public and private family affairs in pharaonic Egypt. Formerly at: *www.uni–koeln.de/phil–fak/afrikanistik/down/insvisible/Morena%20Garcia%20Carlos%20Juan_Articulo%20Colonia%202007.pdf*
Morgan, E. E. (2004), *Untersuchungen zu den Ohrenstelen aus Deir el Medine*. Wiesbaden, Harrassowitz Verlag.
Morkot, R. (1990), '*Nb–M3ʿt–Rʿ* United-with-Ptah'. *Journal of Near Eastern Studies* 49. 323–37.
Morphy, H. (1994), The anthropology of art. In T. Ingold (ed.), *Companion encyclopaedia of anthropology*. London and New York, Routledge. 648–85.
Morris, E. (2002), Review of Lynn Meskell, Private life in New Kingdom Egypt. *Journal of Egyptian Archaeology* 88. 265–7.
Morris, I. (1991), The archaeology of ancestors: the Saxe/Goldstein Hypothesis revisited. *Cambridge Archaeological Journal* 1. 147–69.
Morschauser, S. (1991), *Threat–formulae in ancient Egypt: a study of the history, structure and use of threats and curses in ancient Egypt*. Baltimore, Halgo.
Muhammed, M. A.-Q. (1966), *The development of the funerary beliefs and practices displayed in the private tombs of the New Kingdom at Thebes*. Cairo, General Organisation for Government Printing Offices.
Müller, I. (1991), Damen beim fest (no. 49); Spendenlöffel (no. 147). In K.-H. Priese (ed.), *Ägyptisches Museum*. Mainz, Philipp von Zabern. 82, 241.
Müller, W. M. (1899), *Die Liebespoesie der alten Ägypter*. Leipzig, J. C. Hinrichs.
Müller, V. (1998), Offering deposits at Tell el-Dab'a. In C. J. Eyre (ed.), *Proceedings of the Seventh International Congress of Egyptologists*. Leuven, Peeters. 793–803.
Murnane, W. J. (1995), *Texts from the Amarna period in Egypt*. Atlanta, Scholars Press.
Murray, M. A. (1955), Ancient and modern ritual dances in the Near East. *Folklore* 66, 4. 401–9.
Murray, M. A. (2000), Viticulture and wine production. In P. Nicholson and I. Shaw (eds), *Ancient Egyptian materials and technology*. Cambridge, Cambridge University Press. 577–608.
Nagel, G. (1938), *La céramique du Nouvel Empire à Deir el-Médineh*. Cairo, Institut Français d'Archéologie Orientale.
Naquin, S. (1988), Funerals in North China: uniformity and variation. In J. L. Watson and E. S. Rawski (eds), *Death ritual in Late Imperial and modern China*. Berkeley, Los Angeles, London, University of California Press. 37–70.
Nasr, M. W. (1993), The Theban tomb 260 of User. *Studien zur Altägyptischen Kultur* 20. 173–202.
Naville, E. (1886), *Das aegyptische Todtenbuch der XVIII. bis XX. Dynastie: aus verschiedenen Urkunden*. Berlin, Asher.
Navratilova, H. (2007), *The visitors' graffiti of Dynasties XVII and XIX in Abusir and Northern Saqqara*. Prague, Czech Institute of Egyptology and Set Out.

Navratilova, H. (2009), Graffiti spaces. *First Millennium Workshop*, Prague.

Negm, M. (1997), *The tomb of Simut called Kyky: Theban tomb 409 at Qurnah*. Warminster, Aris & Phillips Ltd.

Negm, M. (1998), Tourist graffiti from the Ramesside Period. *Discussions in Egyptology* 40. 115–23.

Nel, K. (1998), Swazi umntfwana: Swazi evocations of the child. In E. Dell (ed.), *Evocations of the child: Fertility figures of the southern African region.* Cape Town, Pretoria, Johannesberg, Human & Rousseau. 161–71.

Nelson, M. (2003), The Ramesseum necropolis. In N. Strudwick and J. H. Taylor (eds), *The Theban necropolis: past, present and future.* London, British Museum Press. 88–94.

Nicholson, P. T. and Shaw, I. (eds) (2000), *Ancient Egyptian materials and technology.* Cambridge, Cambridge University Press.

Niwinski, A. (1989), *Studies on the illustrated Theban funerary papyri of the 11th and 10th Centuries B.C.* Gottingen, Universitatsverlag Freiberg Schweiz Vandenhoeck & Ruprecht.

Noorani, Y. (1997), A nation born in mourning: The neoclassical funeral elegy in Egypt. *Journal of Arabic Literature*. 28, 1. 38–67.

Nwaoru, E. O. (2000), The motif 'food of life' in Biblical and extra–Biblical traditions. *Biblische Notizen* 105. 16–27.

Ockinga, B. G. (1997), *A tomb from the reign of Tutankhamun at Akhmim*. Sydney, The Australian Centre for Egyptology.

Ockinga, B. G. (2007), Use, reuse, and abuse of 'sacred space': observations from Dra Abu al-Naga. In P. F. Dorman and B. M. Bryan (eds), *Sacred space and sacred function in ancient Thebes*. Chicago, The Oriental Institute of the University of Chicago. 139-62.

O'Connor, D. (1996), Sexuality, statuary, and the afterlife; scenes from the tomb-chapel of Pepyankh (Heny the Black). An interpretative essay. In P. D. Manuelian (ed.), *Studies in honor of William Kelly Simpson.* Boston, Museum of Fine Arts. 621–33.

O'Connor, D. (1997), The elite houses of Kahun. In J. Phillips (ed.), *Ancient Egypt, the Aegean, and the Near East: Studies in honour of Martha Rhodes Bell, Volume II.* New York, Van Siclen Books. 389–400.

O'Donoghue, M. (1999), The 'Letters to the Dead' in ancient Egyptian religion. *Bulletin of the Australian Centre for Egyptology* 10. 87–104.

Ogden, D. (1999), Binding spells: curse tablets and voodoo dolls in the Greek and Roman worlds. In V. Flint, R. L. Gordon and D. Ogden (eds), *The Athlone history of magic and witchcraft in Europe, volume 2: ancient Greece and Rome.* London, The Athlone Press.

Ogden, D. (2001), *Greek and Roman necromancy*. Princeton and Oxford, Princeton University Press.

Ogden, D. (2002), *Magic, witchcraft, and ghosts in the Greek and Roman worlds: a sourcebook*. Oxford, Oxford University Press.

Ogden, J. R. (1998), Studies in ancient Egyptian magical thought, V. A new look at the terminology for 'spell' and related terms in magical texts. *Discussions in Egyptology* 40. 137–45.

Olyan, S. M. (2010), What do we really know about women's rites in the Israelite family context? *Journal of Ancient Near Eastern Research* 10, 1. 55-67.

Orsenigo, C. (2007), La découverte du tombeau de Maiherperi (KV 36) dans les notes inédities de Victor Loret. In J.-C. Goyon and C. Cardin (eds), *Ninth International Congress of Egyptologists, volume II.* Leuven, Paris, Dudley, MA, Peeters & Departement Oosterse Studies, Leuven. 1429–36.

Osing, J. (1992a), *Aspects de la culture pharaonique*. Paris, Diffusion de Boccard.

Osing, J. (1992b), *Das Grab des Nefersecheru in Zawyet Sultan*. Mainz, Phillip von Zabern.

Ossian, C. (1999), The most beautiful of flowers: Water lilies and lotuses in ancient Egypt. *KMT* 10, 1. 49–59.

Otake, E. (1980), Two categories of Chinese ancestors as determined by their malevolence. *Asian Folklore Studies* 39. 21–31.

Otto, E. (1941), Die Anschauung vom *B3* nach Coffin Texts Sp. 99–104. *Miscellanea Gregoriana*. 151–60.

Otto, E. (1942), Die beiden vogelgestaltigen Seelenvorstellungen der Agypter. *Zeitschrift für Ägyptische Sprache und Altertumskunde* LXXVII. 79–91.

Otto, E. (1948), Zur Bedeutung der ägyptischen Tempelstatuen seit dem Neuen Reich. *Orientalia* 17. 448–66.

Otto, E. (1960), *Das ägyptische Mundöffnungsritual*. Wiesbaden, Otto Harrassowitz.

Ouellet, B. (2007), L'Enseignement du Ba à l'Homme Désillusionné: Une praxis en rapport avec le sens de la vie. In J.-C. Goyon and C. Cardin (eds), *Ninth International Congress of Egyptologists, volume II*. Leuven, Paris, Dudley, MA, Peeters & Departement Oosterse Studies, Leuven. 1436–41.

Padgham, J. (2006), Unguent cones: real or representative? *Seventh Current Research in Egyptology Symposium*. University of Oxford.

Padgham, J. (2007), The re-interpretation of the 'unguent' cone as a symbol of cult offerings. *The 68th Annual Meeting of the American Research Center in Egypt*. Wyndham Toledo Hotel, Ohio. http://www.allacademic.com/meta/p175807_index.html.

Padgham, J. (2010a), The interpretation of the 'unguent' cone as a symbol of transition through the possession of cult offerings. *Third British Egyptology Congress*. The British Museum, London.

Padgham, J. (2010b), *The cone on the head of the ancient Egyptian tomb owner – a symbol of transition?* Seminar presented to the Faculty of Oriental Studies, University of Oxford.

Padwick, C. E. (1924), Notes on the jinn and the ghoul in the peasant mind of Lower Egypt. *Bulletin of the School of Oriental Studies* 3, 3 421–46.

Pahl, W. M. (1986), The ritual of Opening the Mouth: Arguments for an actual body ritual from the viewpoint of mummy research. In A. R. David (ed.), *Science in Egyptology: Proceedings of the 'Science in Egyptology' symposia*. Manchester University Press. 212–7.

Palgi, P. and Abramovitch H. (1984), Death: a cross-cultural perspective. *Annual Review of Anthropology* 13. 385–417.

Parker Pearson, M. (1982), Mortuary practices, society and ideology: an ethnoarchaeological study. In I. Hodder (ed.), *Symbolic and structural archaeology*. Cambridge, Cambridge University Press. 99–113.

Parker Pearson, M. (1993), The powerful dead: archaeological relationships between the living and the dead. *Cambridge Archeological Journal* 3. 203–99.

Parker Pearson, M. (1999), *The archaeology of death and burial*. Thrupp, Stroud, Sutton Publishing Limited.

Parkinson, R. B. (1991), *Voices from ancient Egypt: an anthology of Middle Kingdom writings*. London, British Museum Press.

Parkinson, R. B. (1998), *The Tale of Sinuhe and other ancient Egyptian poems, 1940–1640 BC*. Oxford, Oxford University Press.

Parkinson, R. B. (1999), *Cracking codes: The Rosetta Stone and decipherment*. Berkeley, University of California Press.

Parkinson, R. B. (2002), *Poetry and culture in Middle Kingdom Egypt*. New York and London, Continuum.

Parkinson, R. B. (2008), *The painted tomb-chapel of Nebamun*. London, British Museum Press.

Peden, A. J. (1994), *Egyptian historical inscriptions of the Twentieth Dynasty*. Sävedalen, Paul Astroms.

Peden, A. J. (2001), *The graffiti of pharaonic Egypt: scope and roles of informal writings (c. 3100–332 BC)*. Leiden, Brill.

Peet, T. E. (1915a), The great tomb robberies of the Ramesside age. Papyrus Mayer A and B. I Papyrus Mayer A. *Journal of Egyptian Archaeology* 2. 173–177.

Peet, T. E. (1915b), The great tomb robberies of the Ramesside age. Papyrus Mayer A and B. II. Papyrus Mayer B. *Journal of Egyptian Archaeology* 2. 204–6.

Peet, T. E. (1930), *The great tomb-robberies of the twentieth Egyptian dynasty*. Oxford, Clarendon Press.

Peet, T. E. and Woolley, C. L. (1923), *The City of Akhenaten Part I: Excavations of 1921 and 1922 at El-'Amarneh*. London Egypt Exploration Society.

Pendlebury, J. D. S. (1951), *The City of Akhenaten III: the Central City and official quarters*. London, Egypt Exploration Society.

Perry, W. J. (1925), The cult of the sun and the cult of the dead in Egypt. *Journal of Egyptian Archaeology* 11. 191–200.

Petrie, W. M. F. (1894), *Tell el-Amarna*. London, Egypt Exploration Fund.

Petrie, W. M. F. (1903), *Abydos II*. London, Egypt Exploration Fund.

Petrie, W. M. F. (1907), *Gizeh and Rifeh*. London, Egypt Exploration Fund.

Petrie, W. M. F. (1914), *Amulets*. London, Egypt Exploration Fund.

Petrie, W. M. F. and Brunton, G. (1924), *Sedment, volume II*. London, Egypt Exploration Fund.

Piccione, P. A. (1990), Mehen, mysteries, and resurrection from the coiled serpent. *Journal of the American Research Center in Egypt* 27. 43–52.

Piccione, P. A. (1994), The gaming episode in the Tale of Setne Khamwas as religious metaphor. In D. P. Silverman (ed.), *For his ka: Essays offered in memory of Klaus Baer.* Chicago, University of Chicago Press. 197–204.

Pierrat-Bonnefois, G. (2002), Table d'offrandes de Imenemipet et Noubemtekh; Table d'offrandes – bassin à libation d'Amennakhte (nos. 199 and 200). In G. Andreu (ed.), *Les artistes de pharaon: Deir el-Médineh et la Vallée des Rois.* Paris, Turnhout, Reunion des Musées Nationaux/Brepols. 250, 1.

Pierrat-Bonnefois, G. (2003), Cimetière est du village ou cimetière à l'est de Deir el-Médineh? In G. Andreu (ed.), *Deir el-Médineh et la Vallée des Rois: La vie en Égypte au temps des pharaons du Nouvel Empire.* Paris, Éditions Khéops, Musée du Louvre. 49–65.

Pinch, G. (1982), Offerings to Hathor. *Folklore* 93. 138–50.

Pinch, G. (1983), Childbirth and female figurines at Deir el-Medina and el-Amarna. *Orientalia* 52. 405–14.

Pinch, G. (1993), *Votive offerings to Hathor*. Oxford, Griffith Institute.

Pinch, G. (1994), *Magic in ancient Egypt*. London, British Museum Press.

Pinch, G. (2001), Red things: the symbolism of colour in magic. In W. V. Davies (ed.), *Colour and painting in ancient Egypt.* London, British Museum Press. 182–85.

Pinch, G. (2003), Redefining funerary objects. In Z. Hawass and L. Pinch Brock (eds), *Egyptology at the dawn of the Twenty-first Century: Proceedings of the Eighth International Congress of Egyptologists, Volume 2: History, religion.* Cairo, American University in Cairo Press. 443–7.

Pinch, G. and Waraksa, E. A. (2009), Votive practices. In W. Wendrich and J. Dieleman (eds), *UCLA encyclopaedia of Egyptology.* Los Angeles. http://escholarship.org/uc/item/7s07628w.

Pino, C. (2005), The market scene in the tomb of Khaemhet (TT 57). *Journal of Egyptian Archaeology* 91. 95–105.

Pirelli, R. (2007), Les répertoires de scènes des tombeaux privés de la 18ème Dynastie et les scènes de banquet: présentation d'une étude. In J.-C. Goyon and C. Cardin (eds), *Proceedings of the Ninth International Congress of Egyptologists.* Leuven, Paris, Dudley MA, Peeters.

Pischikova, E. V. (1994), Representations of ritual and symbolic objects in late XXVth Dynasty and Saite private tombs. *Journal of the American Research Center in Egypt* 31. 63–77.

Plater, C. (2001), *Aspects of the interaction between the living and the dead.* Ph.D thesis. University of Liverpool.

Pleyte, W. and Rossi, F. (1869–76), *Papyrus de Turin.* Leiden, E. J. Brill.

Polz, D. (1988), *Das Grab Nr. 54 in Theben: Ein Beitrag zur Archäologie thebenischer Felsgräber.* Heidelberg, University of Heidelberg.

Polz, D. (1990), Bemerkungen zur Grabbenutzung in der thebanischen Nekropole. *Mitteilungen des Deutschen Archäologischen Instituts, Abteilung Kairo* 46. 301–36.

Polz, D. (1993), Bericht über die 2. und 3. Grabungskampagne in der Nekropole von Dra' Abu el-Naga/Theben-West. *Mitteilungen des Deutschen Archäologischen Instituts, Abteilung Kairo* 49. 227-38.

Poo, M. C. (1995), *Wine and wine offering in the religion of ancient Egypt.* London and New York, Kegan Paul International.

Porter, B. and Moss, R. L. B. (1937), *Topographical bibliography of ancient Egyptian hieroglyphic texts, reliefs, and paintings V: Upper Egypt: sites.* Oxford, Oxford University Press.

Porter, B. and Moss, R. L. B. (1960), *Topographical bibliography of ancient Egyptian hieroglyphic texts, reliefs, and paintings I: The Theban necropolis Part 1, Private tombs* (second edition). Oxford, Clarendon Press.

Porter, B., Moss, R. L. B. and Malek, J. (1981), *Topographical bibliography of ancient Egyptian hieroglyphic texts, reliefs, and paintings III, Memphis Part 2. Saqqâra to Dahshûr* (second edition). Oxford, Griffith Institute.

Porter, B. A. (1988), North and west walls of burial chamber of Sobek-mose. In S. D'Auria, P. Lacovara and C. H. Roehrig (eds), *Mummies and magic: the funerary arts of ancient Egypt.* Boston, Museum of Fine Arts. 145–7.

Posener, G. (1958), Les empreintes magiques de Gizeh et les morts dangereux. *Mitteilungen des Deutschen Archäologischen Instituts, Abteilung Kairo* 16. 252–70.

Posener, G. (1987), *Cinq figurines d'envoûtement.* Cairo, Institut Français d'Archéologie Orientale.

Posener, G. (1988), Découverte de l'ancienne Égypte. *Bulletin de la Société Française d'Égyptologie* 112. 11–22.

Pumpenmeier, F. (1998), *Eine Gunstgabe von seiten des Königs: ein extrasepulkrales Schabtidepot Qen–Amuns in Abydos.* Heidelberg, Heidelberger Orientverlag.

Pyke, G. (2007), A Christian conversion: the tomb of Panehsy at Amarna. *Egyptian Archaeology* 32. 8–10.

Quack, J. F. (1994), *Die Lehren des Ani: Ein neuägyptischer Weisheitstext in seinen kulturellen Umfeld.* Göttingen, Vandenhoeck and Ruprecht.

Quack, J. F. (2002), Some Old Kingdom execration figurines from the Teti Cemetery. *Bulletin of the Australian Centre for Egyptology* 13. 149–60.

Quack, J. F. (2006), Fragmente des Mundöffungsrituals aus Tebtynis. In K. Ryholt (ed.), *The Carlsberg Papyri 7: Hieratic texts from the collection* Copenhagen, CNI Publication 30. 69–150.

Quack, J. F. (2010), The animals of the desert and the return of the goddess. In H. Riemer (ed.), *Desert animals in the Eastern Sahara: status, economic significance, and cultural reflection in antiquity*. Köln, Henrich-Barth-Institut. 341–61.

Quibell, J. E. and Hayter, A. G. K. (1927), *Excavations at Saqqara: Teti Pyramid, north side*. Cairo, Institut Français d'Archéologie Orientale.

Quirke, S. (1986), The hieratic texts in the tomb of Nakht the Gardiner at Thebes (no. 161), as copied by Robert Hay. *Journal of Egyptian Archaeology* 72. 79–90.

Quirke, S. (1988), Letter to the Dead, no. 39. In S. D'Auria, P. Lacovara and C. H. Roehrig (eds), *Mummies and magic: the funerary arts of ancient Egypt*. Boston, Museum of Fine Arts. 106–7.

Ranke, H. (1935), The origin of the Egyptian tomb statue. *The Harvard Theological Review* 28. 45–53.

Rapoport, A. (1994), Spatial organization and the built environment In T. Ingold (ed.), *Companion encyclopaedia of anthropology: Humanity, culture and social life*. London and New York, Routledge. 460–502.

Raven, M. J. (1983), Wax in Egyptian magic and symbolism. *Oudheidkundige Mededelingen uit het Rijksmuseum van Oudheden te Leiden* 64. 7–47.

Raven, M. J. (1997), Charms for protection during the Epagomenal Days. In J. Van Dijk (ed.), *Essays on ancient Egypt in honour of Herman te Velde*. Groningen, Styx Publications. 275–91.

Raven, M. J. (2001), *The tomb of Maya and Meryt II: objects and skeletal remains*. Leiden and London, National Museum of Antiquities, Leiden/ Egypt Exploration Society.

Ray, J. D. (1999), Dreams before a wise man: a Demotic ostracon in the Nicholson Museum, University of Sydney (inv. R. 98). In A. Leahy and W. J. Tait (eds), *Studies on ancient Egypt in honour of H. S. Smith*. London, Egypt Exploration Society. 241–7.

Redford, D. B. (1961), An unusual stela from Abydos. *Journal of Egyptian Archaeology* 47. 10–8.

Redford, D. B. (1986), *Pharaonic king-lists, annals, and day-books: a contribution to the study of the Egyptian sense of history*. Mississauga Ont, Benben.

Reeves, C. N. (1988), Shrine-stela and offering table of Menmaatre-emheb, no. 108. In S. D'Auria, P. Lacovara, and C. H. Roehrig (eds), *Mummies and magic: the funerary arts of ancient Egypt*. Boston, Museum of Fine Arts. 157.

Reeves, C. N. (1990), *Valley of the Kings: the decline of a royal necropolis*. London, Kegan Paul International.

Reeves, E. B. (1995), Power, resistance, and the cult of Muslim saints in a Northern Egyptian town. *American Ethnologist* 22. 306–23.

Régen, I. (2010), When the Book of the Dead does not match the archaeology: the case of he protective magical bricks (BD 151). *British Museum Studies in Ancient Egypt and Sudan* 15. 267-78.

Reisner, G. A. (1920), Note on the statuette of a blind harper in the Cairo Museum. *Journal of Egyptian Archaeology* 6, 2. 117–8.

Richards, J. E. (1999), Conceptual landscapes in the Egyptian Nile Valley. In W. Ashmore and A. B. Knapp (eds), *Archaeologies of landscape: contemporary perspectives*. Oxford, Blackwell. 83–100.

Richards, J. (2006), The μ50 Group and the Abydos cemeteries during the Middle Kingdom. In K. N. Sowada and B. G. Ockinga (eds), *Egyptian art in the Nicholson Museum, Sydney*. Sydney, University of Sydney. 225–40.

Ricke, H. (1932), *Der Grundriss des Amarna-Wohnhauses*. Leipzig, J. C. Hinrichs.

Ricke, H. (1966), Ein Hausmodell im Kestnermuseum zu Hannover. *Zeitschrift für Ägyptische Sprache und Altertumskunde* 93. 119–23.

Rigault, P. (2002a), Carré de lin peint. In G. Andreu (ed.), *Les artistes de Pharaon: Deir el-Médineh et la Vallée des Rois.* Paris, Turnhout, Reunion des Musées Nationaux/Brepols. 288.

Rigault, P. (2002b), Stèle de Nakhtimen (no.94). In G. Andreu (ed.), *Les artistes de Pharaon: Deir el-Médineh et la Vallée des Rois.* Paris, Turnhout, Reunion des Musées Nationaux/Brepols. 151.

Riggs, C. (2005), *The beautiful burial in Roman Egypt: art, identity and funerary religion.* Oxford, Oxford University Press.

Rinpoche, S. (2002), *The Tibetan Book of Living and Dying (revised and updated).* London, Rider.

Ritner, R. K. (1984), A uterine amulet in the Oriental Institute Collection. *Journal of Near Eastern Studies* 43, 3. 209–21.

Ritner, R. K. (1990), O. Gardiner 363: A spell against night terrors. *Journal of the American Research Center in Egypt* 27. 25–41.

Ritner, R. K. (1993), *The mechanics of ancient Egyptian magical practice.* Chicago, The Oriental Institute, University of Chicago.

Ritner, R. K. (2002), Necromancy in ancient Egypt. In L. Ciraolo and J. Seidel (eds), *Magic and divination in the ancient world.* Leiden, Boston, Cologne, Brill, Styx. 89–96.

Ritner, R. K. (2003), The romance of Setna Khaemuas and the mummies (Setna I). In W. K. Simpson (ed.), *The literature of ancient Egypt: an anthology of stories, instructions, stelae, autobiographies, and poetry.* New Haven and London, Yale Universiy Press. 453–69.

Ritner, R. K. (2008), Household religion in ancient Egypt. In J. Bodel and S. M. Bryan (eds), *Household and family religion in antiquity.* Malden, MA, Oxford, Blackwell. 171–196.

Rizzo, J. (2004), Une mesure d'hygiène relative à quelques statues-cubes déposées dans le temple d'Amon à Karnak. *Bulletin de l'Institut Français d'Archéologie Orientale*104. 511–21.

Robichon, C., and Varille, A. (1936), *Le temple du scribe royal Amenhotep fils de Hapou.* Cairo, Institut Français d'Archéologie Orientale.

Robins, G. (1988), Ancient Egyptian sexuality. *Discussions in Egyptology* 11. 61–72.

Robins, G. (1995), *Reflections of women in the New Kingdom: Egyptian art from the British Museum.* Texas, Van Siclen.

Robins, G. (1997), Women and votive stelae in the New Kingdom. In J. Phillips (ed.), *Ancient Egypt, the Aegean, and the Near East: Studies in honour of Martha Rhodes Bell, Volume II.* New York, Van Siclen Books. 445–54.

Robins, G. (1998), Piles of offerings: paradigms of limitation and creativity in ancient Egyptian art. In C. J. Eyre (ed.), *Proceedings of the Seventh International Congress of Egyptologists.* Leuven, Peeters. 957–63.

Robins, G. (1999), Hair and the construction of identity in ancient Egypt, *c.* 1480–1350 B.C. *Journal of the American Research Center in Egypt* 36. 55-69.

Robins, G. (2008), Male bodies and the construction of masculinity in New Kingdom Egyptian art. In S. H. D'Auria (ed.), *Servant of Mut: Studies in Honor of Richard A. Fazzini.* Leiden, Boston, Brill. 208–15.

Robins, G. (2010), Meals for the dead: the image of the deceased seated before a table of offerings. *Dining and Death: interdisciplinary perspectives on the 'Funerary Banquet' in ancient art, burial and belief.* Conference at the Ioannou Centre for Classical and Byzantine Studies, University of Oxford.

Roehrig, C. H. (1988), Shawabti, no. 102. In S. D'Auria, P. Lacovara and C. H. Roehrig (eds), *Mummies and magic: The funerary arts of ancient Egypt.* Boston Museum of Fine Arts. 155.

Roehrig, C. H. (2003), The Middle Kingdom tomb of Wah at Thebes. In N. Strudwick and J. H. Taylor (eds), *The Theban Necropolis: past, present and future.* London, British Museum Press. 11–13.

Romano, J. F. (1978), *The Luxor Museum of ancient Egyptian art.* Cairo, Egyptian Antiquities Organization.

Romano, J. F. (1982), Headrest. In E. J. Brovarski, S. K. Doll and R. E. Freed (eds), *Egypt's golden age: the art of living in the New Kingdom 1558–1085 B.C.* Boston, Museum of Fine Arts. 75.

Romano, J. F. (1998), Notes on the historiography and history of the Bes-image in ancient Egypt. *Bulletin of the Australian Centre for Egyptology* 9. 89–105.

Romano, J. F. (1999), Small anthropoid bust, and large anthropoid bust, nos. 263, 264. In R. E. Freed, Y. J. Markowitz and S. D'Auria (eds), *Pharaohs of the sun: Akhenaten, Nefertiti, Tutankhamun.* London, Thames and Hudson. 282.

Romano, J. F. (2001), Folding headrest. In E. R. Russmann (ed.), *Eternal Egypt: masterworks of ancient art from the British Museum.* Berkeley and London, University of California Press; British Museum Press. 162–3.

Rose, P. (2003), Ceramics from New Kingdom tombs: recording and beyond. In N. Strudwick and J. H. Taylor (eds), *The Theban Necropolis: past, present and future.* London, British Museum Press. 202–209.

Roth, A. M. (1988), Ancestor bust. In S. D'Auria, P. Lacovara and C. H. Roehrig (eds), *Mummies and magic: the funerary arts of ancient Egypt.* Boston, Museum of Fine Arts. 149.

Roth, A. M. (1992), The *psš-kf* and the 'Opening of the Mouth' ceremony: a ritual of birth and rebirth. *Journal of Egyptian Archaeology* 78. 113–47.

Roth, A. M. (1993), Fingers, stars, and the 'Opening of the Mouth': The nature and function of the *ntrwi* blades. *Journal of Egyptian Archaeology* 79. 57–79.

Roth, A. M. and Roehrig, C. H. (2002), Magical bricks and the bricks of birth. *Journal of Egyptian Archaeology* 88. 121–39.

Roulin, G. (1998), The Book of the Night: a royal composition documenting the conceptions of the hereafter at the beginning of the Nineteenth Dynasty. In C. J. Eyre (ed.), *Proceedings of the Seventh International Congress of Egyptologists*. Leuven, Peeters. 1005–13.

Russmann, E. R. (ed.), (2001), *Eternal Egypt: masterworks of ancient art from the British Museum.* Berkeley and London, University of California Press; British Museum Press.

Russmann, E. R. and Finn, D. (1990), *Egyptian sculpture in Cairo and Luxor*. London, British Museum Press.

Russo, B. (2007), Some notes on the funerary cult in the early Middle Kingdom: Stela BM EA 1164. *Journal of Egyptian Archaeology* 93. 195–209.

Rzepka, S. L. (1995), Some remarks on the rock-cut group-statues in the Old Kingdom. *Studien zur Altägyptischen Kultur* 22. 227–36.

Sadek, A. I. (1984a), An attempt to translate the corpus of the Deir el-Bahri hieratic inscriptions. *Göttinger Miszellen* 71. 67–91.

Sadek, A. I. (1984b), An attempt to translate the corpus of the Deir el-Bahri hieratic inscriptions (part two). *Göttinger Miszellen* 72. 65–87.

Sadek, A. I. (1987), *Popular religion in Egypt during the New Kingdom*. Hildesheim, Gerstenberg Verlag.

Sakurai, K., Yoshimura, S. and Kondo, J. (1988), *Comparative studies of nobles tombs in the Theban Necropolis (Tomb nos. 8,38, 39, 48, 50, 54, 57, 63, 64, 66, 74, 78, 89, 90, 91, 107, 120, 139, 147, 151, 181, 201, 253, 295)*. Tokyo, Waseda University.

Saleh, M. and Sourouzian, H. (1987), *The Egyptian Museum, Cairo: official catalogue*. Mainz and Cairo, Philipp von Zabern; Egyptian Antiquities Organization.
Sandman, M. (1938), *Texts from the time of Akhenaten*. Brussels, Fondation Égyptologique Reine Élisabeth.
Sattin, A. (2000), *The Pharaoh's shadow: travels in ancient and modern Egypt*. London, Victor Gollancz.
Sauneron, S. (1952), *Rituel de l'embaumement: Pap. Boulaq III, Pap. Louvre 5. 158*. Cairo, Imprimerie Nationale.
Sauneron, S. (1960), Les possédés. *Bulletin de l'Institut Français d'Archéologie Orientale* 60. 111–5.
Säve-Söderbergh, T. (1957), *Four Eighteenth Dynasty tombs*. Oxford, Griffith Institute.
Schäfer, H. (1986), *Principles of Egyptian art*, trans. J. Baines. Oxford, Griffith Institute.
Schechner, R. (1994), Ritual and performance. In T. Ingold (ed.), *Companion encyclopaedia of anthropology*. London and New York, Routledge. 613–47.
Scheffler, H. (1966), Ancestor worship in anthropology: or, observations on descent and descent groups. *Current Anthropology* 7. 541–51.
Schiaparelli, E. (1927), *Relazione sui lavori della Missione archeologica italiana in Egitto, anni 1903–1920 II: La tomba intatta dell'architetto Cha nella necropoli di Tebe*. Turin, Giovanni Chiantore.
Schoske, S., Kreissl, B. and Germer, R. (1992), *››Anch‹‹ Blumen für das Leben: Pflanzen im alten Ägypten*. Munich, Staatliche Sammlung Ägyptischer Kunst.
Schott, S. (1950), *Altägyptische Liebeslieder*. Zurich, Artemis.
Schott, S. (1952), *Das schöne Fest vom Wüstentale: Festbräuche einer Totenstadt*. Wiesbaden, Franz Steiner.
Schulman, A. R. (1981), Reshep times two. In W. K. Simpson and W. M. Davis (eds), *Studies in ancient Egypt, the Aegean, and the Sudan: Essays in honour of Dows Dunham* Boston, Museum of Fine Arts. 157–66.
Schulman, A. R. (1984), The iconographic theme: "Opening of the Mouth" on stelae. *Journal of the American Research Center in Egypt* 21. 169–96.
Schulman, A. R. (1986), Some observations on the *ꜣḫ iḳr n rꜥ* stelae. *Bibliotheca Orientalis* 43. 302–48.
Schwartz, G. M. (2007), Status, ideology, and memory in Third-millennium Syria: 'Royal' tombs at Umm el-Marra. In N. Laneri (ed.), *Performing death: social analysis of funerary traditions in the ancient Near East and Mediterranean*. Chicago, Oriental Institute of the University of Chicago. 39–68.
Schweitzer, U. (1956), *Das wesen des Kꜣ im Diesseits und Jenseits der alten ägypter*. Gluckstadt, J. J. Augustin.
Scott, G. D. (1986), *Ancient Egyptian art at Yale*. Yale, Yale University Art Gallery.
Scurlock, J. (2002), Soul emplacements in ancient Mesopotamian funerary rituals. In L. Ciraolo and J. Seidel (eds), *Magic and divination in the ancient world*. Leiden, Boston, Köln, Brill, Styx. 1–6.
Scurlock, J. (2006), *Magico-medical means of treating ghost-induced illnesses in ancient Mesopotamia*. Leiden, Boston, Brill.
Seeber, C. (1976), *Untersuchungen zur Darstellung des Totengerichts im alten Ägypten*, Untersuchungen zur Darstellung des Totengerichts im alten Ägypten. Munich, Deutscher Kunstverlag.
Seeger, A. (1994), Music and dance. In T. Ingold (ed.), *Companion encyclopaedia of anthropology*. London and New York, Routledge. 686–705.

Seele, K. C. (1959), *The tomb of Tjanefer at Thebes (TT 158)*. Chicago, University of Chicago Press.

Seidelmayer, S. J. (2001), Die Ikonographie des Todes. In H. Willems (ed.), *Social aspects of funerary culture in the Egyptian Old and Middle Kingdoms. Proceeedings of the symposium held at Leiden, 6-7 June, 1996*. Leuven, Paris, and Sterling VA, Peeters. 205–53.

Seiler, A. (1993), *Grab und Kult. Zwei 'ungestörte' Schachtgräber in der Nekropole von Dra' Abu el-Naga*. Unpublished MA. Heidelberg.

Seiler, A. (1995), Archäologisch fassbare Kultpraktiken der frühen 18. Dynastie in Dra' Abu el-Naga/ Theben. In J. Assmann, E. Dziobek, H. Guksch and F. Kampp-Seyfried (eds), *Thebanische Beamtennekropolen: neue Perspektiven archäologischer Forchung: Internationales Symposion, Heidelberg, 9.–13. Juni 1993*. Heidelberg, Heidelberger Orientverlag. 185–203.

Seiler, A. (2005), *Tradition und Wandel: Die Keramik als Spiegel der Kulturentwicklung Thebens in der zweiten Zwischenzeit*. Mainz, Philipp von Zabern.

Serpico, M. (2000a), Resins, amber and bitumen. In P. Nicholson and I. Shaw (eds), *Ancient Egyptian materials and technology*. Cambridge, Cambridge University Press. 430–74.

Serpico, M. and White, R. (1998), Chemical analysis of coniferous resins from ancient Egypt using gas chromatography/mass spectrometry (GC/MS). In C. J. Eyre (ed.), *Proceedings of the Seventh International Congress of Egyptologists*. Leuven, Peeters. 1037–48.

Serpico, M. (2000), Oil, fat and wax. In P. Nicholson and I. Shaw (eds), *Ancient Egyptian materials and technology*. Cambridge, Cambridge University Press. 390–429.

Sethe, K. (1906), *Urkunden der 18. Dynastie I-II, vols. 1–4*. Leipzig, J. C. Hinrich.

Sethe, K. (1907), *Urkunden der 18. Dynastie III, vols. 9–12*. Leipzig, J. C. Hinrichs.

Sethe, K. (1909), *Urkunden der 18. Dynastie IV, vols. 13–16*. Leipzig, J. C. Hinrichs.

Sethe, K. (1927-1930), *Urkunden der 18. Dynastie vols. 1–4* (second edition, revised). Leipzig, J. C. Hinrichs.

Sethe, K. (1928), *Ägyptische Lesestücke zum Gebrauch im akademischen Unterricht: Texte des Mittleren Reiches*. Leipzig, J. C. Hinrichs.

Seyfried, K.-J. (1990), Dritter Vorbericht über die Arbeiten des Ägyptologischen Instituts der Universität Heidelberg in thebanischen Gräbern der Ramessidenzeit. *Mitteilungen des Deutschen Archäologischen Instituts, Abteilung Kairo* 46. 341–53.

Seyfried, K.-J. (1995), *Das Grab des Djehutiemhab (TT 194)*. Mainz, Philipp von Zabern.

Seyfried, K.-J. (2003), Reminiscences of the 'Butic burial' in Theban tombs of the New Kingdom. In N. Strudwick and J. H. Taylor (eds), *The Theban Necropolis: past, present and future*. London, British Museum Press. 61–8.

Shafer, B. E. (1997), Temples, priests, and rituals: an overview. In B. E. Shafer (ed.), *Temples of ancient Egypt*. London, New York, I. B. Taurus. 1–31.

Shapiro, W. (1988), Ritual kinship, ritual incorporation and the denial of death. *Journal of the Royal Anthropological Institute (Man)* 23. 275–97.

Shaw, I. (1992), Ideal homes in ancient Egypt: the archaeology of social aspiration. *Cambridge Archaeological Journal* 2.2. 147–66.

Shaw, I. (2004), Identity and occupation: how did individuals define themselves and their work in the Egyptian New Kingdom? In J. Bourriau and J. Phillips (eds), *Invention and innovation: the social context of technological change 2: Egypt, the Aegean and the Near East 1650–1150 BC*. Oxford, Oxbow Books. 12–24.

Shedid, A. G. and Seidel, M. (1996) [1991], *The tomb of Nakht: the art and history of an Eighteenth Dynasty official's tomb at Western Thebes*, trans. M. Eaton-Krauss (*Das Grab des Nacht: Kunst und Geschichte eines Beamtengrabes der 18. Dynastie in Theben-West*). Mainz, Philipp von Zabern.

Sheils, D. (1975), Toward a unified theory of ancestor worship: a cross-cultural study. *Social Forces* 54.2. 427–40.

Sheikholeslami, C. M. (2003), The burials of the priests of Montu at Deir el-Bahri in the Theban necropolis. In N. Strudwick and J. H. Taylor (eds), *The Theban Necropolis: past, present and future.* London, British Museum Press. 131–7.

Sheikholeslami, C. M. (2011), *Hathor's Festival of Drunkenness: evidence from the New Kingdom and Third Intermediate Period.* Paper presented at the Annual Meeting of the American Research Center in Egypt, Chicago.

Sherratt, A. (1991), Sacred and profane substances: the ritual use of narcotics in later Neolithic Europe. In P. Garwood, D. Jennings, R. Skeates and J. Toms (eds), *Sacred and profane: proceedings of a conference on archaeology, ritual and religion; Oxford 1989*. Oxford, Oxford University Committee for Archaeology. 50–64.

Shiffman, J. (2000), Can poor countries surmount high maternal mortality? *Studies in Family Planning* 31, 4. 274–89.

Shimy, M. A.-H. (1997), *Parfums et parfumerie dans l'ancienne Egypte (de l'ancien empire a la fin du nouvel empire)*. Paris, Septentrion.

Shirley, J. J. (2008), Politics of placement: the Theban Necropolis in the Eighteenth Dynasty. *Tenth International Congress of Egyptologists.* Rhodes, University of the Aegean. www.rhodes.aegean.gr/tms/XICE%20Abstract%20book.pdf. 225–6.

Shorter, A. W. (1930), The tomb of Aahmose, Supervisor of the Mysteries in the House of the Morning. *Journal of Egyptian Archaeology* 16. 54–62.

Silverman, D. P. (2000), The threat-formula and biographical text in the tomb of Hezi at Saqqara. *Journal of the American Research Center in Egypt* 37. 1–13.

Simpson, W. K. (1966), The letter to the dead from the tomb of Meru (N 3737) at Nag' ed-Deir. *Journal of Egyptian Archaeology* 52. 39–52.

Simpson, W. K. (1969–1970), A short harper's song of the late New Kingdom in the Yale University Art Gallery. *Journal of the American Research Center in Egypt* 8. 49–51.

Simpson, W. K. (1972), A relief of the royal cup-bearer Tja-wy. *Boston Museum Bulletin* 70. 68–82.

Simpson, W. K. (1976), *The mastabas of Qar and Idu, G7101 and 7102*. Boston, Department of Egyptian and Ancient Near Eastern Art, Museum of Fine Arts.

Simpson, W. K. (1981), The Memphite Epistolary Formula on a jar stand of the First Intermediate Period from Naga ed–Deir. In W. K. Simpson and W. M. Davis (eds), *Studies in ancient Egypt, the Aegean, and the Sudan: Essays in honour of Dows Dunham*. Boston, Museum of Fine Arts. 173–9.

Simpson, W. K. (1982), Egyptian sculpture and two-dimensional representation as propaganda *Journal of Egyptian Archaeology* 68. 266–71.

Simpson, W. K. (1987), *A table of offerings: 17 years of collecting Egyptian and Ancient Near Eastern Art*. Boston, Museum of Fine Arts.

Simpson, W. K. (2003), Three autobiographies of the Old Kingdom. In W. K. Simpson (ed.), *The Literature of Ancient Egypt: An anthology of stories, instructions, stelae, autobiographies, and poetry.* New Haven and London, Yale University Press. 401–17.

Smith, M. (1987), *Catalogue of demotic papyri in the British Museum. Volume 3: the mortuary texts of Payrus BM 10507*. London, British Museum Press.

Smith, M. (1993), *The Liturgy of the Opening of the Mouth for Breathing*. Oxford, Griffith Institute.

Smith, M. (2006), Osiris NN or Osiris of NN? In B. Backes, I. Munro and S. Stöhr (eds), *Totenbuch-Forschungen: gesammelte Beiträge des 2. Internationalen Totenbuch-Symposiums Bonn, 25. bis 29. September 2005.* Wiesbaden, Harrassowitz. 325–37.

Smith, M. (2009), *Traversing eternity: texts for the afterlife from Ptolemaic and Roman Egypt*. Oxford, Oxford University Press.

Smith, S. T. (1992), Intact tombs of the Seventeenth and Eighteenth Dynasties from Thebes and the New Kingdom burial system. *Mitteilungen des Deutschen Archäologischen Instituts, Abteilung Kairo*. 48. 193–231.

Smith, S. T. (1997), State and empire in the Middle and New Kingdoms. In J. Lustig (ed.), *Anthropology and Egyptology: a developing dialogue*. Sheffield, Sheffield Academic Press. 66–89.

Smith, W. S. (1998), *The art and architecture of ancient Egypt*. New Haven and London, Yale University Press.

Snape, S. R. (1994), Statues and soldiers at Abydos in the Second Intermediate Period. In C. Eyre, A. Leahy and L. Montagno Leahy (eds), *The unbroken reed: studies in the culture and heritage of ancient Egypt in honour of A. F. Shore*. London, Egypt Exploration Society. 304–14.

Spalinger, A. J. (1998), The limitations of formal ancient Egyptian religion. *Journal of Near Eastern Studies* 57.4. 241–60.

Spalinger, A. J. (2000), The destruction of mankind: a transitional literary text. *Studien zur Altägyptischen Kultur* 28. 257–82.

Spalinger, G. L. (1982), Bowl with Hathor cow, no. 108. In E. J. Brovarski, S. K. Doll and R. E. Freed, (eds), *Egypt's golden age: the art of living in the New Kingdom 1558–1085 B.C.* Boston, Museum of Fine Arts. 121–2.

Spanel, D. B. (1988), Shawabti, no. 100. In S. D'Auria, P. Lacovara and C. H. Roehrig (eds), *Mummies and magic: The funerary arts of ancient Egypt*. Boston, Museum of Fine Arts. 154.

Sparkes, B. (1989), Classical Greek attitudes to the past. In R. Layton (ed.), *Who needs the past?* London, Boston, Sydney, Wellington, Unwin Hyman. 119–29.

Speleers, L. (1917), *Le papyrus de Nefer Renpet: un livre des morts de la XVIIIeme dynastie aux Musées Royaux du Cinquantenaire à Bruxelles*. Brussels, Vromant.

Spence, K. (2004), The three-dimensional form of the Amarna house. *Journal of Egyptian Archaeology* 90. 123–52.

Spence, K. (2007), A contextual approach to ancient Egyptian domestic cult: the case of the 'lustration slabs' at El–Amarna. In D. A. Barrowclough and C. Malone (eds), *Cult in context: reconsidering ritual in archaeology*. Oxford, Oxbow Books. 285–92.

Spencer, N. (2010), *Life and death in occupied Nubia (Amara West)*. Oxford University seminar. Oriental Studies Faculty, Oxford.

Spencer, P. (2003), Dance in ancient Egypt. *Near Eastern Archaeology* 66, 3. 111–21.

Speigel, J. (1956), Die Entwicklung der Opferszenen in den Thebanischen Gräbern. *Mitteilungen des Deutschen Instituts für Ägyptische Altertumskunde in Kairo* 14. 190–207.

Spieser, C. (2007), Cercueils d'enfants dans l'Egypte ancienne et tardive. *Servei d'Investigacions Arqueòlogiques/ Prehistòriques*. 501–38.

Steadman, L. B., Palmer, C. T. and Tilley, C. F. (1996), The universality of ancestor worship. *Ethnology* 35. 63–76.

Stevens, A. (2003), The material evidence for domestic religion at Amarna and preliminary remarks on its interpretation. *Journal of Egyptian Archaeology* 89. 143–68.

Stevens, A. (2006), *Private religion at Amarna: the material evidence*. Oxford, Archaeopress.

Stevens, A. (2008), South Tombs Cemetery. In B. J. Kemp, Tell el-Amarna, 2007–8. *Journal of Egyptian Archaeology* 94. 1–67 [13–44].

Stevens, A. (2009a), Domestic religious practices. In W. Wendrich and J. Dieleman (eds), *UCLA encyclopaedia of Egyptology*. Los Angeles. http://escholarship.org/uc/item/7s07628w.

Stevens, A. (2009b), South Tombs Cemetery. In B. J. Kemp, Tell el-Amarna, 2008–9. *Journal of Egyptian Archaeology* 95. 1–34 [11–27].

Stevenson, A. (2009a), Social relationships in Predynastic burials. *Journal of Egyptian Archaeology* 95. 175–92.

Stevenson, A. (2009b), *The Pitt Rivers Egyptian flint knife*. http://web.prm.ox.ac.uk/rpr/index.php/object-biography-index/7-farnhamcollection/128-an-egyptian-flint-knife (accessed 06.01.2012).

Stewart, H. M. (1976), *Egyptian stelae, reliefs and paintings from the Petrie Collection*. Warminster, Aris & Phillips.

Stewart, H. M. (1986), *Mummy cases and inscribed funerary cones in the Petrie collection*. Warminster, Aris & Phillips.

Stewart, H. M. (1995), *Egyptian shabtis*. Princes Risborough, Shire Egyptology.

Struble, E. (2010), Ritual engraved: rethinking the meanings of Syro-Hittite mortuary feasts. *Dining and Death: interdisciplinary perspectives on the 'Funerary Banquet' in ancient art, burial and belief.* Conference at the Ioannou Centre for Classical and Byzantine Studies, University of Oxford.

Strudwick, N. (1988), False door of Kha, no. 28. In S. D'Auria, P. Lacovara and C. H. Roehrig (eds), *Mummies and magic: The funerary arts of ancient Egypt.* Boston, Museum of Fine Arts. 95–6.

Strudwick, N. (1994), Change in continuity at Thebes: the private tomb after Akhenaten. In C. J. Eyre, A. Leahy and L. M. Leahy (eds), *The unbroken reed: studies in the culture and heritage of ancient Egypt in honour of A. F. Shore.* London, Egypt Exploration Society. 321–36.

Strudwick, N. (1995), The population of Thebes in the New Kingdom: some preliminary thoughts. In J. Assmann, E. Dziobek, H. Guksch and F. Kampp-Seyfried (eds), *Thebanische Beamtennekropolen: neue Perspektiven archäologischer Forschung: Internationales Symposion, Heidelberg, 9–13 juni 1993.* Heidelberg, Heidelberger Orientverlag. 97–105.

Strudwick, N. (2010), Use and re-use of tombs in the Theban Necropolis: patterns and explanations. In J. C. M. Garcia (ed.), *Elites et pouvoir en Egypte ancienne (Cahiers de recherches de l'Institut de Papyrologie et d'Egyptologie de Lille 28)*. Lille, Université Charles de Gaulle. 239–61.

Strudwick, N. and Strudwick, H. M. (1997), The house of Amenmose in Theban Tomb 254. In R. Tefnin (ed.), *La peinture Égyptienne ancienne: un monde de signes à préserver. Actes du Colloque International de Bruxelles, Avril 1994.* Brussels, Fondation Égyptologique Reine Élisabeth. 37–47.

Strudwick, N. (1996), *The tombs of Amenhotep, Khnummose, and Amenmose at Thebes*. Oxford, Griffith Institute.

Sugi, A. (2003), The iconographical representation of the sun god in New Kingdom Egypt. In Z. Hawass and L. Pinch Brock (eds), *Egyptology at the dawn of the Twenty-first century: Proceedings of the Eighth International Congress of Egyptologists, Volume 2: History, religion.* Cairo, American University in Cairo Press. 514–21.

Sullivan, E. (2002), Stele of Nebnakht and family (cat. no. 12). In E. Hornung and B. M. Bryan (eds), *The quest for immortality: treasures of ancient Egypt.* Munich, London, New York, National Gallery of Art, Washington; United Exhibits Group, Copenhagen; Prestel Publishers. 92–3.

Sweeney, D. (2001a), *Conversation and dialogue: pragmatic factors in Late Ramesside letter writing*. Wiesbaden, Harrassowitz.

Sweeney, D. (2001b), Walking alone forever, following you: gender and mourners' laments from ancient Egypt. *NIN: Journal of Gender Studies in Antiquity* 2. 27–48.

Sweeney, D. (2006a), Review of Lynn Meskell, 'Private life in New Kingdom Egypt'. *NIN: Journal of Gender Studies in Antiquity* 4. 147–58.

Sweeney, D. (2006b), Review of Lynn Meskell, 'Archaeologies of social life: Sex, age, class et cetera in ancient Egypt'. *NIN: Journal of Gender Studies in Antiquity* 4. 159–68.

Szpakowska, K. (2003a), *Behind closed eyes: dreams and nightmares in ancient Egypt*. Swansea, Classical Press of Wales.

Szpakowska, K. (2003b), Altered states: an inquiry into the possible use of narcotics or alcohol to induce dreams in pharaonic Egypt. In A. K. Eyma and C. J. Bennett (eds), *A Delta man in Yebu: Occasional volume of the Egyptologists' Electronic Forum No. 1*. Universal Publishers. 225–37.

Szpakowska, K. (2003c), Playing with fire: Initial observations on the religious uses of clay cobras from Amarna. *Journal of the American Research Center in Egypt* 40. 113–22.

Tainter, J. R. (1978), Mortuary practices and the study of prehistoric social systems. *Journal of Archaeological Method and Theory* 1. 105–41.

Tait, J. (2009), Anger and agency: The role of the emotions in Demotic and earlier narrative. In R. Nyord and A. Kjølby (eds), *'Being in ancient Egypt': Thoughts on agency, materiality and cognition. Proceedings of the seminar held in Copenhagen, September 29–30, 2006*. Oxford, Archaeopress. 75–82.

Tallet, P. (1995), Le shedeh: étude d'un procédé de vinification en Égypte ancienne. *Bulletin de l'Institut Français d'Archéologie Orientale* 95. 459–92.

Tappy, R. (1995), Did the dead ever die in Biblical Judah? *Bulletin of the American Schools of Oriental Research* 298. 59–68.

Taylor, J. H. (1989), *Egyptian coffins*. Princes Risborough, Shire Publications.

Taylor, J. H. (2000), Le rôle symbolique du cercueil égyptien: equipement du mort pour l'éternité. *Dossiers d'Archeologie: Images et rites d'éternité en Egypte* 257. 30–7.

Taylor, J. H. (2001), *Death and the afterlife in ancient Egypt*. London, British Museum Press.

Taylor, J. H. (2003), Theban coffins from the Twenty-second to the Twenty-sixth Dynasty: dating and synthesis of development. In N. Strudwick and J. H. Taylor (eds), *The Theban Necropolis: past, present and future*. London, British Museum Press. 95–121.

Taylor, J. H. (2010), Changes in the afterlife. In W. Wendrich (ed.), *Egyptian archaeology*. Chichester, Wiley-Blackwell. 220–40.

Teeter, E. (1995), Amenhotep son of Hapu at Medinet Habu. *Journal of Egyptian Archaeology* 81. 232–6.

Thomas, A. P. (1981), *Gurob: A New Kingdom town (2 volumes)*. Warminster, Aris & Phillips.

Thompson, S. E. (1988), Death, food, and fertility. In J. L. Watson and E. S. Rawski (eds), *Death ritual in Late Imperial and modern China*. Berkeley, Los Angeles, London, University of California Press. 71–108.

Thompson, S. E. (1994), The anointing of officials in ancient Egypt. *Journal of Near Eastern Studies* 53, 1. 15–25.

Thompson, S. E. (1998), The significance of anointing in ancient Egyptian funerary beliefs. In L. H. Lesko (ed.), *Ancient Egyptian and Mediterranean studies in memory of William A. Ward*. Providence, Department of Egyptology, Brown University. 229–43.

Thompson, S. E. (2001), Cults: an overview. In D. B. Redford (ed.), *The Oxford encyclopaedia of ancient Egypt I*. New York, Oxford University Press. 326–32.

Thomsen, M.-L. (2001), Witchcraft and magic in ancient Mesopotamia. In B. Ankarloo and S. Clark (eds), *Witchcraft and magic in Europe, volume. 1: Biblical and pagan societies*. Philadelphia, University of Pennsylvania Press. 1–95.

Tobin, V. A. (2003), The Maxims of Ptahhotep. In W. K. Simpson (ed.), *The Literature of Ancient Egypt: An anthology of stories, instructions, stelae, autobiographies, and poetry.* New Haven and London, Yale University Press. 129–48.

Toivari-Viitala, J. (2001), *Women at Deir el-Medina: a study of the status and roles of the female inhabitants in the workmen's community during the Ramesside period.* Leiden, Nederlands Instituut voor vet Nabije Oosten.

Tosi, M. (1994), *La cappella di Maia. Un pittore a Deir el-Medina.* Turin, Artema.

Tosi, M. and Roccati, A. (1972), *Stele e altre epigrafi di Deir el-Medina n. 50001 – n. 50262.* Turin, Museo Egizio di Torino.

Trinkaus, K. M. (1984), Mortuary ritual and mortuary remains. *Current Anthropology* 25. 674–9.

Troy, L. (1989), Have a nice day! Some reflections on the calendars of good and bad days. In G. Englund (ed.), *The Religion of the ancient Egyptians: cognitive structures and popular expressions; proceedings of symposia in Uppsala and Bergen, 1987 and 1988.* Uppsala and Stockholm, Almqvist & Wiksell. 127–47.

Tsouli, M. (2010), Testamonia on funerary banquets in ancient Sparta (from the Archaic to the Roman Period). *Dining and Death: interdisciplinary perspectives on the 'Funerary Banquet' in ancient art, burial and belief.* Conference at the Ioannou Centre for Classical and Byzantine Studies, University of Oxford.

Tylor, J. J. (1895), *Wall drawings and monuments of El Kab: The tomb of Paheri.* London, Egypt Exploration Fund.

Tylor, J. J. and Griffith, F. Ll. (1894), *The tomb of Paheri at El Kab.* London, Egypt Exploration Fund.

Ucko, P. J. (1969), Ethnography and the archaeological interpretation of funerary remains. *World Archaeology* 1. 262–90.

Uphill, E. P. (1962), A New Kingdom relief from Memphis. *Journal of Egyptian Archaeology* 48. 162–3.

Valbelle, D. (1985), *'Les ouvriers de la Tombe': Deir el-Médineh à l'époque ramesside.* Cairo, Institut Français d'Archéologie Orientale.

Van Der Toorn, K. (1995), The domestic cult at Emar. *Journal of Cuneiform Studies* 47. 35–49.

Van Dijk, J. (1986), Zerbrechen der roten Töpfe. In C. Meyer (ed.), *Lexikon der Ägyptologie.* Wiesbaden, Harrassowitz. 1390–6.

Van Dijk, J. (1988), The development of the Memphite necropolis in the post–Amarna period. In A.-P. Zivie (ed.), *Memphis et ses nécropoles au Nouvel Empire: Novelles données, nouvelles questions.* Paris, Centre National de la Recherche Scientifique. 37–45.

Van Dijk, J. (1993), *The New Kingdom necropolis of Memphis: historical and iconographical studies.* Groningen, n.p.

Van Dyke, R. M. and Alcock, S. E. (2003), Archaeologies of memory: an introduction. In R. M. Van Dyke and S. E. Alcock (eds), *Archaeologies of memory.* Malden, MA, Oxford, Melbourne, Berlin, Blackwell. 1–13.

Vandersleyen, C. (2005), *Iahmès Sapaïr: fils de Séqénenré Djéhouty-Aa (17 dynastie) et la statue du Musée du Louvre E 15682.* Brussels, Éditions Safran.

Vandier D'Abbadie, J. (1937), *Ostraca Figures de Deir el Médineh Nos. 2001–2722.* Cairo, Institut Français d'Archéologie Orientale.

Vandier D'Abbadie, J. (1939), *Deux tombes de Deir el-Médineh I: la chapelle de Khâ.* Cairo, L'Institut Français d'Archaéologie Orientale.

Vandier D'Abbadie, J. (1946), A propos des bustes de laraires. *Revue d'Égyptologie* 5. 133–5.

Vandier D'Abbadie, J. (1954), *Deux tombes Ramessides à Gournet-Mourraï.* Cairo, L'Institut Français d'Archaéologie Orientale.

Vandier D'Abbadie, J. (1972), *Catalogue des objets de toilette égyptiens au Musée du Louvre.* Paris, Musée du Louvre.
Vandier, J. (1964), Iousâas et (Hathor)–Nebét Hétépet. *Revue d'Égyptologie* 16. 55–146.
Vandier, J. (1969), *Manuel d'archéologie égyptienne V: Bas-reliefs et peintures. Scènes de la vie quotidienne.* Paris, Picard.
Varille, A. (1935), Trois nouveaux chants de harpistes. *Bulletin de l'Institut Français d'Archéologie Orientale* 35. 153–60.
Vassilika, E. (1995), *Egyptian art.* Cambridge, Cambridge University Press.
Verbovsek, A. (2004), '*Als Gunsterweis des Königs in den Tempel gegeben...': Privat Tempelstatuen des Alten und Mittelren Reiches.* Wiesbaden, Harrassowitz.
Verlinden, P. (2008), Child burials in the Dakhla Oasis. *Tenth International Congress of Egyptologists.* Rhodes, University of the Aegean. www.rhodes.aegean.gr/tms/XICE%20Abstract%20book.pdf. 263-4.
Vernus, P. (2003), La piété personnelle à Deir el-Médineh: la construction de l'idée de pardon. In G. Andreu (ed.), *Deir el-Médineh et la Vallée des Rois: La vie en Égypte au temps des pharaons du Nouvel Empire.* Paris, Éditions Khéops, Musée du Louvre. 309–47.
Vértes, K. (2008), 10 years' epigraphy in Theban Tomb 65. *Tenth International Congress of Egyptologists.* Rhodes, University of the Aegean. www.rhodes.aegean.gr/tms/XICE%20Abstract%20book.pdf. 264-5.
Volokhine, Y. (2000), *La frontalité dans l'iconographie de l'Egypte ancienne.* Geneva, Société d'Egyptologie.
Von Pilgrim, C. (1996), *Elephantine XVIII: Untersuchungen in der Stadt des Mittleren Reiches und der Zweiten Zwischenzeit.* Mainz, Philipp von Zabern.
Walker, S. (1983), Women and housing in Classical Greece: the archaeological evidence. In A. Cameron and A. Kuhrt (eds), *Images of women in antiquity.* London and Canberra, Croom Helm. 81–91.
Walter, R., Thomas, T. and Sheppard, P. (2004), Cult assemblages and ritual practice in Roviana Lagoon, Soloman Islands. *World Archaeology* 36. 142–57.
Waraska, E. A. (2009), *Female figurines from the Mut Precinct: context and ritual function.* Fribourg, Academic Press; Göttingen, Vandenhoeck & Ruprecht.
Warburton, D. (2009), Time and space in ancient Egypt: The importance of the creation of abstraction. In R. Nyord and A. Kjølby (eds), *'Being in ancient Egypt': Thoughts on agency, materiality and cognition. Proceedings of the seminar held in Copenhagen, September 29–30, 2006.* Oxford, Archaeopress. 83–95.
Watson, J. L. (1988), The structure of Chinese funerary rites: Elemental forms, ritual sequence, and the primacy of performance. In J. L. Watson and E. S. Rawski (eds), *Death ritual in Late Imperial and modern China.* Berkeley, Los Angeles, London, University of California Press. 3–19.
Watson, R. S. (1988), Remembering the dead: graves and politics in Southeastern China. In J. L. Watson and E. S. Rawski (eds), *Death ritual in Late Imperial and modern China.* Berkeley, Los Angeles, London, University of California Press. 203–227.
Weeks, K. (1979), (ed.), *Egyptology and the social sciences.* Cairo, American University in Cairo Press.
Wegner, J. (2002), A decorated birth–brick from South Abydos. *Egyptian Archaeology* 21. 3–4.
Weiss, L. (2009), Personal religious practice: house altars at Deir el-Medina. *Journal of Egyptian Archaeology* 95. 193–208.
Weiss, L. (2011), Some thoughts on the 'false doors' at Deir el-Medina. In M. Horn, J. Kramer, D. Soliman, N. Staring, C. van den Hoven and L. Weiss (eds), *Current Research in Egyptology 2010: proceedings of the Eleventh Annual Symposium.* Oxford, Oxbow Books. 197–205.

Welsby, D. A. and Anderson, J. R. (eds), (2004), *Sudan ancient treasures: an exhibition of recent discoveries from the Sudan National Museum.* London, British Museum Press.

Wente, E. F. (1962), Egyptian 'make merry' songs reconsidered. *Journal of Near Eastern Studies* 21. 118–28.

Wente, E. F. (1967), *Late Ramesside letters*. Chicago, University of Chicago Press.

Wente, E. F. (1982), Mysticism in pharaonic Egypt? *Journal of Near Eastern Studies* 41. 161–79.

Wente, E. F. (1990), *Letters from ancient Egypt*. Atlanta, Scholars Press.

Wente, E. F. (2003a), A ghost story. In W. K. Simpson (ed.), *The Literature of ancient Egypt: An anthology of stories, instructions, stelae, autobiographies, and poetry (third edition).* New Haven and London, Yale University Press. 112–15.

Wente, E. F. (2003b), The Book of the Heavenly Cow. In W. K. Simpson (ed.), *The Literature of ancient Egypt: An anthology of stories, instructions, stelae, autobiographies, and poetry* (third edition). New Haven and London, Yale University Press. 289–98.

Wenzel, G. (1998), Daily life in the home – the house as a living area. In R. Schultz and M. Seidel (eds), *Egypt: the world of the pharaohs.* Cologne, Könemann. 399–409.

Whale, S. (1989), *The family in the Eighteenth Dynasty of Egypt: A study of the representation of the family in the private tombs*. Sydney, Australian Centre for Egyptology.

Whelan, P. (2007), *Mere scraps of rough wood? 17th–18th Dynasty stick shabtis in the Petrie Museum and other collections*. London, UCL Press.

Whittlesey, S. M. and Reid, J. J. (2001), Mortuary ritual and organizational inferences at Grasshopper Pueblo, Arizona. In D. R. Mitchell and J. L. Brunson-Hadley (eds), *Ancient burial practices in the American Southwest: Archaeology, physical anthropology, and native American perspectives.* Albuquerque, University of New Mexico Press. 68–96.

Whyte, M. K. (1998), Death in the People's Republic of China. In J. L. Watson and E. S. Rawski (eds), *Death ritual in Late Imperial and modern China.* Berkeley, Los Angeles, London, University of California Press. 289–316.

Wickett, E. (2010), *For the living and the dead: the funerary laments of Upper Egypt, ancient and modern*. London and New York, I. B. Tauris.

Wiebach, S. (1986), Die Begegnung von Lebenden und Verstorbenen im Rahmen des thebanischen Talfestes. *Studien zur Altägyptischen Kultur* 13. 263–91.

Wikgren, H. (2005), The festival calendar at Deir el-Medina. In K. Piquette and S. Love (eds), *Current Research in Egyptology 2003: Proceedings of the Fourth Annual Symposium, University College London, 2003.* Oxford, Oxbow Books. 179–200

Wildung, D. (1969), *Die Rolle ägyptischer Könige im Bewusstsein ihrer Nachwelt I, Posthume Quellen über die Könige der ersten vier Dynastien*. Berlin, Bruno Hessling.

Wildung, D. (1977a), *Egyptian saints: deification in pharaonic Egypt*. New York, New York University Press.

Wildung, D. (1977b), *Imhotep und Amenhotep: Gottwerdung im alten Ägypten*. Munich and Berlin, Deutscher Kunstverlag.

Wildung, D. (1999), *Egyptian art in Berlin* (second edition). Mainz, Philipp von Zabern.

Wilfong, T. G. (1999), Menstrual synchrony and the 'Place of Women' in ancient Egypt (Oriental Institute Museum Hieratic Ostracon 13512). In E. Teeter and J. A. Larson (eds), *Gold of Praise: studies on ancient Egypt in honor of Edward F. Wente.* Chicago, The Oriental Institute, University of Chicago. 419–34.

Willems, H. (1990), Crime, cult and capital punishment (Mo'alla Inscription 8). *Journal of Egyptian Archaeology* 76. 27–54.

Willems, H. (2001), The social and ritual context of a mortuary liturgy. In H. Willems (ed.), *Social aspects of funerary culture in the Egyptian Old and Middle Kingdoms: proceedings of the symposium held at Leiden, 6–7 June, 1996.* Leuven, Paris, and Sterling VA, Peeters. 253–372.

Williams, H. (2003a), Introduction. In H. Williams (ed.), *Archaeologies of remembrance: death and memory in past societies.* New York, Springer. 5–11.

Williams, H. (2003b), Remembering and forgetting the medieval dead. In H. Williams (ed.), *Archaeologies of remembrance: death and memory in past societies.* New York, Springer. 227–54.

Williams, M. (2003), Tales from the dead: remembering the bog bodies in the Iron Age of North-Western Europe. In H. Williams (ed.), *Archaeologies of remembrance: death and memory in past societies.* New York, Springer. 89–112.

Williams, R. J. (1962), Reflections on the *Lebensmüde. Journal of Egyptian Archaeology* 48. 49–56.

Winthrop-Young, G. (2005), Memories of the Nile: Egyptian traumas and communication technologies in Jan Assmann's theory of cultural memory. *New German Critique* 96. 103–33.

Wood, M. (1998), The sorghum child. Nguana modula: South Sotho child figures. In E. Dell (ed.), *Evocations of the child: fertility figures of the southern African region.* Cape Town, Pretoria, Johannesberg, Human & Rousseau. 36–51.

Woodburn, J. (1982), Social dimensions of death in four African hunting and gathering societies. In M. Bloch and J. Parry (eds), *Death and the regeneration of life.* Cambridge, Cambridge University Press. 187–210.

Wright, J. C. (2004), A survey of evidence for feasting in Mycenean society. *Hesperia* 73, 2. 133–78.

Žabkar, L. V. (1968), *A study of the ba concept in ancient Egyptian texts.* Chicago, University of Chicago Press.

Zakovitch, Y. (2000), Song of Songs – riddle of riddles. In K. Modras (ed.), *The art of love lyrics.* Paris, J. Gabalda & Co. 11–23.

Zandee, J. (1960), *Death as an enemy according to ancient Egyptian conceptions.* Leiden, E. J. Brill.

Zibelius-Chen, K. (2002), Stèle de Séankhaptah et Ramosé (no. 189). In G. Andreu (ed.), *Les artistes de Pharaon: Deir el-Médineh et la Vallée des Rois.* Paris, Turnhout, Reunion des Musées Nationaux/Brepols. 233.

Ziegler, C. and Rutschowscaya, M-H. (1990), *The Louvre: Egyptian antiquities.* Paris, Editions Scala.

Zillhardt, R. (2009), *Kinderbestattungen und die soziale Stellung des Kindes im Alten Ägypten: Unter besonderer Berucksichtigung des Ostfriedhofs von Deir el-Medine.* Göttingen, Göttinger Miszellen.

Zivie, A. (2002), A pharaoh's peacemaker. *National Geographic* October 2002. 26–31.

Zivie, A. (2003), Un détour par Saqqara: Deir el-Médineh et la nécropole memphite. In G. Andreu (ed.), *Deir el-Médineh et la Vallée des Rois.* Louvre, Paris, Éditions Khéops. 67–82.

Zivie, C. M. (1975), À propos de quelques reliefs du Nouvel Empire au musée du Caire I. La tombe de Ptahmay à Giza. *Bulletin de l'Institut Français d'Archéologie Orientale* 75. 285–310.

Zivie, C. M. (1976), À propos de quelques reliefs du Nouvel Empire au musée du Caire II. La tombe de Khaemouas, chef des charpentiers du roi, à Giza. *Bulletin de l'Institut Français d'Archéologie* 76. 17–36.

Zonhoven, M. J. (1979), The inspection of a tomb at Deir el-Medîna (O. Wien Aeg. 1). *Journal of Egyptian Archaeology* 65. 89–98.

Index